Prophetic Statements on

FOOD STORAGE

for Latter-day Saints

"If ye are prepared ye shall not fear"
—D&C 38:30

*"The revelation to produce and store food may be
as essential to our temporal welfare as boarding the
ark was to the people in the days of Noah."*
—President Ezra Taft Benson

Prophetic Statements on

FOOD STORAGE

for Latter-day Saints

NEIL H. LEASH

Second Printing: May, 2005

International Standard Book Number:
0-88290-665-8

Horizon Publishers' Catalog and Order Number:
C1255

Printed and distributed
in the United States of America by

Address:
925 North Main Street
Springville,Utah 84663

Local Phone: (801) 489-4084
Toll Free: 1 (800) SKYBOOK
FAX: (800) 489-1097

CONTENTS

6. A PROPHET DISCUSSES CONCERNS FOR THE 21ST CENTURY . . 73

7. PROPHETIC STATEMENTS ABOUT EVENTS
PRECEDING THE SECOND COMING OF CHRIST 84

8. THE PREPAREDNESS RESPONSIBILITIES
OF LOCAL CHURCH LEADERS 95

9. THE SAINTS ARE NOT PREPARED 111

10. WHERE SHOULD LATTER-DAY SAINTS LIVE
DURING TIMES OF TRIBULATION? 117

DEDICATION

This book is dedicated to Velma, my beloved wife and sweetheart who diligently labored to enable this book to be written. Her wisdom, insight, and her knowledgeable attention to details polished the manuscript so that it could be published. It truly would have never been completed without her.

And it is dedicated to my children:

Neil A., who has always challenged me to think deeply and consider life's many dimensions.

Deborah, whose excellence in her own written work set a standard for me to follow.

Moroni, whose publishing and technical skills, along with persistent encouragement, helped me to not weary in a good thing. His willingness to labor with the manuscript, while under stress from his Ph.D. studies and even when he was ill, went far beyond what I could have hoped for.

This book is also dedicated to special members of *First* and *Fourth Wards* of the Sacramento Stake, who struggled to follow their bishop's counsel to become a prepared people before the Lord.

ACKNOWLEDGMENTS

I gratefully acknowledge David Whitmer and Elaine Hinds for their willingness to offer suggestions after reading a developing manuscript.

Cliff Collins and Kent Larson who, in spite of their ". . . I can't believe what you did . . ." comments, patiently worked on my computer when I had really messed it up.

Don Schanz, who often was unaware of the new material he gave me and the inspiration he shared.

President John H. Huber, whose example of dedicated labor to compile two books at an age when most seek the comfort of a soft chair and television, inspired me to persist until this task was completed.

Duane S. Crowther, editor and publisher, for his willingness to assist a novice in completing a manuscript that could eventually be published. And the work of his staff at Horizon Publishers is acknowledged for their efforts in bringing the book to completion.

CHAPTER

1
EDITOR'S AND PUBLISHER'S FOREWORD
BY
DUANE S. CROWTHER

Brother Neil H. Leash, the author of this compilation, invited me to write a brief foreword and to include some suggestions for family emergency preparedness which I wrote years ago in a book titled *Inspired Prophetic Warnings*. I feel honored by his invitation and am happy to comply with his request.

Let me first say, as the President and Senior Editor of Horizon Publishers, that it pleases me to see an extensive compilation of the counsel of Latter-day Saint Church leaders concerning food storage being made available to the Saints. I am pleased to have a part in the editing, shaping and publishing of the book because I know it has the potential to accomplish much good within the Church.

I know some last-days events which lie ahead are frightening because of their tremendous scope and severity, so I appreciate Brother Leash's approach in presenting the prophetic warnings pertaining to them: he counsels us to avoid fear and anxiety by making sound preparations, and he proposes that we approach this important subject with an attitude of "urgent calm" rather than a spirit of anxiety and alarm—a wise approach!

I also appreciate the maxim he has coined—a saying we would all do well to memorize and often include in our communications to one another:

The degree of our preparation will equal the extent of our obedience, which will determine the measure of our peace of mind.

Without further comment I will include the several pages of counsel which Brother Leash requested, hoping that its message will serve as a level of beginning guidance for many—a foundation to which they can add the words of admonition found throughout this book. I quote the following items from my book, *Inspired Prophetic Warnings*:[1]

---

[1] Duane S. Crowther, *Inspired Prophetic Warnings*. (Bountiful, Utah: Horizon Publishers & Distributors, Inc., 1987, pp. 287-292). Used by permission. *Inspired Prophetic Warnings* is a sequel and companion volume to *Prophecy—Key to the Future*, also by Duane S. Crowther. (Bountiful, Utah: Horizon Publishers & Distributors, Inc., 1962. Thirty-second printing, 1998, updated and revised.) *Prophecy—Key to the Future* is based on Brother Crowther's BYU Masters Thesis written in 1960 as he concluded his studies for a M.A. degree in Old and New Testament.

Information concerning these and other books on the last days and on food storage and emergency readiness can be found on Horizon Publishers' home page on the internet. See http://*www.horizonpublishers.com*.

ANTICIPATE PHYSICAL NEEDS:
STORE FOOD, CLOTHING, FUEL

The Saints have been counseled repeatedly to store the supplies needed to preserve life in times of shortage and want. Theirs is the responsibility to prepare for their own personal and family needs, and also to anticipate the needs of many who will gather together in times of future distress. As Heber C. Kimball explained, *"This is a part of our religion—to lay up stores and provide for ourselves and for the surrounding country; for the day is near when they will come by thousands and by millions, with their fineries, to get a little bread."*

Many events can cause shortages and scarcity of necessary commodities. Besides the obvious dangers of crop failure and war, consider other possibilities: strikes, transportation breakdowns, economic upheavals, energy shortages, disruption of farming, quarantine against pestilence, etc. The supply of basic commodities is directly dependent upon manpower, equipment, and profit. If it becomes unprofitable to manufacture, distribute, or sell commodities, the items will either disappear from the stores or exorbitantly increase in price until the average family cannot afford to purchase them.

Serious difficulties can develop overnight. Food stores were suddenly left bare in many parts of the nation, for instance, as the "Cuban crisis" developed. The "great depression" erupted in a matter of hours as the stock market collapsed. The "energy crisis" emerged abruptly, with no meaningful advance warning to the general public.

Because of the possibility of rapid changes, and because of the prophetic warnings of future hardships, it is vital that an effective preparedness program be established in every family unit.

Several brief suggestions might prove helpful.

A. Anticipate emergency situations:

Think what would happen in a variety of situations such as a prolonged power failure, an extended transportation strike which would leave stores bare, a major disaster such as an earthquake, etc. What would you need if you were unable to buy anything from local merchants? Record your observations and analyze them in terms of preparatory actions required.

B. Inventory present needs and supplies:

No meaningful storage program can be developed without proper assessment of current inventory and needs and the setting of realistic goals and timetables. No comprehensive, long-range storage program can be maintained without a record-keeping system. The inventory should include food, clothing, fuel, and household necessities. Anticipate family growth and needs for years to come.

C. Store medical and sanitation supplies:

If severe shortages occurred, people would soon feel particular need for basic medicinal goods to ward off the typical minor ailments with which families are beset. There would also be need for disinfectants, first aid supplies, home pesticides, etc.

D. Buy home maintenance supplies:

If difficult times come, there is a definite possibility of extended periods in which basic services such as power and fuel supply are maintained, but in which many necessary items are unavailable from merchants. There is wisdom in storing a basic supply of nuts and bolts, nails, faucet washers, toilet parts, electrical switches, light bulbs, etc. Every home, should have basic tools for repair and construction available.

E. Involve the neighborhood in storage activities:

Latter-day Saints have been commanded to warn their neighbors and to prepare them for coming judgments. In no situation is this command more imperative than in the area of storage of survival commodities. In a time of real shortage, unprepared neighbors could cause serious dilemmas of both a moral and temporal nature.

F. Avoid the "hoarding" mentality:

In times of scarcity, the "have nots" tend to accuse the "haves" of hoarding. The publicity they generate can sometimes place a viable storage program in an unfavorable light, causing discouragement and even persecution. Systematically-spaced buying, rather than "panic buying," tends to dispel this attitude. Prior emphasis and community publicity on the advantages of food storage and preparedness will help place the practice in better prospective.

G. Plant a garden:

Prepare to be self-supporting to as great a degree as possible. Successful gardening requires skill and experience which cannot be learned overnight, and it often requires long-range soil development. Tools should be acquired. Seeds should be stored. Water rights should be obtained. Records should be kept.

H. Obtain a survival library:

Many books explain helpful techniques for self-sufficient living. Building a basic library on food storage and preservation, gardening, home repair, and outdoor survival is a wise precaution.

I. Provide emergency heating and cooling facilities:

Emergency ability to maintain warmth in even one room could be the means of averting severe discomfort and suffering in a fuel shortage or power outage. There should also be provision for emergency cooking on the stove or fireplace. A supply of wood or coal should be on hand. There should be some provision for the emergency refrigeration of foodstuffs in case of prolonged power failure.

J. Insulate homes:

Advance effort to properly insulate homes would be of particular value in times of fuel shortage. Adding insulation, upgrading window quality, installing weather stripping and storm doors—all are effective preparedness measures as well as hedges against rapidly-rising fuel costs.

K. Repair, paint homes:

A vital aspect of preparedness is to have the home in good repair. Plumbing, heating, electrical items, the roof, exterior surfaces—every aspect of a home should be maintained in good condition. Homes should be painted. Once hard times come, it is difficult to meet the costs of such repairs.

L. Replace worn appliances:

Old stoves, refrigerators, toilets, and other necessary appliances should be upgraded while supplies are plentiful.

M. Provide for home security from theft:

Scarcity of food and other necessary supplies would cause a serious increase in the danger of theft. Preparations should be made to maintain the security of the home.

N. Safe storage of important records:

In the event of major disruptions or emergencies, there might be increased need for ready access to vital family records. Such records should be cataloged and preserved in a safe place, protected from fire and water damage and from theft. There might also be a need for ready access to addresses of family members and other important directions for distant geographical areas.

O. Maintain mobility and travel potential:

In case of serious emergency, families might find it necessary to travel relatively long distances to reach shelter in the homes of other family members and acquaintances. An automobile should be maintained in good working order, and an adequate supply of gas should be safely stored in portable containers. An emergency travel kit should be planned and prepared. Maps should be on hand.

P. Pre-arranged emergency travel plan:

The chance of having to rapidly leave an area and travel to another increases as the possibility of future war and anarchy increases. Contingency decisions should be made, and all family members should be made aware of them.

ANTICIPATE THE DANGER OF ECONOMIC UPHEAVAL: BE FREE FROM DEBT

As the world enters the trauma of the last days, economic stability may become increasingly fragile. Shortages of supplies may occur. Production may cease. Transportation and distribution systems may become inoperative. There continues to be the dual dangers of inflation and depression. War always influences the economy.

With the potential for economic instability looming ever more ominous as perilous times approach, there is wisdom in proceeding cautiously in matters of personal finance. These suggestions are offered:

A. Be free from debt:

This counsel has been given to Latter-day Saints by their leaders on many occasions. It is wise instruction. In times of difficulty, indebtedness becomes financial bondage, and those who are in debt are not in full control of either their lives or their property. Set a course which will repay all indebtedness as soon as possible. That may not be the most profitable course for "good" times, but the freedom and security it offers for troubled times far outweighs the profit lost.

B. Place preparation for security before pleasure and profit:

In establishing personal priorities, recognize the value of proper food storage, home care, and other basics of personal security over the many luxury items which are available. Preparations for future family well-being should take precedence over boats, campers, and speculative financial ventures.

C. Be self-sustaining:

Every effort should be made for able-bodied individuals to provide for their own needs, and to resist the temptation to draw from government welfare programs. Those who do not provide for their own needs are not free, and are locked into unproductive situations which will not allow them to make adequate preparations for the future, nor enjoy life fully in the present. There is no effective substitute for personal effort and the development of individual skills and abilities.

D. Provide for financial emergencies:

A family needs a cushion of readily-available capital to serve as protection against sudden emergencies. An amount equal to six month's income is often recommended. There is also need for the protection available through insurance programs.

E. Recognize that money has value only in a working economy:

Money is only a means of exchange and has no value in and of itself. It can be used to obtain goods and services in normal times, but may be worthless in times of economic distress. There is wisdom in obtaining needed and desired items before periods of instability arise.

ANTICIPATE COMMUNICATION DISRUPTION: MAKE LONG-RANGE EMERGENCY PLANS

Communication and transportation networks could be seriously disrupted or destroyed in the event of war or internal strife. Many of today's families are scattered across the nation. There is wisdom in establishing a family emergency plan, specifying what steps that family would take to be reunited or maintain family ties in the event of major problems in the nation, fixing dates and places for future meetings, proposing alternate communication systems, etc. A formal family organization would strengthen the emergency plans.

* * *

The above is but a limited portion of a quite extensive chapter in *Inspired Prophetic Warnings.* I hope the pages cited in this context have provided insights which will be of value to all who read this book.

I share Brother Leash's strong belief that the message found herein is truly essential to the future well-being of millions of Latter-day Saints scattered all around the globe. May they read, give heed, and obey the counsel the Lord has repeatedly revealed through his inspired servants is my desire and oft-repeated prayer.

Sincerely,

Duane S. Crowther

CHAPTER

2
AUTHOR'S INTRODUCTION

Over the years my wife, Velma, and I have worked diligently to put together our food storage. We have had the opportunity to address the Saints on a number of occasions concerning the Lord's counsel regarding the need for food storage preparation for themselves and their families.

Through the years we have been blessed to know many faithful Saints who diligently, and at times with considerable sacrifice, have gathered together their food storage. We have rejoiced in their testimonies regarding the value, deepened security and personal delight that comes to those who accomplish what the Lord and his prophets have instructed them to do.

During this same time we have also become aware how very negligent others have been in carrying out this assignment to prepare. A 1986 study reported by the Church confirmed our experience. The report indicated that most members thought food storage was a "good idea," but few had actually done anything about it.

THE SAINTS ARE GRATEFUL
FOR FOOD-STORAGE COUNSEL

Even so, as a people it would seem that the Saints have generally felt grateful for food storage counsel, recognizing that we belong to a Church so divinely led that many essential aspects of our life and well-being are specifically addressed and accounted for. Yet for some, it seems sufficient only to know that the Lord loves them, as though feeling content in this knowledge will somehow be sufficient protection should days of tribulation overtake them. Perhaps they feel that since Heavenly Father loves us so much, should any of us not prepare as counseled, He will in some way see that we are left unharmed.

That is in direct contrast to the Lord's promise: "I, the Lord, am bound when ye do what I say: but when ye do not what I say, ye have no promise" (D&C 82:10).

There are others, perhaps the majority of the Saints, who seem to feel, "I agree with the principle of food storage, and someday—when it's more convenient or more easily affordable, I will certainly prepare." They are stalwart members of the "Almost Club," they almost do it—*almost*! It is not so much that as a people we don't believe it should be done, it is simply relegated to a position far down on the list of our priorities, if it's on the list at all. Many have fallen into the same snare as did King Agrippa, who told Paul, "*almost* thou persuadest me to be a Christian" (Acts 26:28).

A Commandment We Can Fulfill, Completely and Perfectly

It is interesting, however, that this revealed directive is one of the few instructions from the Lord that we can nearly all fulfill, completely and perfectly. Food storage is very much like the law of tithing—if we set our minds to it and act aggressively, most of us can bring ourselves into full compliance and obedience to the Lord's counsel. Conversely, if we don't act in accordance with this revealed direction, we leave ourselves with little excuse but to stand fully exposed to the judgments of God which will eventually be poured out upon the world, and consequently also upon ourselves and our loved ones.

These concerns have initiated in me a desire to gather together into one body some measure of the Lord's counsel, given through his prophets, regarding the temporal and spiritual welfare of His children. In this way, perhaps each of us may come to see more clearly our Heavenly Father's great love for His children and His desires for our protection.

Hopefully, you will come to recognize, as you read this book, that the Lord has *not* been casual about food storage and preparedness. On the contrary, He has been amazingly persistent—with over 150 years of regular reiteration, encouragement, emphasis and direction in this dispensation alone. Thus, in as much as we can only be protected to the degree of our obedience, it is my earnest prayer that each of us will now take the Lord's instructions and counsels to heart and act upon them.

The Lord is clear about the relationship between obedience and blessings:

> There is a law, irrevocably decreed in heaven before the foundations of this world, upon which all blessings are predicated—
> And when we obtain any blessing from God, it is by obedience to that law upon which it is predicated (D&C 130:20-21).

A Dream Worth Contemplating

With this thought in mind, I would like to relate an experience shared with me many years ago by a close friend, which brought to me a meaningful measure of personal motivation to follow the Lord's counsel to be prepared. Hopefully, it will touch your heart similarly to the way it touched mine.

Many years ago Kenneth Holbrook, an older high priest in my Sacramento, California Ward, approached me regarding a dream he had experienced which left him very perplexed. The dream seemed so real to him that he had been unable to dismiss it; consequently he felt a need to share it. The following is what he related to me, to the best of my recollection.

In this dream Ken found himself in what profoundly impressed him as being a real-life situation. At the outset, he observed members of the Church anxiously engaged in making preparations to leave their homes because a directive had been received from Church Headquarters that all the Saints in his area were to emigrate to Utah. To assist them in this endeavor, a train had been chartered by the Church to provide transportation for all those who could quickly leave.

Brother Holbrook stated that he somehow became aware that the requirement for being allowed to board this train was for each individual to have his year's supply of food with him. Apparently, those who were making this journey to Utah had to be able to provide for themselves during the first year after their arrival. It seemed to him that provisions, after the year's supply was exhausted, would then be available in the Salt Lake Valley.

He related to me that in this dream he saw people greatly exercised and rapidly putting things together because this instruction to move had come at such short notice. Because of limited time and space there was a need to decide what could be taken, and then everything had to be quickly transported to the railroad station in time to meet the train's scheduled stop.

In his dream, upon arrival at the train station Brother Holbrook found himself greatly troubled because, as he wandered through the large crowds there assembled, many anticipated faces were missing. He felt a need to look for them. He named to himself dedicated stake and ward leaders who were not present, as well as many active members who were missing. Ken also expressed surprise to find families there whom he would never have expected to see, since they had not been outwardly active members in their own wards.

However, what was most troubling to him in the dream were those whom he did not see, and who in spite of his best efforts, he was unable to locate. He again reiterated to me, in an obvious state of disbelief, that many stake and ward leaders were not present, and many of the most faithful members of the ward were not to be found, no matter how hard he searched for them.

Brother Holbrook then expressed to me how stressful this dream had been to him, stating that he had no idea what its true meaning was, or what—if anything—he could or should do about it. He continued by stating that it was not like any other dream he had ever experienced, it being so very real and profound that he had been unable to dismiss it as one generally does with troubling dreams. The intensity with which he shared this experience made such a strong impression upon my mind that what he shared has stayed with me these many years.

Frankly, I have no personal knowledge regarding the "realness" or "predictive nature" of Ken's dream, but I do know that this faithful high priest was deeply moved; therefore I have not taken his experience lightly. I have always been impressed by its implications, one of which is that we should never casually dismiss nor ignore the counsel to obtain and maintain at least a year's supply of food.

When I think of Brother Holbrook's dream, I'm reminded of an interesting dream reported by President *Heber C. Kimball*:

I will tell you a dream which Brother Kesler had lately. He dreamed that there was a sack of gold and a cat placed before him, and that he had the privilege of taking which he pleased, whereupon *he took the cat,* and walked off with her. Why did he take the cat in preference to the gold? Because *he could eat the cat, but could not eat the gold* (*Journal of Discourses,* vol. 3, p. 262).

A MAJOR CALAMITY WOULD DEMONSTRATE OUR DEGREE OF OBEDIENCE

None of us know when the Lord may personally call on us to use our food storage, nor the circumstances under which its use may be required. No one knows what the Lord has in mind for those who are thus prepared, nor do we know the specific price that will be paid by those who fail to prepare—all we know for certain is that we have been "repetitively" told to prepare. An element of faith is required. Moroni speaks of it this way: "I would show unto the world that *faith is things which are hoped for and not seen;* wherefore, *dispute not because ye see not, for ye receive no witness until after the trial of your faith*" (Ether 12:6).

The obvious and positive temporal aspects of the Food Storage Program are seldom misunderstood. But to the Lord, all things are spiritual, and it is in this area that the obvious becomes less clear. It is possible that when we reach the point in our preparation that we have a year's supply of food, that it is a key—a "moment in time" which the Lord clearly sees as reflective of each individual's commitment to obedience—another one of life's small but not-so-insignificant tests.

Often, when looking at ourselves and others, we assume that righteousness and faithfulness are measured by attendance at ward meetings, the strength of expressed testimonies regarding the prophet, significant positions held in the Church, etc., seeing these as major indicators that define obedience. To some extent this may be true, but who can really say how the Lord will sum up our obedience in the end? He may very well use rather simple, straight-forward ways of communicating to us what our standing before Him really is, such as a major calamity which would require that we subsist on just our prepared resources. This would uniformly demonstrate our degree of obedience, no matter what our position in the Church or the world may be— regardless of whether we be one of his Saints, a Ward or Stake officer or leader, or a General Authority. When the need for use of our food storage comes, it will show us.in no uncertain terms that before the Lord all His children are equal.

Man often forgets that the criteria by which the Lord knows and decides our standing before Him are not position, wealth, opportunity, education, prestige, etc.. His judgments are made by things of much greater importance, such as obedience, sacrifice, love for one another, and our personal relationship with Him and our Heavenly Father. Obedience, and those things which make up our character, are truly His points of measurement.

Thus, perhaps one of the Lord's ways of measuring the level of our obedience and commitment to Him may be to merely hold us accountable for our response towards

His instructions, given consistently over some 150 years, to be prepared with food storage.

He has instructed us to live each day as though He were coming *today*—we are to "watch and be ready." Our awareness of His directives and the simplicity and opportunity of fulfilling this counsel, especially in America, a land of plenty, certainly cannot be seriously argued. With very few exceptions, every member of the Church could have *something* stored which would demonstrate, to some degree, their willingness to be obedient to such extensive and repetitive counsel from the Lord to prepare.

Think for a moment how clearly a famine of just one year's duration would demonstrate to each of us how obedient we truly were in following the Lord's counsel through his prophets. The message we would individually receive from such an experience would certainly be painfully plain and self-explanatory. Indeed, consider carefully the clarity of the following excerpts:

Bishop **H. Burke Peterson**, in the April 12, 1975 *Church News*, said of the food storage program: "It is a serious issue. *Let's not forget one of the most important lessons learned through the year's supply program is the lesson of obedience.*" And President **Ezra Taft Benson** said,

> *Should the Lord decide at this time to cleanse the Church*—and the need for that cleansing seems to be increasing—*a famine in this land of one year's duration could wipe out a large percentage of slothful members,* including some ward and stake officers. *Yet we cannot say we have not been warned* (*Teachings of Ezra Taft Benson*, p. 265).[1]

As you read this compilation of prophetic instructions and counsel, I have great hope that it will give added insight, momentum, and motivation to action that will in turn become a blessing of peace and security to you and your family. Remember, the Lord has promised to help us when we put forth an honest effort to be obedient to His instructions.

THIS BOOK'S OBJECTIVE:
TO AWAKEN A BURNING DESIRE UNTO ACTION

This book has been compiled with the hope of awakening in the hearts of the Saints a burning desire . . . a desire unto *action* . . . to be prepared for the coming of our Lord and Savior so that we are a people who in very deed are (as in the parable of the five wise and five foolish virgins) *Saints, with our "lamps trimmed."*

---

[1] Throughout this book, the author and editor have placed key passages in italics to add emphasis and to focus the reader on the important concepts set forth in the quotations cited. If emphasis was placed in the original source, it will be noted in the reference citation.

May the Spirit of the Holy Ghost bare witness to our hearts that the Lord requires a prepared people, a people who live every day as though it is the day of His coming.

This has been in accordance with His instructions to the Saints since the days when He walked upon the earth and taught in person. For even in the meridian of time, He told his disciples about the troubles that would proceed His coming and instructed them to "watch and pray," to "prepare for that which is to come," to be "ready for the trials and tribulations that will be poured out upon the earth," that they "not be caught unawares."

It is consistent with the scriptures that He has always wanted to protect His children and make life easier for them, but the even greater aspect of His instructions seems to be escaping the understanding of many of the Saints at large. He wants— no, requires—of His people that we sacrifice our time, funds, space, thought, effort, and even acceptance of the world, if so required, to be obedient to Him.

The food storage program is not given just to protect us, it is also given to consistently confirm before the Lord, ourselves, and all people that the things which He has instructed His people to do . . . they will do! Even when the reasons for doing them don't immediately seem important, or even understandable.

If the Lord's only goal was to have His Saints prepared with food, clothing and the necessities of life for the disasters that will come, He could simply let his people know that He would warn us to get prepared through his prophets a short time before the difficulties were to arise. After all, in the eternal economy of things, that would leave us free to use our earthly time and means more effectively, would it not? It would certainly be an efficient way to take care of all concerns regarding being prepared for mass destructions, trials, tribulations, etc.

And as far as individual challenges such as loss of jobs, health, etc., which would not involve large groups of people, He could simply let His children know to stay in tune and He would inspire them individually to prepare just before personal or family needs would occur. We could reason that, after all, it would still require obedience on the part of the Saints, and those who were willing to hear and follow His prophets would reap the reward of safety.

THE GOAL: AN OBEDIENT, PREPARED PEOPLE WHO PUT THE LORD BEFORE SELF

However, the above misses the entire point of an *obedient, prepared, people* who are putting the Lord before self and living each day as though it is the day of His coming. Indeed, we are only among the five wise virgins who are allowed to go in to the Bride Groom if we *are* (not if we *will become*) daily prepared. And it is important to be prepared, since none of us know if today we may die, having thus been left with no "preparation time" before we stand before Him.

Obviously, the five foolish virgins would not have had difficulty if the Lord had stated that "three months from now I will be coming," but such is not the Lord's way.

Remember, the five foolish virgins were not only members of the Church; they were people who fully expected that they would be allowed in to the wedding. They even presented themselves at the door. Yet their "lamps were not trimmed," and the Lord said unto them, "ye never knew me." And the doors were closed before them. Notice that they had full intentions (in the future) of buying oil for their lamps. How sad for them! Their love for the Lord had not been strong enough to move their hearts to obedient action so that they would be consistently prepared.

As you read the pages of this book, pay close attention to how often, how consistently, even how constantly He instructed and re-instructed through his servants this principle of food storage and preparedness. It would behoove us to notice that, of all the instructions the Lord has given His Saints, the directives related to food storage and preparedness are among those *most often stressed* of all His counsels:

> We are to watch and be ready.
> We are to live obediently and be ready to meet Him.
> We are to be prepared for the calamities that will come upon the earth.
> We are to be prepared for famines and pestilences.
> We are to be prepared for wars and rumors of wars.
> We are to be prepared for personal and family crises.
> We are to be prepared for local, regional and national emergencies.
> We are to be prepared for world calamities.
> We are to be prepared for the turbulent times which are to precede His coming.
> We are to be prepared for the day of His return.
> Again, we are to "Watch" and "Be ready!"

Consider how fervently the Lord desires our spiritual and physical safety. Obviously, to have our "lamps trimmed" requires spiritual preparation, but we are fooling ourselves if we think we can be spiritually prepared without having sacrificed enough to be obedient to the requirement of physical preparation. Perhaps we had better reevaluate ourselves to see if we are that righteous a people after all. As we take individual inventory of our preparation and of where we are today in our obedience, let us look inwardly and determine if we really are ready to meet Him.

Have we made the kinds of preparations that will enable us to endure the difficulties the nations and the earth must endure, so that we can stand among those left to greet Him at His coming? The Lord will help us to do so if we do our part; to this end let us labor and pray for ourselves and each other. Remember, *"The Lord giveth no commandments unto the children of men, save he shall prepare a way for them that they may accomplish the thing which he commandeth them"* (1 Nephi 3:7).

CHAPTER

3

LIFE-SHAPING MOMENTS ALTER THE COURSE OF OUR LIVES

Before we enter into a review of the Lord's counsel of why, how and what we should prepare to provide security for the future, let's look first at several events from the past to help us appreciate the need for divine counsel.

In each of our lives, there are significant defining "moments in time"—author Karl Mannheim called them "crystallizing moments"—which have such profound impact upon us that they alter the course of our entire lives. Some of these moments are large and dramatic; others seem small and insignificant. Yet all of them make up the sum of our existence and are therefore profound in their results.

Whether or not we pay an honest tithe, keep the word of wisdom, get baptized, go on a mission, marry in the temple, get an education, or obtain a year's supply of food, these are a few examples of "moments in time" where we make choices that will affect us for the rest of our earthly, even eternal lives. Since past moments can't be retrieved, at least some of the results of their effect upon us becomes fixed. As one of our hymns attests, "time flies on wings of lighting, we cannot call it back. . . ." The blessings and/or negatives attendant to our choices therefore, are set in motion so that we constantly either dam or bless ourselves, depending upon our decisions regarding things we do or don't do.

There are also effects from other "moments in time" which are fully outside our scope of influence or realm of choice. Decisions are set in motion that we must reckon with which are made by someone or something else, yet our life is affected none-the-less by them. A brief review of recent world history reveals a number of "moments in time" after which the future from that point on was markedly different. Yet the vast majority of people had no choices in whether or not they occurred.

For example, on **June 28, 1914,** mankind unknowingly awoke to the beginning of a different world. On that date, a student from Serbia shot and killed Archduke Ferdinand of Austria who was visiting in Sarajevo. This was the defining moment which set in motion the events that resulted in *World War I*.

On **October 24, 1929** the *Stock Market crashed*. The majority of the people in America went to bed on the night of the 23rd totally unaware that on the morrow they would awake to the beginning of a terrible world-wide depression, the effects of which would impact their lives for some 25 years.

In like manner, the **summer of 1935** started out hot and dry like many other summers, but ended up being the *beginning of the Dust Bowl*. Some of the richest and most productive farming soil in the nation simply dried up. Seventy thousand American refugees abandoned their homes after watching their lands become parched, their crops fail and their cattle die.

At 10:00 p.m. on **March 12, 1938,** Germany annexed Austria, thereby breaking Article 88 of the Treaty of Versailles. This was the significant "moment in time" which resulted in *World War II*. In the seven years which followed, about 50 million men, women and children were to die, and thousands of cities were to be turned into ashes and dust.

In corollary impact, Americans arose on **December 7, 1941**, and went about their routine daily tasks, yet they were nearing a "moment in time" that was about to change their lives in ways they had not foreseen. Tens of thousands of America's young men went about their lives that day completely unaware that they were to die, sometime during next four years, in lands with strange, unknown names. That morning the Japanese launched their war planes into the air and pointed them towards *Pearl Harbor*.

The first *atomic bomb was tested* on **July 16, 1945**. On the eve of that day, millions of Japanese people finished their labors and retired quietly to their beds completely unaware that in about three weeks hundreds of thousands of them were going to die or be horribly scared from a weapon they had never even heard of. Two atomic bombs were dropped, one on *Hiroshima* on **August 6th** and another on *Nagasaki* three days later , on **August 9th**.

There are, however, other more significant "moments in time" that go equally unrecognized by the world as a whole. Consider, for example, that it was on a beautiful morning in the **spring of 1820** when an obscure young man named *Joseph Smith went into a grove and prayed*. He was an entirely unrecognizable figure by the world's standards. And yet, because of his humble and earnest prayer and its answer, modern man's concept of God would never be the same, and an entire dispensation would be opened to the world. In continuation of that event, on **April 6, 1830** the *Church of Jesus Christ was restored* to the earth, an event that has changed and will yet change the lives of many millions of Heavenly Father's children.

THE SIGNIFICANCE OF MOST "DEFINING MOMENTS" USUALLY IS UNRECOGNIZED UNTIL LATER

The impact of virtually all significant events can easily be seen from an historical perspective, i.e. hindsight. But the significance of most "defining moments" is overlooked because of their immediate obscurity. Thus, for most such "moments," we could never expect to be prepared. Obviously, if we knew the end from the beginning we would always be prepared, even if only at the last moment. But such foreknowledge as this is reserved solely to our Heavenly Father and His son, Jesus Christ. However, in the case of food storage preparation, we have received knowledge both through the words of the Savior and through His ordained spokesmen. Hence, our opportunities to prepare continue even to this very moment. But they can be lost if we ignore this knowledge and decline to follow the Lord's counsel just because we don't understand the present or eventual impact it might have on our lives.

INSPIRED GUIDANCE NEEDED TO AVOID POTENTIALLY DISASTROUS "MOMENTS IN TIME"

If we are to avoid potentially disastrous "moments in time" (whether they be externally or self imposed), it is crucial that we receive personal revelation and/or prophetic guidance—and act upon it. How frustrating it must be to our Creator to witness our public testimonies that we believe in a prophet, acknowledge the inspired nature of his calling and counsel, and then observe us ignore his prophetic guidance! We hear this frustration in the Lord's incriminating statements to ancient Israel:

> O Jerusalem, Jerusalem, thou that killest the prophets, and stonest them which are sent unto thee, how often would I have gathered thy children together, even as a hen gathereth her chickens under her wings, *and ye would not!* (Matthew 23:37).

If we were to paraphrase this lament to fit the poor preparatory responsiveness of this generation, it might be:

> O Israel, Israel, thou that *denieth and setteth for naught the counsel of the prophets,* and ignoreth them which are sent unto thee, how oft would I have gathered you, my children, together *that ye would have food,* even as a hen gathereth her chickens together to feed them, *but ye would not prepare!*

The truth is, without prophetic guidance, it is nearly impossible for any of us to anticipate or understand how to respond, or to know what to prepare for when we are, or will be, personally caught up in the throes of a crisis. As we consider both present and future "defining moments in time," we should ponder that from the very beginning of man's sojourn upon earth, the Lord has always given counsel, instructions and warnings through His prophets as a means of preserving and blessing the obedient, thereby keeping them safe.

He has taught them, "If ye are prepared ye shall not fear," and has told them how to be prepared, both through righteous living and by specific preparatory instructions. However, during both ancient and modern times, more often than not, the Lord's people have elected not to heed His warnings or have only half-heartedly followed His instructions. Yet, history has always shown that the only sure safety available to us is to be found in obedience to His instructions and to the counsel of His prophets.

Consider, for example, Christmas day **December 25, 1832**. On that day the Lord revealed, to His prophet, Joseph Smith, the fore-knowledge that this nation was shortly to experience a terrible *Civil War*, starting with the rebellion of South Carolina. As always on that day families throughout this country went about their Christmas festivities unaware that in a few short years nearly a million of them would die in a "war between brothers" which was to begin on **April 12, 1861**, when the South fired on Fort Sumter. Yet by the time this war commenced, having obediently followed His prophets, the Saints were safely tucked away in the protective arms of the Rocky Mountains.

Notice, however, that the event was revealed years in advance, and required that a journey of over a thousand miles be carried out upon the basis of sacrifice and faith alone. In regard to the counsel to gather our food storage, most of us seem content to wait until something apparent makes it 'reasonable' to believe we might need it. We fail to understand that most circumstances which could make having our food storage necessary *will not come with obvious advance notice*. The Lord knows this as well, and He has asked that we simply become and remain prepared.

Even as you read this book it is not unlikely that there could be some event in the making, of which you are completely unaware, but which will have a profound effect upon you and your family in the months or years ahead.

PREPARE FOR EARTH'S "SATURDAY-NIGHT BATH"

Your need for a dependable food supply in the near future is certainly not outside the realm of possibility, and the possibility of such a need increases with each passing year as incidents preceding the Second Coming unfold.

Elder *Orson F. Whitney* commented on the earth's approaching Sabbath:

> Earth's long week is now drawing to a close, and we stand at the present moment in the *Saturday Evening of Time, at or near the end of the sixth day of human history*. Is it not a time for thought, a season for solemn meditation? Morning will break upon the Millennium, the thousand years of peace, the Sabbath of the World! (*Saturday Night Thoughts*, rev. ed. 1927, p. 12)

Whether we wish it or not, we now stand at the beginning of a pivotal period in world history, the *beginning of the Millennial Era*. It is a profound "moment in time" in which the *telestial* world where we now reside has begun to move inexorably from its current existence into a *terrestrial* state. This journey requires that all wickedness be completely wiped off the face of the earth as it was in the days of Noah.

Elder *Bruce R. McConkie* indicates the coming destruction of the wicked:

> This earth is now in its fallen or telestial state, in which condition wickedness prevails on its surface. When our Lord comes to usher in the millennial era, there will be a new heaven and a new earth. See Rev. 21:1-6. The earth will be renewed and receive it paradisiacal glory; it will return to that edenic state which prevailed before the fall. *The wicked, meaning those who live a telestial law, shall either be destroyed before the Second Coming or be burned at that time.* None will remain who do not live at least a terrestrial law (*Doctrinal New Testament Commentary*, vol. 3, p. 587).

The cleansing of the earth preparatory to the Lord's reign has been the subject of many prophetic utterances in all dispensations of time. This preparatory time will be its "Saturday night bath," so to speak. Then, freshly cleaned, the earth will be prepared to enter into its terrestrial period—the scriptural Millennium—and receive its Lord and Savior as King of Kings.

Our only certain protection for dealing with the challenging "moments in time" which tomorrow will bring is to follow the prophets, heed their counsel and keep the Lord's commandments. Draw your family close to you and be prepared to care for each other, and for others, as distressing times come—for they surely will come—the Lord Jesus Christ has explicitly told us so.

For those who are obediently prepared, the Second Coming of the Savior with all the attendant tribulations, will not bring feelings of heavy apprehension, for the obedient shall have come to know the signs of the times and will have been looking forward to that great event.

> And it shall come to pass that *he that feareth me shall be looking forth for the great day of the Lord to come, even for the signs of the coming of the Son of Man* (D&C 45:39).

> And he that believeth shall be blest with signs following, even as it is written. And *unto you it shall be given to know the signs of the times, and the signs of the coming of the Son of Man* (D&C 68:10-11).

"IF YE ARE PREPARED, YE SHALL NOT FEAR"

The scriptures describe events that clearly indicate the Lord has always watched over his people. The story of Joseph who was sold into Egypt is a simple story of obedience to revelation received from the Lord. Interestingly, as the Lord prepared to feed the children of Jacob through his son Joseph, the Egyptian Pharaoh's heart was also prepared to hear, believe, and act on the prophetic interpretation of his dream by Joseph.

Now, several thousand years later, Israel is again faced with the choice of whether or not to follow the revelations received by the prophets. From the beginning of this dispensation the Lord has been perfectly clear that the Saints are required to be a prepared people. A visit from Moroni to Joseph Smith set the stage for the challenging times that were to come.

Joseph Smith, in 1823, stated that Moroni "informed me of *great judgments* which were coming upon the earth, with *great desolations* by *famine, sword,* and *pestilence;* and that these *grievous judgments* would come on the earth in this generation" (*Joseph Smith–History,* 1:45).

Yet, the Lord's foreknowledge will indeed become a blessing to us if we follow His Prophets:

> Wherefore the voice of the Lord is unto the ends of the earth, that all that will hear may hear: *Prepare ye, prepare ye* for that which is to come, for the Lord is nigh. . . .
>
> Wherefore, I the Lord, *knowing the calamity* which should come upon the inhabitants of the earth, called upon my servant Joseph Smith, Jun., and spake unto him from heaven, and gave him commandments (D&C 1:11-12, 17).

However, failure to prepare can have devastating consequences, for the Lord has made it clear that He will first hold His own people accountable:

> Behold, *vengeance cometh speedily* upon the inhabitants of the earth, a day of wrath, a day of *burning,* a day of *desolation,* of *weeping,* of *mourning,* and of *lamentation;* and as a whirlwind [suddenly] *it shall come upon all the face of the earth,* saith the Lord. And *upon my house shall it begin, and from my house shall it go forth, saith the Lord* (D&C 112:24-25).

President *Joseph F. Smith* emphasized that if Latter-day Saints fail to live their religion, they cannot expect to avoid the Lord's judgments:

> . . . I further testify, that unless the Latter-day Saints will *live their religion, keep their covenants* with God and their brethren, *honor the Priesthood* which they bear, and try faithfully to bring themselves into subjection to the laws of God, *they will be the first to fall beneath the judgments of the Almighty, for his judgment will begin at his own house* (*Conference Report,* April, 1880, p. 96).

Indeed, the Lord indicates that the Saints are to "hardly escape" and, then, only if they are obedient:

I have sworn in my wrath, and decreed wars upon the face of the earth, and the wicked shall slay the wicked, and *fear shall come upon every man; And the Saints shall hardly escape;* nevertheless, *I, the Lord am with them* (D&C 63:33-34).

The Lord's scourge shall pass over by night and by day, and the report thereof shall vex all people; yea, it shall not be stayed until the Lord come; For the indignation of the Lord is kindled against their abominations and all their wicked works. Nevertheless, *Zion shall escape if she observe to do all things whatsoever I have commanded her.*

But if she observe not to do whatsoever I have commanded her, I will visit her according to all her works, with sore affliction, with pestilence, with plague, with sword, with vengeance, with devouring fire (D&C 97:23-26).

In case we are "hearing" the Lord but are not "listening" to what He is saying to us, He gave the parable of the ten virgins so that the active membership of the Church will not mistake the message. Concerning that well-known parable (see Matthew 25:1-13), note carefully the following interpretive remarks:

President *Spencer W. Kimball* identified who the Ten Virgins are in the Church:

I believe that the Ten Virgins represent the people of the Church of Jesus Christ and not the rank and file of the world. All of the virgins, wise and foolish, had accepted the invitation to the wedding supper; they had knowledge of the program and had been warned of the important day to come.

They [the foolish] knew the way but gave only a small measure of loyalty and devotion. I ask you: *What value is a car without an engine, a cup without water, a table without food, a lamp without oil?*

Hundreds of thousands of us today are in this position. *Confidence has been dulled and patience worn thin. It is so hard to wait and be prepared always. But we cannot allow ourselves to slumber. The Lord has given us this parable as a special warning.*

The foolish asked the others to share their oil, but spiritual [and temporal] preparedness cannot be shared in an instant. The wise had to go, else the bridegroom would have gone unwelcomed. *They needed all their oil for themselves;* they could not save the foolish. *The responsibility was each for himself* (*Faith Precedes the Miracle*, p. 253).

It is not the Lord's intention to do for the Saints what they can do for themselves. All the tribulation attendant to the Second Coming of the Savior cannot and will not be modified to meet the needs of a people adequately warned but who refuse, or otherwise fail, to prepare.

Because the Lord loves us he has sent us warnings and counseled us through his prophets, who have informed us of the way of "escape" he then leaves it to our right of agency to choose the course of action each feels inclined to take. Although the Lord has rarely disclosed the exact date when a significant event will come to pass, He will give his chosen people time to set their lives in order. Always remember a people prepared really have no need to fear. In short, the Lord apparently desires that we remain diligent and display a willingness to keep all His prophetic instructions, even—or perhaps especially—when we do not know how, when, or where they may be fulfilled.

Obviously, it does not take a prophet to comment on what should have been done after the opportunity for preparation has passed. Therefore, would not wisdom dictate that the warning to prepare should come at a time and season conducive to preparation? Yet, because there would seem, at that moment, no discernable need to make preparation, a natural response would be to put the matter off.

A true test of one's testimony of a prophet is whether or not he will follow his counsel, even if there seems at that moment no logical reason to do so. The only way is to live obediently, every day of our lives, so that we stay ready to meet our Lord and Savior.

Elder *Neal A. Maxwell* discussed being appropriately moved to prepare:

It has been asked, and well it might be, how many of us would have jeered, or at least been privately amused, by the sight of Noah building his ark: Presumably, the laughter and the heedlessness continued until it began to rain—and kept raining! How wet some people must have been before Noah's ark suddenly seemed the only sane act in an insane, bewildering situation! *To ponder signs without becoming paranoid, to be aware without frantically matching current events with expectations, using energy that should be spent in other ways, these are our tasks* (*For the Power is in Them*, p. 20).

Please note carefully: It was obedience, not rain, that motivated Noah to build an ark. Are we any less willing to be obedient? Have we been told any less plainly to be prepared than was Noah—to build our own "ark" even in the absence of rain? Do we want to be the cause of our own suffering, or cause our loved ones to suffer for our failures to "build"? If we answer no, it requires, then, that we act upon the words of counsel from the prophets to become properly prepared.

President *James E. Faust* gave this testimony—a warning with assurance:

It is my testimony that we are facing difficult times. We must be courageously obedient. *My witness is that we will be called upon to prove our spiritual stamina, for the days ahead will be filled with affliction and difficulty.* But with the assuring comfort of a personal relationship with God, *we will be given a calming courage.* From Divine so near we will receive the quiet assurance (See D&C 121:7-8. *Ensign*, January 1999, p. 5).

Again, the key to our future well-being lies in the Lord's instruction that "If ye are prepared, ye shall not fear" (D&C 38:30). Since we have been "warned and forewarned," and amply counseled concerning how we should prepare, note the following maxim:

*The degree of our preparation will equal the extent of our obedience,
which will determine the measure of our peace of mind.*

NOT WITH FEAR, BUT WITH "URGENT CALM"

There is much in the following pages that speaks of dire circumstances, dramatic hardship, troubling and catastrophic events. This often has been the theme of many of the prophetic utterances of the leadership of the Church since its inception, when speaking of events surrounding the latter days, the second coming of the Savior, and the need for the Saints to be prepared.

Even so, it is not the author's intent to incite readers to feelings of fear and anxiety. Neither do I believe that to be the Lord's intent, nor the intent of the leaders of His church. Fear is not in keeping with the Spirit and design of the Lord. Indeed, the entire premise of the Lord's counsel is that the Saints "need not fear" if only they are prepared. Even back in Biblical times, the Lord's servant *Timothy* wrote that "*God hath not given us the spirit of fear; but of power, and of love, and of a sound mind*" (2 Timothy 1:7).

Thus, rather than creating fear, it seems the Lord's intent is to encourage us to use our "sound minds" to *avoid fear* by making equally sound preparations. Prophets of this dispensation have gone out of their way, when speaking of the need to be prepared, to approach the task rationally without being motivated by fear. Elder *Neal A. Maxwell*, for example, urged us to "*ponder signs without becoming paranoid*, to be aware without frantically matching current events with expectations, using energy that should be spent in other ways . . ." (*For the Power Is In Them*, p. 20)

Likewise, in a recent conference talk, President *Gordon B. Hinckley* used quiet, firm, caution not to unduly excite the Saints as he spoke about issues of finance, the history of the Great Depression, etc., when he noted: "Now, brethren, I want to make it clear that *I am not prophesying,* that *I am not predicting* years of famine in the future. But I am suggesting that the *time has come to get our houses in order.*" He closed his talk with this quiet but firm exhortation: "That's all I have to say about it, but I wish to say it with *all the emphasis of which I am capable*" (*Ensign*, November 1998, p. 53).

I would herein to propose that we approach this important subject with an attitude of "urgent calm." As Elder *Neal A. Maxwell* has put it so well, when speaking of the signs of the times, "Thus *what I have said is not said to alarm* at all, but, rather, so that we might be *noticing and preparing*" (*Ensign*, May 1988, p. 8).

THE "FOOD STORAGE WINDOW IN TIME" MAY BE FAST CLOSING

As you read further you will see that this is truly a day of preparation. Time is short, perhaps much shorter than any of us are willing to acknowledge. The Church of Jesus Christ of Latter-day Saints is a worldwide church, and if you look carefully at conditions in the world today you will find that for some Saints, in some nations, the "moment in time" regarding food storage preparation may well have already past.

For the rest of us, the "window" of *our* "significant moment in time," the opportunity for us to obtain our food storage, may well be fast closing. No one knows the exact time when this window will close for each individual or family. What we do know is, a regret will not feed us or our families if we are unprepared.

But I would also emphasize that I do not believe it to be the Lord's intent for us to be ever preparing for a day of need that never comes. Rather, we should be carefully preparing for a day of need that for many will indeed come, and that by so doing we may secure a much greater sense of peace, happiness and safety for ourselves and those we love.

If in the brief period of our lives we are never personally called upon to use our food storage, let us find satisfaction in that special blessing and rejoice in the fact that, regardless of the outcome, we have been ever willing to be obedient.

CHAPTER

4

SOME INSIGHTS ON FOLLOWING A PROPHET

Where there is no vision, the people perish (Proverbs 29:18).

Of all of Heavenly Father's creations, man is the only one that struggles to know the future. But generally speaking, individuals seek to know the future only so long as it conforms to their desires. Therefore, when true prophets give counsel contrary to the wishes of the recipients, many elect to ignore it, while others turn away in ridicule or rebellion. The call then, is for us to listen better, to take heed, and then to act.

President *J. Reuben Clark* noted that what is needed is a people that is willing to listen. He said, "What we need today is not more prophets. We have the prophets. But *what we need is more people with listening ears.* This is the great need of our generation" (*Conference Report*, October 1948, p. 82).

President *Harold B. Lee* elaborated on a similar idea, stating that the Brethren's comments on how to prepare and be ready should be regarded as the Lord's words:

Brothers and sisters, this is the day the Lord is speaking of. You see the signs are here. Be ye therefore ready. *The Brethren have told you in this conference how to prepare to be ready.*

Let us not turn a deaf ear now, but *listen to these as the words that have come from the Lord, inspired of him, and we will be safe on Zion's hill,* until all that the Lord has for his children shall be accomplished (*Ensign*, January 1974, p. 129).

THE PURPOSE OF PROPHECY

It cannot be emphasized enough that the purpose of prophecy is to affect our understanding, our testimony, and most importantly, our behavior. President *Joseph Fielding Smith* reviewed some prophetic statements regarding our day and then added that it was our duty to read and understand them:

Is not our duty to read these things and understand them? Don't you think the Lord has given us these things that we might know and *we might prepare ourselves through humility, through repentance, through faith, that we might escape from these dreadful conditions* that are portrayed by these ancient prophets? . . . I feel just as keenly as you do about the conditions, and I pray for it to come to an end, but I want it to come to an end right (*The Signs of the Times*, p. 155).

President *Joseph Fielding Smith* also taught that the Brethren repeatedly counsel the way that will offer protection, if the Saints are willing to be obedient:

> We hear occasionally somebody make the statement that things are as bad as they could be, that they could not be worse.
>
> I want to tell you *they could be worse, a great deal worse.* If I read the signs of the times, *we have not suffered yet as much as we are going to suffer, unless we repent.*
>
> From this stand men have prophesied in the name of the Lord for many decades. President Brigham Young, President John Taylor, President Wilford Woodruff, and others of our leading brethren and presidents of the Church, have raised the warning voice. They have called attention to these present conditions. The Lord has also prophesied of these things, and they have been mentioned by ancient seers and prophets. *We have had ample warning. We have been told of the calamities that are coming. We have been taught how we might avoid them, how we might be protected,* if we would only hear the counsels that come to us, heed the testimony of truth. *If we fail we cannot escape . . .*
>
> Do not think we have reached a condition where things could not be worse. *Unless there is repentance they will be worse (Doctrines of Salvation,* vol. III, p. 31).

Elder *Neal A. Maxwell* spoke, in 1988, of the importance of prophecy, and also emphasized one of its essential purposes. He said, "Prophecies are given, in part, that we might know and remember that these things had been made known beforehand, *to the intent that [we] might believe"* (*Ensign,* May 1988, p. 8).

EVALUATING OUR INDIVIDUAL RESPONSES TO THE WORDS OF THE PROPHETS

From the earliest pleadings of the prophets in ancient scriptures to those of our day, one of their greatest concerns has been that we might, after learning the teachings of the Lord through the words of His prophets, yet take no action in our own personal lives. *"For of him unto whom much is given much is required"* (D&C 82:3). They thus seek through persistent counsel to help us avoid condemnation. But President *Harold B. Lee* has cautioned that though the Lord speaks clearly, some still will hear selectively:

> The trouble with us today, *there are too many of us who put question marks instead of periods after what the Lord says.* I want you to think about that. We shouldn't be concerned about why he said something, or whether or not it can be made so. Just *trust the Lord* (*Ensign,* January 1973, p. 108).

Elder *Henry B. Eyring* outlined the processes the Savior uses to counsel through His living prophets, and cautioned about our choices in responding:

> *He calls by more than one means* so that it will reach those willing to accept it. And those means always include sending the message by the mouths of His prophets,

whenever people have qualified to have the prophets of God among them. *Those authorized servants are always charged with warning the people, telling them the way to safety.*

In 1838, a record of the time includes this: "Brother Joseph had sent word by Haun, who owned the mill, to inform the brethren who were living there to leave and come to Far West, but Mr. Haun did not deliver the message."

Later, the Prophet Joseph recorded in his history: "*Up to this day God had given me wisdom to save the people who took counsel.* None had ever been killed who [had abided] by my counsel."

Each of us who listen has heard President Kimball give counsel . . . and then heard President Benson quote him, and we [have] heard President Hinckley quote them both. The Apostle Paul wrote that "*in the mouth of two or three witnesses shall every word be established*" (2 Cor. 13:1). One of the ways we may know that the warning is from the Lord is that *the law of witnesses, authorized witnesses, has been invoked. When the words of prophets seem repetitive, that should rivet our attention* and fill our hearts with gratitude to live in such a blessed time.

Looking for the path to safety in the counsel of prophets makes sense to those with *strong faith.*

When a prophet speaks, those with *little faith* may think that they hear only a wise man giving good advice. Then if his counsel seems comfortable and reasonable, squaring with what they want to do, they take it. If it does not, they consider it either faulty advice or they see their circumstances as justifying their being an exception to the counsel.

Those *without faith* may think that they hear only men seeking to exert influence for some selfish motive.

Another fallacy is to believe that the *choice* to accept or not accept the counsel of prophets is no more than deciding whether to accept good advice and gain its benefits or to stay where we are. *But the choice not to take prophetic counsel changes the very ground upon which we stand. It becomes more dangerous. The failure to take prophetic counsel lessens our power to take inspired counsel in the future.* The best time to have decided to help Noah build the Ark was *the first time he asked.*

Every time in my life when I have chosen to delay following inspired counsel or decided that I was an exception, I came to know that I had put myself in harm's way. *Every time that I have listened to the counsel of prophets, felt it confirmed in prayer, and then followed it, I have found that I moved toward safety.*

We are blessed to live in a time when the priesthood keys are on the earth. We are blessed to know where to look and how to listen for the voice that will fulfill the promise of the Lord that He will gather us to safety (*Ensign*, May, 1997, pp. 24-25).

President *Spencer W. Kimball* cautioned about rejecting a prophet because of undue familiarity:

The trouble with rejection because of personal familiarity with the prophets is that the prophets are always somebody's son or somebody's neighbor. They are chosen from among the people, not transported from another planet, dramatic as that would be! (*Ensign*, May 1978, p. 77).

Before us lies a new era, one never before trod by man, an era fraught with great difficulties which will require considerable courage on our part and the guiding light of a prophet of God combined with the whisperings of the Spirit. Each of us continually has a choice. If we follow the prophet we have the assurance that the Lord is with us and will indeed bless us, but if we elect to follow our own way, or the ways of the world, we do so at great personal and family risk.

There is an old saying that goes something like this: "To decide not to decide is to decide." One can fail to follow a prophet by deciding not to obey, but more often the disobedient merely postpone their decision. In either case, a decision has been made.

As you read on you will become further acquainted with the "mind and will of the Lord" through many prophets who will speak to you "repetitively" on the subject of food storage. As you move forward in your reading you will become aware you cannot escape accountability for what has been made known to you. The Lord is not a "doom and gloomer," yet what he shares with us is true and will be fulfilled regardless of our feelings about it.

This is indeed a day of warning, a day of repentance, and a day of preparation. The Millennial Era is upon us. Hopefully, by the time the tumultuous events ushering in the Lord's coming begin to more fully unfold, each of us will have our houses in order.

Hopefully, we shall avoid the attitudes manifested by the Book of Mormon people just prior to the Savior's birth:

> . . . the *people began to harden their hearts*, all save it were the most believing part of them, . . . and *began to depend upon their own strength and upon their own wisdom*. . . . And *they began to reason and to contend among themselves*, saying: That it is not reasonable that such a being as a Christ shall come (Hel. 16:15, 17-18).

Then the scriptures conclude: "Satan did get great hold upon the hearts of the people upon all the face of the land" (Hel. 16:23).

Now there are many who would count themselves amongst the "most believing part" but have yet to "follow the prophets" in such a simple and understandable thing as planning and acquiring their food storage. Should you wish to determine where you really stand, among the pertinent questions to ask yourself are: (1) Am I a full tithe payer, and (2) do I have my food storage preparations complete? As with the Word of Wisdom, the above two questions are simple principles—"adapted to the capacity of the weak and the weakest of all saints, who are or can be called saints" (D&C 89:3). Yet if we can't give an unqualified "yes" response to both of them, we should feel deep concern. Remember, *just as tithing is "fire insurance"* (D&C 64:23), *food storage is "famine insurance."*

RECEIVING THE COUNSEL OF THE PROPHETS

It is critical that the Saints read, take into their hearts, and make a part of their family plans the counsel of the prophets. The Lord expects that we will familiarize ourselves with His word, and then take the appropriate steps to be in compliance with His will and design. The following comments made by prophets of God illustrate this point more fully. For instance, President *Harold B. Lee* emphasized that we need to attend conferences or at least read the conference addresses of the Brethren:

> A man came in to see me and said that he had heard that some man appeared mysteriously to a group of temple workers and told them, "You had better hurry up and store a year, or two, or three, because there will come a season when there won't be any production." He asked me what I thought about it, and I said, "Well, were you in the April conference of 1936?" He replied, "No, I couldn't be there." And I said, "Well, you surely read the report of what was said by the Brethren in that conference?" No, he hadn't. "Well," I said, "at that conference the Lord did give a revelation about the storage of food. *How in the world is the Lord going to get over to you what He wants you to do if you are not there when He says it, and you do not take the time to read it after it has been said?* (*Stand Ye in Holy Places*, p. 159).

Lest there should be any confusion, modern prophets continue to speak with ever greater clarity regarding the Lord's wishes that His people become prepared with an understanding of gardening and with having secured unto themselves an appropriate storage of food. In recent years He has even come to portend the outcome that may befall those who do not become so prepared. For instance, President *Ezra Taft Benson* further emphasized his counsel regarding food storage with a clear, unmistakable comparison:

> *The revelation to produce and store food may be as essential to our temporal welfare today as boarding the ark was to the people in the days of Noah* (*Ensign*, November 1980, p. 33).

At the time the prophet spoke these words, it seemed that many responded to his admonition, but there were still a sizeable number that seemingly paid but little attention. Yet, what more could the prophet have said? The comparison between boarding the ark and gathering food storage is beyond plain. One would do well to ask himself, "What actually happened to those who did not board the ark? Was their day of accounting hard to understand? Was their decision to consistently ignore Noah's prophetic warnings, apparently so casually made, equally "casual" in its ultimate consequences?

We are readily able to recall and visualize the results experienced by those who failed to follow Noah's counsel because we are so well versed with the outcome of this particularly famous biblical story. But what of the coming scenarios in which the prophets have described the outcome but we do not know specifically the role we shall play in them? Is there a way for those of us who desire to be obedient to enter into the "Ark," so to speak, and move ourselves to safety?

Elder *Richard G. Scott* [1989] noted that the Lord has not left us alone; if we prayerfully seek his direction answers do come to us, and he explained how they may come:

> Most often what we have chosen to do is right. *He [Heavenly Father] will confirm the correctness of our choices His way.* That confirmation generally comes *through packets of help found along the way.* We discover them by *being spiritually sensitive.* They are like notes from a loving Father as evidence of His approval. *If, in trust, we begin something which is not right, He will let us know before we have gone too far.* We sense that help by recognizing troubled or uneasy feeling (*Ensign*, November 1989, p. 32).

There are those who may contend, as did Laman and Lemuel of old, ". . . the Lord maketh no such thing known unto us" (1 Nephi 15:9). To these, the prophet *Brigham Young* offered the following counsel:

> *If I ask him [the Lord] to give me wisdom concerning any requirement in life*, or in regard to my own course, or that of my friends, my family, my children, or those that I preside over, *and get no answers from him, and then do the very best that my judgment will teach me, he is bound to own and honor that transaction, and he will do so to all intents and purposes* (*Discourses of Brigham Young*, p. 43).

It is clear that food storage is not just a matter of "accepting good advice." Rather, it is a matter of whether we are going to exercise "wisdom" and "strong faith" or whether we are going to seek ways to make ourselves exceptions to the revealed will of the Lord. Such tendencies, particularly as relevant to food storage, were spoken of by President *Spencer W. Kimball* when he noted the following:

> *We encourage families to have on hand this year's supply; and we say it over and over and over and repeat over and over* the scripture of the Lord where he says, 'Why call ye me, Lord, Lord, and do not the things which I say?' (Luke 6:46) How empty it is as they put their spirituality, so-called, into action and call him by his important names, but *fail to do the things which he says* (*The Teachings of Spencer W. Kimball*, p. 375).

Elder *Neal A. Maxwell* adds this thought regarding intentional disobedience to the counsel given by the prophets, and uses food storage and debt in illustration:

> *Disobedience to the counsel of prophets, of course, is often a cumulative thing—a cumulative failure to listen to counsel.* This failure may be spread over many years,

rather than sudden disobedience to a single declaration. We cannot, [when] offered so many opportunities to do so, get oil for our lamps at the last minute. *Nor can most of us suddenly acquire a year's supply of food, nor can we break free of debt in a moment—especially when it has taken us years to get so deeply in debt* (*All These Things Shall Give Thee Experience*, p. 117).

NOT A MATTER OF CHOICE WITHOUT CONSEQUENCES

Adherence to the Lord's Food Storage Program is not one of those matters of "choice" that comes without consequence; it was not created by some group that felt it merely "a good idea." This program came by revelation from the Lord, through his prophets, with the intent that we should be obedient and prepare ourselves as counseled. To ignore this counsel is to personally assume responsibility for the ultimate outcome.

I'm sure it is also a major part of the obedience process to "watch and be ready." This, then, is one of the few very tangible ways in which we can demonstrate our faith before the Lord—that we are willing to be in a constant state of preparation to welcome the Savior in His ultimate return to the face of this earth.

As members, we come to assume that because the Lord's directive has been given so many times, and over the course of so many years, perhaps its real efficacy and value can be cast into doubt. To such thinking, however, the prophets and apostles offer important caution and concern. As Elder **Henry B. Eyring** noted, "When the words of prophets seem repetitive, that should rivet our attention and fill our hearts with gratitude to live in such a blessed time" (*Ensign*, May, 1997, p. 25).

Thus, while the teaching to store reserve foods has a long and "repetitive" history, its importance has never diminished in the eyes of the Lord, and should be an occasion for us to express "gratitude" rather than disbelief or merely tune out the counsel of the Lord.

RECENT DISASTERS HAVE PRE-TESTED THE FOOD STORAGE PLAN

Early on in the Church, the Brethren began teaching the necessity of self-reliance. They clearly taught that there would be times of plenty, even to excess, and then there also would be times when food production would be scarce and, eventually, even times of serious famine. That extended repetition over time portends even greater importance, need, and concern today. It would seem that the past 150 years has been something akin to a schooling, a preparatory time leading to the far more demanding "final exam"—the tumultuous pre-millennium era and the ushering in of the scriptural millennium. President **Harold B. Lee** spoke of this idea definitively:

During the last eleven years, there have been *occasional "dress rehearsals" in the Welfare Program with floods and disasters, wars and overwhelming destructions,* all no doubt, looking to a day when *greater problems confronting this people may demand greater abilities and facilities to meet them* (*Church News*, December 20, 1947, p. 7).

Over the years, many who have been obedient and put up a supply of emergency food have been blessed in very real ways. Individuals, families and communities have experienced traumatic events where the food and water which had been stored met essential, even life-threatening needs. Again, these scattered events seem much like the process of pre-testing a program destined to fill a much greater need in the future. It is as though the Lord has been preparing his Saints by giving mini-classes as a means of teaching us the very real value of, and need for, being prepared.

The Lord and his prophets over many generations have focused considerable attention on the events leading up to the Millennium. They have described in detail the great turmoil and tribulation that will occur during that time. Realizing that only a prepared people will be able to safely survive the events that will unfold, we have been given instructions, preparatory experiences, opportunity and—with some sacrifice—the financial means necessary to become a prepared people.

THE LORD WILL EVENTUALLY LEAVE HIS PEOPLE WITHOUT EXCUSE

In all of this the Lord will eventually leave His people without excuse. The destruction of the wicked and the cleansing of the earth cannot be a casual event; we know from prophecy that it will consist of many terribly tumultuous events. Neither can it be postponed, modified or altered to meet the needs of those who may have elected to ignore the counsel to be prepared. The fact is, all the events planned in the pre-mortal council for this world's transition from a telestial to a terrestrial state will unfold on schedule, exactly as outlined, regardless of their effects on those volitionally unprepared, however regrettable that lack of preparation may be.

Obviously, this is not an exercise in fun and games, it is serious business! For many, how they respond to the Lord's counsel may be the difference between life and death for them and their family. It makes little difference if we do not want to participate, if we disagree with what will take place, or for that matter if we decide not to believe that the prophesied events will ever occur. Whether we like it or not, we are all involved.

However, because we have a loving and caring Heavenly Father who knows in exact detail what will take place for each of his children both collectively and individually, he has told us how and when to prepare—even in proportional detail. Even so, because our Heavenly Father always honors agency, he will not force his children to prepare for what he has told them will most assuredly occur. On the other hand, because he loves us he has clearly and consistently instructed us regarding the means whereby we might "escape."

We again find ourselves back at the point clearly stated by Elder Henry B. Eyring, we will either be found amongst those manifesting "strong faith," "little faith," "without faith," or believing that it really is nothing more than a "choice to accept or not accept the counsel of prophets." Regarding this, the Lord has been explicitly clear concerning where he stands and who we should follow:

> What I the Lord have spoken, I have spoken, and I excuse not myself; and though the heavens and the earth pass away, *my word shall not pass away, but shall all be fulfilled, whether by mine own voice or by the voice of my servants, it is the same* (D&C 1:38).

With the Lord there is no equivocation on what is expected of us. As you read the following counsel given by many prophets, you will find that they have clearly and plainly outlined exactly what the Lord expects us to do. In this matter the prophets' words have been "repetitive" and, indeed, demand that our attention be "riveted" on the prophetic counsel that has been so consistently given by the First Presidency and the Quorum of Twelve Apostles and the many others who have filled these offices before them.

CHAPTER
5
LESSONS FROM CHURCH HISTORY
ON PREPAREDNESS AND OBEDIENCE

In March, 1829, the Lord set the direction that his prophets have consistently followed to this day. They are to warn the people whereby they might repent and prepare for those things which will surely come. Equally surely, should we refuse to follow His counsel, the Lord is prepared to eventually require our complete destruction:

> For a desolating scourge shall go forth among the inhabitants of the earth, and shall continue to be poured out from time to time, it they repent not, until the earth is empty, and the inhabitants thereof are consumed away and utterly destroyed by the brightness of my coming (D&C 5:19).

THE EXPULSION OF THE SAINTS FROM NAUVOO; THE JOURNEY WESTWARD BEGINS

There are lessons to be learned from the experiences of the early Mormon pioneers. Consider the heart-wrenching experiences of the Saints who were expelled from Nauvoo, Illinois by anti-Mormon mobs in the frigid temperatures of mid-winter, 1846. For months they had known that expulsion was coming in the spring, and they had been given detailed instructions from the Brethren as to what food supplies and other equipment they were to accumulated in preparation for their departure. Many of the Saints were not fully prepared when the exodus began, and those unprepared were counseled to wait. Elder Willard Richards described the circumstances on February 19th of that year of those who had left and were camped on the west bank of the Mississippi River. It was a terrible winter day. The wind blew steadily from the northwest accompanied by a wet snow that fell to the depth of about eight inches. The storm raged all day. Elder Willard Richards recorded in his journal,

> The evening was very cold, which caused *much suffering in the camp*, for there were many who had no tents or any comfortable place to lodge: many tents were blown down, some of them were unfinished and had no ends.
>
> Friday it became even colder. Ice formed on the edges of the Mississippi River and considerable ice floated on the river. The apostles voted to buy 300 bushels of corn to feed the hungry in the camp as *many Saints had left Nauvoo without taking enough*

food as they had been instructed. Already the corn, potatoes, turnips and other veg-etables and grain that had been part of the "tithing" had been consumed by the camp. Food shortages became a pressing concern (*Church News*, March 2, 1996, p. 11).

With their sudden expulsion, weeks before the agreed-upon date, most of the Saints did not have all of the food and supplies they were supposed to have accumulated in preparation for their journey. The following is what each family had been instructed to acquire, as an "18 month supply of food" for five people:

One good strong wagon well covered with a light box; two or three good yoke of oxen between the age of four and ten years; two or more milch cows; one or more good beefs; three sheep if they can be obtained; one thousand pounds of flour or other bread stuffs in good sacks; one good musket or rifle to each male over the age of twelve years; one pound powder; four pounds lead; one pound tea; five pounds coffee; one hundred pounds sugar; one pound cayenne pepper; two pounds black pepper; one-half pound mustard; ten pounds rice for each family; one pound cinnamon; one-half pound cloves; one dozen nutmegs; twenty-five pounds salt; five pounds saleratus; ten pounds dried apples; one bushel of beans; a few pounds of dried beef or bacon; five pounds dried peaches; twenty pounds dried pumpkin; twenty-five pounds of seed grain; one gallon alcohol; twenty pounds of soap for each family; four or five fish hooks and lines; fifteen pounds of iron and steel; a few pounds of wrought nails; one or more sets of saw or grist mill irons to a company of one hundred families; one good seine and hooks for each company; two sets of pulley blocks and ropes to each company for crossing rivers; from twenty-five to one hundred pounds of farming and mechanical tools; cooking utensils to consist of bake kettle, frying pan . . . plates, knives, forks, spoons and pans as [few] as will do; a good tent and furniture to each two families; clothing and bedding to each family, not to exceed five hundred pounds; ten extra teams for each company of one hundred families (*Ensign to the Nations*, p. 7).

Nine months later, after most of the Saints had finally left Nauvoo, crossed the Mississippi, and started to wend their way west, the anti-Mormon mobs rose up once again and expelled the final stragglers who were still in Nauvoo, doing so in October, 1846. These Saints who had remained behind in Nauvoo, after the main body of Saints had moved west, were mainly the elderly, the handicapped, and women and children who were either physically unable to travel or lacked the means to purchase wagons and animals, or to provide for themselves in the wilderness. President **Brigham Young** describes what those late-departing Saints had to endure, saying, "There remained behind a few of the very poor, the sick and the aged, who *suffered again from the violence of the mob; they were whipped and beaten, and had their houses burned*" (*Discourses of Brigham Young*, pp. 473-74).

It was this group, the last remnant, that was driven out of Nauvoo by the mob in their final effort to obtain the remaining property of the Saints. This group of poverty-stricken Saints found themselves on the west bank of the Mississippi River late in the fall of the year, subjected to storms, without adequate shelters to protect them from the elements and without food to eat.

President *Brigham Young* described the struggle almost all the Saints experienced as they tried to move westward because they lacked the necessary food and supplies to sustain themselves:

> *We were migrating, we knew not whither, except that it was our intention to go beyond the reach of our enemies.* We had no home, save our wagons and tents, and *no stores of provisions and clothing;* but had to earn our daily bread by leaving our families in isolated locations for safety, and going among our enemies to labor (*Discourses of Brigham Young*, p. 478).

SURVIVING IN THE SALT LAKE VALLEY, 1848

The last part of the journey and settling into the Valley itself was a pure exercise in faith since there was no external access to food—they either had sufficient with them or, of necessity, grew it if they were to stave off starvation. President *Brigham Young* made this observation as he commented on the status of the Saints as they entered the Great Salt Lake Valley:

> [When] we arrived here . . . we found a few . . . Indians, a few wolves and rabbits, and any amount of crickets; but as for a green tree or a fruit tree, or any green field, we found nothing of the kind, with the exceptions of a few cottonwoods and willows on the edge of City Creek. For some 1200 or 1300 miles we carried every particle of provision we had when we arrived here. When we left our homes we picked up what the mob did not steal of our horses, oxen and calves, and some women drove their own teams here. *Instead of 365 pounds of breadstuff when they started from the Missouri river, there was not half of them had half of it.*
>
> We had to bring our seed grain, our farming utensils, bureaus, secretaries [desks], sideboards, sofas, pianos, large looking glasses, fine chairs, carpets, nice shovels and tongs and other fine furniture, with all the parlor, cook stoves, etc., and we had to bring these things piled together with some women and children, helter skelter, topsy-turvy, with broken-down horses, . . . oxen with three legs, and cows with one teat. This was our only means of transportation, and if we had not brought our goods in this manner we would not have had them, for there was nothing here (*Discourses of Brigham Young*, p. 480).

President Young later continued:

> [The Saints] picked up a few buckskins, antelope skins, sheep skins, buffalo skins, and made leggings and moccasins of them, and wrapped the buffalo robes around them. *Some had blankets and some had not; some had shirts, and I guess some had not. One man told me that he had not a shirt for himself or family.* I will venture to

say that not one in four out of my family had shoes to their feet when we came to this valley (*Discourses of Brigham Young*, pp. 475-76).

After the Saints had settled into their new homes, they immediately began the task of plowing and planting because their very lives depended upon raising sufficient food to sustain them.

The season was so far advanced when the pioneers arrived in the summer of 1847 that little resulted from the planting, except to obtain some seed potatoes. Their salvation depended on the success of their crops in 1848. They had built three saw mills in the mountains and one grist mill. Their planted fields consisted of five thousand one hundred and thirty-three acres, of which nearly nine hundred acres were planted in winter wheat (*Essentials In Church History*, p. 467).

In May, 1848, the pioneers were gaunt, malnourished and hungry to the point that they "could eat anything!" Pioneer doctor Priddy Meeks described the winter of 1847-48 for the Meeks family:

My family went several months without a satisfying meal of vittals. I went sometimes a mile up Jordan to a patch of wild roses to get the berries to eat, which I would eat as rapid as a hog, stems and all. I shot *hawks* and *crows* and they eat well. I would go and search the mire hole and find *cattle dead*, and would fleace off what meat I could and eat it. We used *wolf* meat, which I thought was good. I made some wooden spades to dig *seagoes* with, but we could not suply our wants. . . . I would take a grubing hoe and sack and start by sunrise in the morning and go, I thought six miles, before coming to where the *thisel roots* grew, and in time to get home I would have bulshel and sometimes more. . . . I would dig until I grew weak and faint, and sit down and eat a root and then begin again (*Journal of Priddy Meeks*, p. 17, spelling as in original. See *Church News*, May 16, 1998).

In the months of May and June they were menaced by a danger as devastating as any from the persecution of mobs, when myriads of crickets came down the mountain sides into the valley. The first mention of crickets coming in hordes was made in the spring of 1848 by John Taylor, who wrote on May 22 of their arrival. The pests evidently continued their crop destruction through most of June. It is recorded that the first gulls came early in June, and returned each day for about three weeks (*Journal History*, June 21, 1848).

Like a vast army marshaled for battle, the ravenous insects began to methodically destroy the fields. They passed rapidly from one field to another, and in a few moments could leave that field as barren as a desert waste. Something had to be done, or the inhabitants must perish. The community was aroused, and every soul entered the unequal conflict. Trenches were dug around the fields and filled with water in the hope of stopping the invaders, but without result. Fire was equally unavailing. An attempt was made to beat them back with clubs, brooms and other improvised weapons, but nothing that man could do was able to stop the steady onward march of the voracious insects. The settlers were helpless before them.

Another historical account summarized the coming of the gulls in this way:

> When all seemed lost, and the Saints were giving up in despair, the heavens became clouded with gulls, which hovered over the fields, uttering their plaintive scream. Was this a new evil come upon them? Such were the thoughts of some who expected that what the crickets left the gulls would destroy; but not so, the gulls in countless battalions descended and begin to devour the crickets, waging a battle for the preservation of the crops. They ate, they gorged upon the pest, and then flying to the streams would drink and vomit and again return to the battle front. This took place day by day until the crickets were destroyed (*Essentials In Church History*, p. 468).

In 1848 the sea gulls saved several thousand Saints who would have likely perished from famine had they not come and eaten the crickets and grasshoppers, and they were to reduce their suffering on a number of occasions thereafter. As one pioneer recorded in her journal:

> The pioneers had no further trouble with crickets that year. The sea gulls also fought *marauding plagues of crickets in 1849*, and in succeeding years and in other places. The pioneers noted that *crops were lost to crickets in 1851*, but that the *sea gulls did come again in 1852 and destroyed the insects* (*Zera Pulsipher Autobiography*, p. 4, see *Church News*, May 16, 1998).

As we see from the above account, the Saints were blessed with "miracles" only after they had done all that they could do for themselves, or when they were clearly unable to do for themselves. If we carry this principle forward and apply it to our own lives, we learn that the Lord will most likely leave his people to fend for themselves if they have been counseled to prepare and have elected not to obey. President **Brigham Young** taught,

> While we have a rich soil in this valley, and seed to put in the ground, *we need not ask God to feed us, nor follow us round with a loaf of bread begging of us to eat it. He will not do it, neither would I, were I the Lord.* We can feed ourselves here; and *if we are ever placed in circumstances where we cannot, it will then be time enough for the Lord to work a miracle to sustain us* (*Discourses of Brigham Young*, p. 294).

By the early 1850's the Saints had learned enough about the climate and systems of irrigation to produce food sufficient for their needs, and at times they were blessed with some excess. But they were still subjected to excessively dry weather and insect infestations which would greatly limit food production periodically. Because of these eventualities, they were consistently counseled to store food for times of emergencies—a counsel that has persisted to this day.

Hardships During the Expansion into Other Mormon Settlements

It is difficult for some of the affluent and sophisticated Saints of today to visualize how hard life can be when one must be completely self-reliant and must literally struggle to survive. Perhaps the following comments recorded by two Utah pioneers, James Brown and Charles W. Nibley, can convey an understanding of just how difficult that process of living is at this level.

James Brown, a member of the Mormon Battalion, returned to Utah with sufficient gold to purchase Ogden Valley, and in 1948 located a settlement there called Brownsville (now called Ogden). He offered this observation regarding conditions in 1855:

> It will be remembered by the early residents of Utah that *the year 1855 was a grasshopper year, as well as a season of great drought,* and therefore *one of the hardest years that many of the people had ever experienced,* both for man and beast. *Hundreds of horses and cattle starved to death, and many of the people barely escaped the same sad fate.* I could do no better than to let my horses go out on the range to die of starvation and cold, and turn my hand to anything I could get to do to earn a honest dollar (*Pioneer Stories,* p. 66).

In spite of these hardships, the Saints were yet reluctant (even as we are today) to heed the counsel of their leaders to store food in sufficient quantities to reduce the burdens of famine or times of personal difficulty. And this in spite of the fact that they were, by and large, faithful in the gospel and attentive to their leaders. One can see the necessity of a "schooling" process intended to lead to greater preparedness in our day.

Charles W. Nibley related how the Saints survived in Cache Valley during the winter of 1860. When he was about 10 years old, his family arrived in Cache Valley in September to find only a few families living in log cabins. They immediately set about to obtain land, for which they traded their heating and cooking stove. They built a log cabin, gathered the winter's wood, built a corral for the cattle and got what grass they could to feed their cattle during the winter.

> I recollect that the very first day after we arrived and got our camp permanently pitched, my mother . . . took me with her into the adjoining field to glean wheat. . . . We two gleaned close to one-half bushel of wheat a day.
>
> *Our breakfasts were of the scantiest kind, a little wheat porridge without much milk and a little of the brown or black bread without butter.* In the morning I was furnished a piece of bread for my dinner, as I would start off on the hills with the cows, but my dinner was devoured before I got half a mile away from our camp and *I had to go hungry until evening.* . . . I can remember that when I was very hungry at din-

ner time, about the only thing I could do to help my stomach was to tighten my rope [his belt].

There was not a window of any kind whatever in our house. Neither was there a door. *My mother hung up an old quilt or piece of an old quilt, which served as a door for the first winter.*

It was a scramble of the severest kind for a mere existence. How to begin at the very beginning of things and make the earth produce your food and shelter was such a new experience and such a severe one that the older folks never forgot it.

Somehow we managed to trade for some wheat and we built a little bin with some boards in one corner of the [12' x 16'] dugout and put our wheat in this bin and on the wheat made our beds. Wheat is about the hardest stuff to sleep on that I have ever experienced.

My mother used to go out and do a day's washing here and there and *take flour for her pay. Usually 12½ pounds of flour was payment in full for a hard day's washing.* . . . It helped to keep us eating and that was the main struggle just at that time.

Eggs and butter were the chief currency of the country. There was no such thing as money. I don't think we saw a dollar in money in the first two years we were in Cache Valley. *Wheat was $2.00 a bushel and it was considered that a bushel of wheat was payment for a good day's work. ".* . . Mother was extra thrifty and the eggs and most of what little butter was made, had to be kept to exchange for a little thread or a little calico or perhaps a pair of shoes when some peddler wagon should come along. (*Pioneer Stories*, pp. 87-98).

COUNSEL ON FOOD STORAGE DURING THE PIONEER ERA

The early years spent settling in the Utah valleys taught the Saints much about what was required to secure economic and food security when times of change in the elements and circumstances arose. These lessons were not lost on the leadership of the Church, who regularly counseled the membership regarding storing food stuffs, the value of what was produced, and building a practical storehouse:

In March, 1856, President *Heber C. Kimball* cautioned the Church that the Saints must do more than live from hand to mouth:

Take this people as a people, throughout the valleys of the mountains, and I presume that they are the best people upon the face of the earth, and *even here there is hardly a person but what takes a course to live from hand to mouth, that is, they will never lay up anything.* This course will not answer for us, *we must lay up grain against famines that will prevail upon the earth* (*Journal of Discourses*, vol. 3, p. 227).

That same year President *Brigham Young* offered similar comment:

We never ought to be without three or five years provisions on hand. But when you see men run to hell to sell a bushel of wheat for sixty cents, instead of laying it up in their granaries for a day of scarcity, you are forced to conclude that they would trade with the very devil, to get his coat and shoes in exchange for their wheat. I hope they will learn wisdom in the future (*Journal of Discourses*, vol. 3, p. 196).

On April 6, 1857, President **Brigham Young** gave this counsel to the members attending conference:

I will now present a subject which will be a text for the brethren to preach upon from this stand, viz., *the necessity of building store houses in which to preserve our grain. . . . until they [the members] have enough to last them seven years. You can fig-ure at that, and learn how much grain you ought to lay up.* If we have, as I believe we shall, a few seasons fruitful in grain, the staple article that we can cure and pre-serve, *it is our indispensable duty to safely store it for a time to come* (*Journal of Discourses*, vol. 4, p. 307).

Elder **Orson Hyde**, in 1857, also observed that when they had a plentiful food supply it was taken lightly, and he commented that the Saints were ill prepared for a time of scarcity:

We have been told to store up our grain and to take care of it. The history of the past forms ample ground for advice of this kind. We have not only seen, but felt the folly of placing too low an estimate upon the productions of the earth. When they were plentiful, they have been thought of little value. We have found ourselves *com-paratively destitute* at times, in consequence, and, in the time of this scarcity, have suf-fered in our feelings—*have been pinched with hunger*; and it *does seem that the subject of laying up our grain has been presented under circumstances that cannot fail to impress every heart with its importance* (*Journal of Discourses*, vol. 5, p. 14).

Heber C. Kimball, in the same conference, [April 6, 1857] admonished the Saints to build solid storehouses and to stock them well:

Every man who has a farm needs a storehouse—one made of rock and lime, that will guard your grain against the mice, rats and all other four-legged vermin; also against the two-legged ones. I have more fears of the two-legged one than I have of the four-legged ones.

Plan to build a good storehouse, every man who has a farm, and never cease until you have accomplished it. And do not forget to pay your tithing before you put the grain into the storehouse. *Lay up enough for seven years, at a calculation for from five to ten in each family; and then calculate that there will be in your families from five to ten persons to where you now have one, because you are on the increase.*

Where a family now requires only a hundred bushels a year, let the head of that family lay up a hundred bushels the first year, two hundred the next, and increase the amount every year in proportion to their probable requirements.

When we have stored away our grain we are safe, independent of the world, in case of famine, are we not? Yes, we are; for, in that case, we will have the means for subsistence in our hands. *When the famines begin upon the earth, we shall be very apt to feel them first.*

If Judgement must need begin at the house of God, and if the righteous scarcely are saved, how will it be with the wicked? *Am I looking for famines? Yes, the most terrible and severe that have ever come upon the nations of the earth.* These things are right before us, and some of this people are not thinking anything about them; they do not enter their hearts.

Be wise, listen to counsel, and obey the voice of the head, and you will prosper and never want for bread; but as the Lord liveth, you will feel it, if you do not continue in the line of duty.

There are a great many things that we can save and take care of, as well as we can *wheat, barley,* and *oats.* We can dry *pumpkins, squashes, currants, apples, peaches,* etc., and save them; we can also save *beans, peas,* and like articles, and *keep them for seven years.* And if you will take the right care of your wheat, you can save it just as long as you may wish to (*Journal of Discourses*, vol. 5, pp. 20-21).

Lessons were also learned, during this period, about the spiritual impact of terrestrial concerns and the need of food to improve our telestial conditions. President **Brigham Young**, in 1860, suggested that the failure to adequately provide for temporal needs, such as food, could compromise the acquisition of "heavenly things."

I wish to ask the strong-minded men—the talented men . . . *How many of you have had wisdom enough to procure and lay up for yourselves produce enough to last until harvest?* You may call this a small matter. *How many of you have wheat or flour to last you a year?* If you are without bread, how much wisdom can you boast, and of what real utility are your talents, if you cannot procure for yourselves and *save against a day of scarcity those substances designed to sustain your natural lives?* . . .

If you have not attained ability to provide for your natural wants, and for a wife and a few children, what have you to do with heavenly things? (*Ensign*, November 1980, p. 33).

That same year, President **Heber C. Kimball** said,

Let it not be said that any portion of the people of this Territory have not wheat enough to last them until harvest. Let them be sure to do one thing, if God permit it—*secure well the coming harvest, and be sure to lay up enough to last one, two, or three years.* . . . It is hard to improve when there is no bread. When a man has no bread, and his neighbours have none, he must have terrible feelings (*Journal of Discourses*, vol. 8, p. 89).

In 1863 President *Brigham Young* complained that when grain was plentiful and of little value it was given for tithe, but when it was scarce and had more value, people sold so much they risked hunger:

> Brother Samuel W. Richards had a good deal to say, this afternoon, about grain. We have talked about it for a long time, and *we have tried to get the people to build store houses to save it.* When grain could not be sold for money the Tithing Office was full of it; but now we have none to hand out to the poor who depend upon us for bread.
>
> *Our granaries are empty, and scarcely grain enough in the Territory to bread our own population* until another harvest, yet some will sell their grain to go out of the country. What a lamentable fact (*Journal of Discourses*, vol. 10, p. 89).

As time progressed, direction from their leaders clearly expanded well beyond the goal of simple survival in a difficult land, to reflect a clear and growing awareness of future events and trials to befall the Saints in later years. Particularly note the following:

In May, 1857 President *Heber C. Kimball* warned of a future time when the United States would be without food:

> We have done first rate; but we can wake up more, and keep waking up, and attend to the things you have been told to attend to; and one of them is, to *lay up stores of corn, wheat, oats, peas, beans, buck wheat, and every thing else that can be preserved;* for you will see a day when you will want it; and *it will be when we shall feel the effects of famine, and when the United States have not any food* (*Journal of Discourses*, vol. 4, p. 330).

A month later President *Heber C. Kimball* again taught that the Saints should prepare a seven-year supply, and warned of a time of trouble which would someday come upon the world:

> Brethren, go and build your storehouses before your grain is harvested, and lay it up, and *let us never cease until we have got a seven year supply.* You may think that we shall not see times in which we shall need it. Do you not comprehend how comfortable it will be for us to know that we *have grain enough to last seven years?*
>
> *Will you be slack, brethren, and let the evil come upon us, when we forewarn you of the future events that are coming?*
>
> We are telling of what the prophets have said—of what the Lord has said to Joseph. Wake up, now, wake up, O Israel, and lay up your grain and your stores. *I tell you that there is trouble coming upon the world* (*Journal of Discourses*, vol. 4, pp. 337, 338).

President *Brigham Young* in June, 1857 admonished the Saints to prepare for that which the prophecies say will surely come:

> Let us go, then, and lay up in our store-houses, *and prepare for the day of famine, of sorrow, and of trouble;* for all those things written in the prophecies, in ancient days

and in this our day, *will surely come upon the inhabitants of the earth* (*Journal of Discourses*, vol. 4, p. 343).

In July, 1857 President **Heber C. Kimball** again instructed the Saints to provide for themselves or else they would become servants:

> *You will also see the day that you will wish you had laid up your grain*, if you do not do it now; for you will see the day, if you do not take care of the blessings God has given to you, that you will become servants, the same as the world will (*Journal of Discourses*, vol. 5, p. 10).

Two years later, in 1859, President **Heber C. Kimball** again warned that if they are not prepared, the Saints will see hard times:

> With regard to *grain*, I will say, If you do not *lay it up and keep it*, you will be sorry in a day to come; for you will see *hard times, trying times, plagues, and famines, and bloodshed.* Be advised and *provide in time, and while you have the opportunity* (*Journal of Discourses*, vol. 7, p. 234).

COUNSEL ON FOOD STORAGE
DURING AND FOLLOWING THE CIVIL WAR

During the U.S. Civil War, 1861-1865, President **Brigham Young** repeatedly counseled the Saints to store food in large quantities. In 1864 he said,

> The clouds are gathering; the *distant thunders can be heard;* the grumblings and mutterings in the distance are audible, and tell of destruction, want and famine. But mark it well, *if* we live according to the Holy Priesthood bestowed upon us, while God bears rule in the midst of these mountains, *I promise you, in the name of Israel's God, that he will give us seed-time and harvest.*
>
> *Let us live our religion, and hearken to the counsel given to us.*
>
> I have no doubt but He [the Lord] will provide for His Saints, but if you do not take his counsel and be industrious and prudent, you will not long continue to be one of His Saints; *sow, plant, buy a half a bushel of wheat here, and a bushel there, and store it up till you get your five or seven years' provisions on hand* (*Journal of Discourses*, vol.10, pp. 292, 294).

Further, the brethren began to re-emphasize that failure to heed the Lord's counsel about these affairs could readily leave the Saints as destitute as any other peoples within the world. Note particularly the following:

In May, 1864, President **Brigham Young** said,

> Now you, my brethren and sisters, who have been in the habit of coming here for the last twelve, or fifteen years, *have you not been told all the time, at least as often as once a month, that the time would come when you would see the necessity of taking counsel and laying up grain?*

We have had a cricket war, a grasshopper war, and a dry season, and now we have a time of need. Many of the inhabitants of this very city, I presume, have not bread-stuffs enough to last them two days; and *I would not be surprised if there are not seven-eights of the inhabitants who have not breadstuffs sufficient to last them two weeks.* Has the Lord stayed the heavens? No. Has He withdrawn His hand? No. . . . He has provided for his Saints.

Then why are we destitute of the staff of life? Comparing the people with their sub-stance, we might say *we have sold ourselves for nought. We have peddled off the grain which God has given us freely, until we have made ourselves destitute.* Has this been told us before? Yes, year after year (*Journal of Discourses*, vol. 10, p. 291).

Commenting on whether this was the end of scarcity *President Young* stated:

Is this the last season we are to have scarcity? I will say I hope it is, but *I cannot say that it is, if the people are not wise.* Some sow their wheat, and after the Lord has given one hundred-fold of an increase, they sell that at one-fourth of its value, and *leave themselves wanting.*

He further indicated that the sisters had neglected the counsel to prepare:

What was told you last harvest? "Sisters, you had better get a chest, or a little box, for there is plenty of wheat to be had—it is not worth a dollar a bushel—and *you had better fill your box with it.*" "Oh, there is plenty of it; there is no necessity for my emp-tying the paper rags out of my box, or my clothes out of the large chest where I have them packed away; my husband can go and get what he wants at the Tithing Store." *They would not get the wheat and flour that was then easy to be obtained, and now they are destitute. Why could they not believe what they were told?* (*Journal of Discourses*, vol. 10, p. 291).

The Prophet felt so strongly about the Saints needing to store food that he not only counseled them to become prepared, but he even provided more explicit instructions on how they might accomplish this:

If you love brother Brigham, brother Heber and the Twelve, do as they tell you. As fast as possible, *secure a year's supply of breadstuff,* and then *try to sustain yourselves without using any of the supply;* and take the same course in the harvest of 1865-6-7, and so on, *until you have a supply for seven years, then you are prepared either for a famine of that duration, or to feed the thousands who will come here hungry* (*Journal of Discourses*, vol. 10, p. 338).

And, all the while, the leadership of the Church continued to regularly impress upon the membership of the Church the need to be prepared, and to warn of the con-sequences of their deliberate failures to heed counsel and become prepared.

Elder *George A. Smith*, in June, 1867 said,

President Kimball has been urging us strongly to store our bins with wheat and flour. This may sound like strange counsel to those who, during most of their lives, have been in the habit of receiving their wages every Saturday, and, then, without further care, laying in their week's provisions. *But in this country, where we are liable to seasons of scarcity, it is requisite to prepare for such emergencies; hence the counsel to store up food is frequently given, and is absolutely necessary.* Yet, as a people, we are apt to neglect it, for the sun rises and sets, the seasons come and go with unfailing regularity, and we expect that every year will bring plenty; yet *we have had years of scarcity, and may have again, and we are not safe unless we provide against them, and be prepared for a day of hunger.* Hence, in this respect and in many others, the Latter-day Saints have many things to learn (*Journal of Discourses*, vol. 12, p. 25).

In August, 1867 President **Brigham Young** again instructed the Saints to prepare for all contingencies and promised them if they did so they would never see a famine:

> So this people *if they will take the counsels which the Lord gives to them through His servants with regard to their grain, and prepare all contingencies* to which they are subject in this mountainous country, *we shall never see a famine;* but if we neglect his counsel, refusing to hearken to good advice, *we shall, by taking this course, bring distress upon ourselves and upon all who depend upon us for a subsistence. Let us pursue a course to preserve ourselves and avert every calamity.* This we can do. *It is not necessary for calamity to come upon us, if we will only take a course to prevent it* (*Journal of Discourses*, vol. 12, p. 121).

Elder **George A. Smith**, in October, 1867, stressed that the Saints need to follow counsel given by the prophet. He used the loss of half their crops that year to grasshoppers as a reminder of the need to follow counsel on the matter:

> A few years ago President Young gave counsel to the people of the Territory—most of whom agreed to it—*to lay by seven year's provisions. We were to have commenced three years ago, and were to have laid up one year's bread over and above the year's supply. The following year we were to add another year's supply, and so have continued until we had our seven years' supply laid up.*
>
> How faithful the people have been in keeping this counsel I am not prepared to say, but I am afraid that *few men in Israel, . . . had three years' bread laid aside when the grasshoppers made their descent this season and swept off half the grain, vegetables, and fruit raised in the Territory.*
>
> A good many of us claim our descent from Joseph who was sold into Egypt. He was the instrument of the Almighty in saving the Egyptians, through the interpretation of the King's dream of the seven fat and the seven lean kine, and the seven full and the seven blighted ears of corn. He prescribed the means by which the storehouses of Egypt were filled with corn, and when the seven years of famine came the whole people were actually saved from death through the wisdom of Joseph in laying up bread.
>
> *We all exercise faith that God may give to our President wisdom and understanding to foresee the evils with which we may be threatened, and to take measures to*

avert them. Suppose that he comes forward and tells us how to prepare, and we neglect his counsel, then the watchman is clear, and we are liable to the dangers and difficulties resulting from disobedience.

. . . those who did not obey Joseph's counsel were under the necessity of selling all their property, and ultimately themselves, for slaves to the king, *in order to obtain that bread which they could have laid up during the seven years of plenty (Journal of Discourses,* vol. 12, pp. 141, 142).

On May 17, 1868 President **Brigham Young** again reaffirmed the 1864 seven-year food-storage plan, saying that "Brother Kimball counseled the people to lay up two year's provisions, and then enough *for four, and for six and for seven years.* I have it now, and I'm dealing it out *(Journal of Discourses,* vol. 12, p. 219).

President **Brigham Young**, speaking on July 25, 1868, told the Saints that there will be no famine for the obedient if we have saved our grain as directed by the spirit:

I have never promised a famine to the Latter-day Saints, if we will do half right. You have never heard it drop from my lips that a famine would come upon this people. *There never will, if we will only do half right,* and we expect to do better than that. There is not another people on the earth whose *faith and works are directed for the accomplishment of good* like the Latter-day Saint. But we do not obey counsel as we should.

We must learn to listen to the whisperings of the Holy Spirit, and the counsels of the servants of God, until we come to the unity of the faith. *If we had obeyed counsel we would have had granaries to-day, and they would have been full of grain; and we would have had wheat and oats and barley for ourselves and our animals, to last us for years.*

The people have also been counseled to take their straw and stack it up, making nice beautiful ricks of it. You may see the day your cattle will want it or perish.

Is the hay kept? No: it must be sold . . . even if there is nothing—comparatively speaking—got for it. Save your hay; save your chaff; save your straw; save your wheat; save your oats; save your barley, and everything that can be saved and *preserved against a day of want.*

Who is deserving of honor or glory from God? Those who have preserved their substance or those who have wasted it? Those who preserved it; for they know how to preserve those things which the Lord places in their hands (Journal of Discourses, vol. 12, pp. 241, 242).

Even as late as 1868 there was pressure on many of the Saints to seek out riches by pursuing the search for gold. *President Young* re-focused the Saints by emphasizing the need to labor in the field to produce food that truly enriches life and then to store it up for future need:

Those among us who are anxious to find rich gold deposits, are equally anxious to destroy themselves, and we are no wiser than our little children are in handling sharp-edged tools. They would not only destroy themselves but all around them if they had the power to do it. Instead of hunting gold, *let every man go to work at raising wheat, oats, barley, corn and vegetable and fruit in abundance, that there may be plenty in the land* (*Journal of Discourses*, vol. 12, pp. 202, 203).

In the mid-1870s President *Wilford Woodruff* spoke out repeatedly on the necessity for adequate food production and to warn that the prophecies on coming famines were yet to be fulfilled. In 1874 he said,

> *There are certain events awaiting the nations of the earth as well as Zion;* and when these events overtake us . . . we will be preserved if we take the counsel that is given us and *unite our time, labor and means, and produce what we need for our own use; but without this we shall not be prepared to sustain ourselves* (*Journal of Discourses*, vol. 17, p. 70).

In 1875 President *Wilford Woodruff* again taught that the time will come when the prophecies will be fulfilled and all will need to be prepared:

> I want to ask you if you ever heard brother Kimball tell about laying up wheat? "Yes," say some "we have heard him, but the famine has not come yet." No, but *it will come. The Lord is not going to disappoint either Babylon or Zion, with regard to famine, pestilence, earthquakes or storms,* he is not going to disappoint anybody with regard to any of these things, they are at the doors.
>
> I feel to exhort the brethren, and to say to them—*lay up bread*, do not sell it for a song; let your wives and daughters go for awhile without ribbons and ornaments, *let your wheat stay in your bins;* let us try to get along with old coats and old hats, and *keep the wheat*, and in a little while you will see the reason why this counsel has been given. *Lay up your wheat and other provisions against a day of need, for the day will come when they will be wanted, and no mistake about it* (*Journal of Discourses*, vol. 18, p. 121).

PROPHETIC COUNSEL DURING THE FINAL QUARTER OF THE NINETEENTH CENTURY

On July 21, 1878, President *George Q. Cannon* said that there is great wisdom in storing grain in anticipation of the prophesied events which will surely come:

> Do not forget, my brethren and sisters, the teachings you have heard and which have been repeated in our hearing for so many years; I refer to *the saving and storing of grain;* for the day will come when you will see the wisdom of doing so, and many of you will doubtless wish you had profited by it. For *I tell you that wars and desolation will cover the land just as Prophets have declared they would; and these are coming, coming, coming as plainly and as surely as the light comes in the morning*

before the sun rises above the summit of yonder mountains and before we see its rays (*Journal of Discourses*, vol. 25, pp. 258-259).

President *Joseph F. Smith*, in 1879, spoke of the future day when the Saints will be left to fend for themselves:

> We shall be prepared, not only *to manufacture* our own *wearing apparel*, but also to make all our *mechanical and agriculture implements*, our house-hold *furniture*, our *building materials*, our *wagons, carriages and equipment*, with all that is necessary for the righteous and legitimate use of man, that *when Babylon shall fall we may be prepared for it*, and not be found among those who shall wail and lament because "no man buyeth her merchandise any more (*Journal of Discourses*, vol. 20, p. 347).

President *George Q. Cannon* continued the theme in November, 1891, warning that although it is difficult to believe, a famine will come, and wisdom dictates preparation:

> It seems scarcely possible, in so fruitful a land as America that there should be famine; yet we have good reason to believe that *sooner or later even this country*, now so bountifully supplied with every product of nature, *may be visited by famine;* and we should not waste the bounties of the earth because of their abundance and their cheapness. We should *garner our grains and fruits of the earth and preserve them so that we may have on hand sufficient to meet our wants should crops fail for one or more seasons*. This is true prudence on our part and *should be acted upon by every wise man and woman in this country, especially those who have faith in the predictions of God's servants* (*Juvenile Instructor*, vol. 26, p. 666).

Speaking in the Tabernacle on the subject, "The Need For a Food Storage Program," Elder *John Morgan, in* August, 1893, made the following observation:

> We read in tonight's paper of events that transpired this morning in the furthermost parts of the earth. This all demonstrates that *the world is moving very rapidly. It does not take years to bring about a crisis, financially, politically, socially, or otherwise.* They invade our homes before we know it. The watchmen upon the towers in the financial world gave us to understand that it was only a flurry, and that it would be over in a week or two.
>
> Well, it may be that it will not last as long as some anticipate; but are we prepared for that which will follow after? *Are we in a position to meet the next wave that shall come, let its character be what it will?* I believe the Latter-day Saints are in a better position to meet it than the balance of the world; but *are we in the position that the Lord desires us to be in?* We have been told ever since the location of the Latter-day Saints in these valleys of the mountains that *there shall come into our midst not alone a famine for money, but also a famine for bread.* I know that it is easy enough for us to argue that we have a bounteous harvest, that grain throughout the country is cheaper today than ever.

Possibly therein lies the great danger. But abundant as the harvests are, as easily as they can be transported from one portion of the land to the other, as numerous and as perfect as the appliances are which exist for the supply of the human family with food, the echo has scarcely died out in our ears of the clamor of the hungry mob in one of our neighboring cities for bread, when the municipal and state authorities had to establish places where they could get food to prevent them from looting the city; and yet within a few hours' ride of Denver there were thousands and thousands of bushels of grain and all the necessaries of life!

How easily these things can come upon us! Are we prepared for them? There is an official appointed by the municipality of the city of New York whose duty it is to compile statistics of the food supply of that city, and he startled the people a short time ago by notifying them through his statistics that *if the lines of communication that carry the supplies into that city were disconnected and no food carried within the boundaries of New York, it would require just four days to use up all the food that they had.* Certainly not much preparation for a time of scarcity! Although it would seem incredible that such an event should transpire in the midst of such bounteous harvests as we have at the present time, *I believe it behooves the Latter-day Saints to act wisely and prudently, and look forward for such a time, and be prepared for it* (*Collected Discourses,* 1886-1893, vol. 3, p. 335).

President *George Q. Cannon* continued the counsel to store food in an 1893 address in which he said,

Many may think this will never come, that it is folly to talk about famine in this land. . . . If grasshoppers were let loose, they could soon spoil the prospects for crops in those regions where food has hitherto been so plentiful. But whether this shall come or not, *I think it a wise precaution for the Latter-day Saints to keep a year or two's bread stuff on hand* (*Deseret News Weekly,* vol. 47, p. 347).

COUNSEL ON FOOD STORAGE IN THE TWENTIETH CENTURY: 1901-1950

Lest we come to feel that the previous directives from the prophets and other leaders within the Church only applied to the Saints when they lived in precarious circumstances during the early days in the Utah area, we now move to the counsel of the Brethren as provided during challenges of this, the 20th century. Included in this section is a representative sample of the counsel which has been given through the Prophet leaders of the Church. Obviously, much more has been said, as will be seen in later chapters.

In 1916, Elder *Charles W. Nibley* called on the Saints to be wise in temporal things:

Let me advise you in another point. *Do not sell all the wheat you have, but keep enough for your local demands. It is good to have enough wheat on hand for bread, so that we will not be obliged to call on some other country to feed our own people.* I know when I went on a mission, forty years ago . . . I provided a bin full of wheat for my wife and two children before I left. *In those days we used to make a point to have a year's bread-stuff on hand. That was President Young's counsel, and it is mighty good counsel today.* It will not hurt you to keep a little of your wheat at home and not sell it all. So be wise in these temporal things. They are small things but, as I said before, *the counsel is just as good as in spiritual things, and we need to lay it well to heart (Conference Report,* October 1916, p. 151).

President *David O. McKay* [1936], speaking during the darkest days of the great depression, conveyed the great suffering the Saints shared with others across the nation:

> *During the last few years practically all the world has been passing through a critical period of depression. People in this inter-mountain region have been hit, in some respects, more severely than others. . . .* When the *mines closed,* many men were thrown out of employment. *When the springs and rivers dried, products of farms shriveled and died.* The price of cattle dropped below the cost of raising them. As a result many people are worried and disheartened. *They have lost not only their farms or business interests, but also their homes.* Day by day *men have vainly searched for honest work.* After fruitless searching and inquiry, they return home almost with bitterness in their hearts. Wives with a fortitude sublime encourage their husbands even though it is more difficult for wives to struggle continually to keep up appearances and to supply food and nourishment for their children. It is embarrassing to such men and women, accustomed to independence, comfortable living, even opulence, to accept help either from the government or the Church *(Gospel Ideals,* p. 200).

The Welfare Plan of the Church had its beginning in 1937, and further references will be made to it throughout this book. On April 19, 1937, President *J. Reuben Clark* instructed the Saints to prepare for tribulation by having essentials on hand:

> What may we as a people and as individuals do for ourselves to prepare to meet this *oncoming disaster, which God in his wisdom may not turn aside from us?*
> *Let every head of every household see to it that he has on hand enough food and clothing, and, where possible, fuel also, for at least a year ahead (Conference Report,* April 1937, p. 26).

A message from the First Presidency (President *Heber J. Grant,* President *J. Reuben Clark,* President *David O. McKay*), given in 1942 during the perilous early days of World War II, spoke of the need for producing essential food storage:

> As the Church has always urged since we came to the Valleys, *so now we urge every Church householder to have a year's supply of essential foodstuffs ahead.* This should, so far as possible, *be produced by each householder and preserved by him.* This course will not only relieve from any impending distress those households who so provide themselves, but will release just that much food to the general national

stores of foodstuff from which the public at large must be fed (*Conference Report.*, April 1942, p. 89).

Statements made during the latter period of World War II and the decade that followed stressed the need for the Saints to be self-sustaining. President **Harold B. Lee** said, "By the power of the living God *we can and we will be self-sustaining and be the most independent creatures* under the celestial world" (*Church News*, February 12, 1944, p. 8).

Two years later, in 1946, Elder **Albert E. Bowen** again asserted that the Saints are under obligation to become self-sustaining:

> The only way the Church can stand independent is for *its members to stand independent, for the Church IS its members.* It is not possible to conceive of an independent church made up of dependent members—members who are under the inescapable obligation of dependency (*Gospel Doctrine*, 1946 course manual, p. 77).

COUNSEL ON FOOD STORAGE: 1951-1980

The instruction from the Church leaders to maintain at least a year's supply of food and other necessary items on hand continued after the end of World War II, during the "Cold War" era, but it tended to broaden in its scope. For instance, in 1953 President **J. Reuben Clark** warned of the danger of valueless money:

> . . . where food is scarce or there is none at all, and so with clothing and shelter, money may be no good for *there may be nothing to buy, and you cannot eat money, you cannot get enough of it together to burn to keep warm, and you cannot wear it* (*Church News*, November 21, 1953, p. 4).

The next year Bishop **Carl W. Buehner** related food storage to general health needs, joking that we should avoid storing food on the body:

> I am also thoroughly *converted to the welfare program in which we are admonished to put away a year's supply.* No one has ever indicated that we should carry around a half a year of it and put the other half year's supply in the basement; but many of us do it just that way. I am sure our doctor would tell us that it is well to be converted to these great programs but that we would be healthier and much better off if we would *put the full year's supply in the basement and get our blood pressure down* (*Conference Report*, April 1954, p. 81).

During the 1960s, 1970s and 1980s, when Elders Lee, Benson and Kimball were serving in the Twelve and the Quorum of the First Presidency, the counsel concerning food storage was shaped and enunciated by the Welfare program of the Church. All three of them were quite vocal on the subject having dealt with the sufferings of large groups of distillate church members both in the United States and in Europe. It was in this era that the concept of reducing food storage from many items down to "what it would take to keep us alive" took shape, under the guidance of Harold B. Lee.

At a welfare conference in October 1966, President *Harold B. Lee*, while discussing the four food groups, introduced the "keep us alive" concept to the Church::

> Perhaps if we think not in terms of a year's supply of what we ordinarily would use, and *think more in terms of what it would take to keep us alive in case we didn't have anything to eat, that last would be very easy to put in storage for a year . . . just enough to keep us alive if we didn't have anything else to eat.* We wouldn't get fat on it, but we would live; and *if you think in terms of that kind of annual storage rather than a whole year's supply of everything that you are accustomed to eat which, in most cases, is utterly impossible for the average family,* I think we will come nearer to what President J. Reuben Clark advised us way back in 1937 (*Welfare Conference*, October 1966).

In 1969 President *Ezra Taft Benson* spoke of the need to protect and provide for our families:

> The scriptural parable of the five wise and the five foolish virgins is a reminder that *one can wait too long before he attempts to get his spiritual and temporal house in order.* Are we prepared? A man should not only *be prepared to protect himself physically,* but he should also *have on hand sufficient supplies to sustain himself and his family in an emergency* (*Conference Report,* April 1967, p. 61).

In a First Presidency Message issued October 6, 1973 Presidents *Harold B. Lee, N. Elder Tanner* and *Marion G. Romney* approved the release of a message on food storage that was prepared by the Church Welfare Services Department. This was reported in the *Church News:*

> Let every head of every household see to it that he has on hand enough food and clothing, and where possible fuel also, for at least a year ahead.
>
> Planned storage in the home will assist the membership to be self-sustaining in times of need. . . . The likelihood of such eventualities as accidents, illness, and underemployment face nearly every family at one time or another.
>
> *Wars, depressions,* and *famines,* as well as *earthquakes, floods,* and *tornadoes,* loom as possibilities to be considered in looking ahead and planning for the care and protection of the family.

Then President *Harold B. Lee*'s 1966 counsel was restated:

> Perhaps if we think not in terms of a year's supply of what we ordinarily would use, and *think more in terms of what it would take to keep alive in case we didn't have anything to eat, that last would be very easy to put in storage for a year:*

The Presidency's message contained recommendations for storage of fabrics, thread, needles and other sewing material along with a reserve of fuel and some first aid items. The *four basic foods* which were suggested for storage, with the amount needed were *grains (wheat, rice or other grass cereals) 300 lbs;* along with *nonfat powdered milk, 100 lbs; sugar or honey, 100 lbs;* and *5 lbs. of salt for each adult per year.*

These items, used exclusively, provide a diet that supplies approximately 2,300 calories per day which is recommended for an average woman 25 years old. [A small child will use 1,000 calories less and an adult male 1,000 calories more, per day.]

Those in *highly mobile situations,* such as being in the armed services or enrolled in school, or who have small homes with little storage area, may find it more difficult to store a year's supply of food, clothing and fuel. [However,] *this does not release them from the obligation of doing their best to be prepared for an emergency.*

It was further noted that the four basics can be stored in a very limited space, following which he commented,

It is better to have food storage sufficient for a few months than to have no storage at all.

Also, in home storage planning, some *water reserve* may be considered. *The approximate requirement per person on a two-week basis is 14 gallons (seven gallons for drinking and seven gallons for other uses). . . .*

Security through the home storage program can be strengthened by the observance of further counsel that (1) *we live righteously;* (2) *we avoid debt;* (3) *we practice thrift;* and (4) *we have a willingness to work. . . .*

All members are encouraged to participate in the home storage program to provide for their own.

This message from the First Presidency gave a concluding quote from 1 Timothy 5:8, which unmistakably summarizes their counsel: "*If any provide not for his own, and specially for those of his own house, he hath denied the faith . . .*" (*Church News,* October 6, 1973, p. 14).

In President *Harold B. Lee*'s last public address (December 13, 1973—he died 13 days later), he again asked the Saints what have we done about food storage:

We are the inheritors of what they [our pioneer forefathers] gave to us. But what are we doing with it? Today we are basking in the lap of luxury, the like of which we've never seen before in the history of the world. . . .

As I read the papers today and the talk about food shortage, energy crises, the talk of war and the possibility of entering into a world conflict if things don't change, I wonder now if we are beginning to see the tip of the iceberg as it were. I'm wondering if we beginning to see what the brethren were talking about when they said, way back in 1937, to *put aside in storage for at least a year food, fuel, clothing and enough to tide one over during an emergency.* And we've said, "*Now don't think of storing all that you are accustomed to having. But store enough of what would keep you alive if you didn't have anything else to eat. Think of storing that for a year's supply . . .*"

How many of our Saints listen to that counsel? Do all of you folks . . . listen to the Brethren who said that to you, and have been trying to urge you to do that? Have you done it today? (*Pure Religion*, p. 370).

President *Ezra Taft Benson*, in 1973, moved the counsel beyond just food storage, reminding the Saints that essential clothing and cloth goods also needs to be obtained and stored:

Concerning clothing, we should anticipate future needs, such as *extra work clothes* and *clothes that would supply warmth during winter months* when there may be shortages or lack of heating fuel. *Leather and bolts of cloth could be stored*, particularly for families with younger children who will outgrow and perhaps outwear their present clothes. [He then quoted President Wilford Woodruff:]

"The day will come . . . when, as we have been told, we shall all see the necessity of making our own shoes and clothing and raising our own food."

He next quotes President Joseph Fielding Smith: "The pioneers were taught by their leaders to *produce, as far as possible, all that they consumed. . . .*" This is still excellent counsel. President Benson continues:

Wood, coal, gas, oil, kerosene, and even candles are among these items which could be reserved as fuel for warmth, cooking, and light or power.

It would also be well to have on hand some *basic medical supplies* to last for at least a year.

I have seen a hungry woman turn down food for a spool of thread. I have seen grown men weep as they ran their hands through the wheat and beans sent to them from Zion—America (*Conference Report*, October 1973, pp. 91-93).

In 1974 President *Spencer W. Kimball* warned that the increasing calamities require the Saints to be prepared:

We have had many calamities in this past period. It seems that every day or two there is an earthquake or a flood or a tornado or distress that bring trouble to many people. I am grateful to see that our people and our leaders are beginning to catch the vision of their self-help . . .

Now I think the time is come when *there will be more distresses*, when *there may be more tornadoes, and more floods, . . . more earthquakes . . . I think they will be increasing probably as we come nearer to the end, and so we must be prepared for this* (*Conference Report*, April 1974, pp. 183-84).

The next year, President *Marion G. Romney* counseled that it is necessary for the welfare program to organize the Church members because we will likely have to live on food that we produce:

I do not want to be a calamity howler. I don't know in detail what's going to happen in the future. I know what the prophets have predicted. But I tell you that *the welfare program, organized to enable us to take care of our own needs, has not yet performed the function that it was meant to perform. We will see the day when we live on what we produce (Conference Report*, April 1975, p. 165).

The following year, **Marion G. Romney** quoted President Brigham Young's admonition for seven years of storage readiness:

> If we are to be saved in an Ark, as Noah and his family were, it will be because we build it . . . My faith does not need me to think the Lord will provide us with roast pigs, bread already buttered, etc., *He will give us the ability to raise the grain, to obtain the fruits of the earth, to make habitations, to procure a few boards to make a box, and when harvest comes, giving us the grain, it is for us to preserve it—to save the wheat until we have one, two, five or seven years' provisions on hand*, until there is enough of the staff of life saved by the people to bread *themselves* and *those who will come here seeking for safety (Ensign*, May 1976, p. 123).

Later, President **Spencer W. Kimball** forthrightly expressed his deep concern that the Saints as a people may have developed an attitude that we need not be overly concerned about food storage because we feel we can care for ourselves without it:

> Brethren and sisters, we've gathered here this morning to consider the *important program which we must never forget nor put in the background.* As we become more affluent and our bank accounts enlarge, there comes a feeling of security, and we feel sometimes that we do not need *the supply that has been suggested by the Brethren.* It lies there and deteriorates, we say. *And suppose it does? We can reestablish it.* We must remember that conditions could change and *a year's supply of basic commodities* could be very much appreciated by us or others. So we would do well to listen to what we have been told and to follow it explicitly . . .

> *Develop your skills in your home preservation and storage. We reaffirm the previous counsel the Church has always given, to acquire and maintain a year's supply— a year's supply of the basic commodities for us (Ensign*, May 1976, pp. 124, 125).

President **Boyd K. Packer**, in 1978, noted that food storage is more functional in the home than at the chapel:

> We have been taught to *store a year's supply of food, clothing, and, if possible, fuel*—at home. There has been no attempt to set up storerooms in every chapel. We know that in the crunch our members may not be able to get to the chapel for supplies (*Ensign*, May 1978, p. 91).

President **Marion G Romney** said, in 1979:

> Now, I would like to repeat what you have heard a thousand times, more or less, about taking care of yourselves. You ought to now, more than at any previous time, *make sure that you are prepared to go through a period of stress on the resources you have provided for yourselves.* The necessity to do this may come any day. I hope it will not come too soon. In fact I hope it doesn't come in my lifetime. *But it will come sooner or later.*

Never forget this matter of providing for yourselves, even though you don't hear as much about it now as you did a few years ago. Remember that it is still a fundamental principle, one that has been taught the Saints ever since they came to these valleys of the mountains. We have always been urged to *provide for ourselves, in the day of harvest, enough to last until the next harvest*. Be sure that you do so now. *Be prepared to take care of yourselves through a period of need* (*Ensign*, May 1979, pp. 94, 95).

But in 1980 Bishop **Victor L. Brown** expressed the concern of the Brethren that far too many Saints are ill prepared to care for themselves in difficult times, even though they have been instructed to prepare for years:

However, *we still have a great concern that as a people we are far short of truly being prepared.* The heart of welfare services' success is not church preparedness but *member preparedness.* The increased call by bishops on the resources of the storehouse system is an indication that *many of our people do not have their reserves and consequently are unable to take care of their own basic needs.*

I am afraid some members are laboring under the illusion that in difficult times the Church will take care of them. This is not so. The Church is prepared to take care of a limited number of members for a relatively short period of time.

There should be no misunderstanding on this point. The fundamental principle of welfare services is that I provide for our own needs. If serious economic disruption were to occur, the Church would do all in its power to alleviate suffering by supplementing member efforts. *But it would not be able to do for the Saints what we have been taught to do for ourselves for over forty years—that is, to have a year's supply of food, clothing, and, where possible, fuel; to have savings in reserve; and to possess basic production skills.*

This counsel has been given at least twice a year for all these years. Some have followed the counsel of the Brethren and are prepared, as were the five wise virgins. Some, like the foolish virgins, do not have enough oil in their lamps (*Ensign*, May 1980, p. 89).

But throughout the twentieth century, the Brethren have not wavered from their firm belief that scriptural prophecies clearly warn of difficult times which still lie ahead. This statement from President **Ezra Taft Benson** is typical:

In the light of these prophecies (abomination of desolation), there should be no doubt in the mind of any priesthood holder that *the human family is headed for trouble. There are rugged days ahead. It is time for every man who wishes to do his duty to get himself prepared—physically, spiritually, and psychologically—for the task which may come at any time, as suddenly as the whirlwind* (*Teachings of Ezra Taft Benson*, p. 107).

There can be no doubt left that the Lord has amply advised the membership of the Church to remain fully prepared in both temporal and spiritual affairs throughout the last century and a half, and that the accumulation and storage of at least a year's food supply continues to appear as a part of that ongoing preparation.

However, we might ask ourselves, "Why has this counsel continued to be given for so many years?" and, "To what end does it continue to be given to us today?" even some 150 years after its earliest utterance.

Could it be that the Lord has a greater, overriding purpose and need for us to become ever more thoroughly prepared? Could there actually be a culminating objective and intention that underlies the protracted design of the Lord in this matter?

When one considers the careful economy of heaven in planning and purpose, it should appear obvious to each of us that the Lord does not engage in frivolous communications with the Brethren or with members of the Church. That being true, then *we must assume the storage of food is unusually critical, since so much emphasis has been placed on it for such a long period of time.* Because of this, there ultimately has to be a day of accounting, a day when we will look back and know why the council was given—a "significant moment in time." The problem for us is that when we become keenly aware of the "why's," it will also be obvious that it is too late to prepare!

COUNSEL FROM PROPHETS DURING THE LAST TWO DECADES

President *Ezra Taft Benson* gave a talk entitled "Prepare for the Days of Tribulation" in the October 1980 General Conference of the Church. This talk was sent to all the bishops of the Church under the title *Basic Welfare Principles*. I quote segments from President Benson's talk, but every family would do well to review the entire talk. It is found in the *Ensign*, November 1980, pp. 32-34. Bold paragraph headings have been inserted by the author).

Warning. We do not know when a crisis involving sickness or unemployment may affect our circumstances. We do know that *the Lord has decreed global calamities for the future and He has warned us and forewarned us to be prepared. For this reason the Brethren have repeatedly stressed a "back to basics" program for temporal and spiritual welfare.*

Serious crises will come. Have you ever paused to realize what would happen to your community or nation *if transportation were paralyzed or if we had a war or depression?* How would you and your neighbor obtain food? How long would the corner grocery store—or supermarket—sustain the needs of the community?

Gardens. No more timely counsel, I feel, has been given by President Kimball than his repeated emphasis to grow our own gardens. *"We encourage you to grow all* *the food that you feasibly can on your own property.* Berry bushes, grapevines, fruit trees. . . . Grow vegetables and eat them from your own yard."

Rationalization. [Some] have rationalized that they had no time or space. May I suggest you do what others have done. Get together with others and seek permission to use a vacant lot for a garden, or rent a plot of ground and grow your gardens.

Obtain food storage. Plan to build up your food supply just as you would a savings account. *Save a little for storage from each pay-check. . . . Make storage a part of your budget. . . .* If you are saving and planning for a second car or a television set or some item which merely adds to your comfort or pleasure you may need to *change your priorities.* We urge you to do this prayerfully and do it now. I speak with a feeling of great urgency.

Be self-sustaining during days of tribulation. *The Lord wants us to be independent and self-reliant because these will be days of tribulation. He has warned us and forewarned us of the eventuality.*

For over forty years . . . members of the church have been counseled to be thrifty and self-reliant; to avoid debt; pay tithes and a generous fast offering; be industrious; and have sufficient food, clothing, and fuel on hand to last at least one year. Today there are compelling reasons to re-emphasize this counsel.

In his discourse, President Benson confirmed the words of other prophets, applying the law of witnesses. He quotes Orson Hyde, who said, "There is more salvation and security in wheat, . . . than in all the political schemes of the world." President Benson then quotes counsel from President Brigham Young: "If you are without bread, how much wisdom can you boast, and of what real utility are your talents, if you cannot *procure for yourselves and save against a day of scarcity* those substances designed to sustain your natural lives?" He goes on to quote President Harold B. Lee's 1966 counsel: "Perhaps if we think not in terms of a year's supply of what we ordinarily would use, and think more in terms of what it would take to keep us alive in case we didn't have anything else to eat, that last would be very easy to put in storage for a year . . . just enough to keep us alive if we didn't have anything else to eat." President Benson Continues: "Those families will be fortunate who, in the last days, have an adequate supply of food because of *their foresight and ability to produce.*"

.   **Urgency.** Plan to build up your food supply just as you would a savings account. . . . We urge you to do this prayerfully and do it now. I speak with a feeling of great urgency. I have seen hunger stalk the streets of Europe. I have witnessed the appalling, emaciated shadows of human figures. I have seen women and children scavenge army garbage dumps for scraps of food.

Complacency. Too often we bask in our comfortable complacency and rationalize that the ravages of war, economic disaster, famine, and earthquake cannot happen here. Those who believe this are either not acquainted with the revelations of the Lord, or they do not believe them. *Those who smugly think these calamities will not* *happen, that they somehow will be set aside because of the righteousness of the Saints, are deceived and will rue the day they harbored such a delusion.*

The Lord's warning. The Lord has warned and forewarned us against a day of great tribulation and given us counsel, through His servants, on how we can be prepared for these difficult times. Have we heeded his counsel? (*Conference Report*, November 1980, pp. 45-48).

Other comments made by President Benson on a later occasion should be set forth in this context:

A Father's Responsibility. Fathers, another vital aspect of providing for the material needs of your family is the provision you should be making for your family in case of an emergency. Family preparedness has been a long-established welfare principle. It is even more urgent today. *I ask you earnestly, have you provided for your family a year's supply of food, clothing, and, where possible, fuel?* (*Conference Report*, October 1987, p. 61).

The essential nature of this counsel. The revelation to produce and store food may be as essential to our temporal welfare today as boarding the ark was to the people of Noah (*Conference Report*, October 1987, p. 61).

None should have any doubts concerning the critical nature of food storage after reviewing President Benson's straight-forward, urgent counsel to prepare.

WARNINGS FROM OTHER MODERN PROPHETS

There has been a consistent effort by recent prophets to urge repentance and offer encouragement for us not to procrastinate but to prepare *now*. President **Joseph Fielding Smith** clearly noted the unprepared status of the Latter-day Saints with these observations:

The Lord made the promise to the Latter-day Saints that if they would keep his commandments, they should escape *when these destructions like a whirlwind should come suddenly.*

We are not keeping his commandments. . . . We are covenant-breakers; we violate the Sabbath day, we will not keep it holy; we do not keep our bodies clean; I do not believe we pray—a large part of us, I mean. As far as the fast day is concerned, we have forgotten it. *We are not half as good as we think we are. We need repentance, and we need to be told to repent. We need to have our attention called to these conditions that we might repent and turn to the Lord with full purpose of heart lest these destructions come upon us.* We do not pay our tithing—some of us pay tithing . . . and some of us pay donations and call it tithing; some of us do not pay at all (*Doctrines of Salvation*, vol. III, p. 44).

Bishop **Vaughn J. Featherstone** expressed the concern of the Brethren that the Saints are unresponsive to counsel:

"[He] spoke on food storage, and *the concern the General Authorities have* concerning those church members who won't heed the counsel of the leaders on this subject" (*Church News*, April 3, 1976, p. 9).

President *Spencer W. Kimball* taught that rationalization precedes disobedience:

The Lord has urged that this people save for the rainy days, prepare for the difficult times, and put away for emergencies, *a year's supply or more* of bare necessities so that *when comes the flood, the earthquake, the famine, the hurricane, the storms of life, our families can be sustained through the dark days.* How many of us have complied with this? We strive with the Lord, finding many excuses: We do not have room for storage. The food spoils. We do not have the funds to do it. We do not like these common foods. It is not needed—there will always be someone to help in trouble. The government will come to the rescue. And *some intend to obey but procrastinate.*

. . . As we become more affluent and our bank accounts enlarge, there comes a feeling of security, and we feel sometimes that we do not need the supply that has been suggested by the Brethren. . . . *We must remember that conditions could change and a year's supply of basic commodities could be very much appreciated by us or others.* So we would do well to listen to what we have been told and to follow it explicitly (*The Teachings of Spencer W. Kimball*, p. 374).

Elder *F. Enzio Busche*, who endured the ravages of the Second World War in Germany, spoke of his experiences in a 1982 address, as follows:

Since my conversion and because of my World War II experiences, I now have a deep appreciation for the revealed plan of a year's supply for each member.

Frequently I am asked, "What were the most valuable items in the days of starvation in Germany?" The answer is difficult to believe, because some of the experiences we had seem to be totally illogical and contrary to human nature. *The items of highest value were tobacco and alcohol,* because people who live in fear and despair, who have not learned the principles of self-control, tend to need in times of panic some drug to escape the dreadful awareness of reality.

How fortunate we are as members of the Church that we learn to develop a feeling for the true values of life and the necessity of self-control, so that in times of need there will be no panic, but we will be prepared.

As for what we needed, *the food item we relied on most was vegetable oil. With a bottle of vegetable oil, one could acquire nearly every other desirable item.* It has such value that with a quart of vegetable oil one could probably trade for three bushels of apples or three hundred pounds of potatoes. *Vegetable oil has a high calorie content, is easy to transport and in cooking can give a tasty flavor to all kinds of food items that one would not normally consider as food—wild flowers, wild plants, and roots from shrubs and trees.*

For me and my family, a high-quality vegetable oil has the highest priority in our food storage, both in times of daily use and for emergency usage. When vegetable oil is well-packed and stored appropriately, it has a long storage life without the necessity of refrigeration. We found ours to be in very good condition after twenty years of storage, but circumstances may vary.

The second highest priority item for me and my family is *grain in all forms, preferably wheat and rye,* When grain is well-packed and well-preserved, it too is easy to transport, easy to store, and will last for generations.

A third priority item is honey. Its value in daily usage is immeasurable. My family prefers honey rather than sugar because our experience supports some of the research finding regarding the preeminence of honey. Another reason I prefer honey is because during the starvation period in postwar Germany, *honey could be traded for three times as much as sugar; its value was considered that much greater* . . . A fourth important food storage product is *powdered milk.*

When we think in terms of our own year's supply . . . we may feel we have to store everything." "However, let me offer this comforting idea based on past experience. We need to take into consideration that in difficult times, *so long as there survives more than one family, there will be trading of valuable items.* A free market will begin immediately to satisfy the needs of people, and items in greatest demand will set the price, bypassing the use of money. The ingeniousness of mankind become evident in times of need (*Ensign,* June 1982, pp. 17-18).

President *James E. Faust* in 1986, taught the Church:

Strive to have a year's supply of food and clothing. The counsel to have a year's supply of basic food, clothing and commodities was given fifty years ago and has been repeated many times.

It is therefore necessary that each home and family do what they can to assume the responsibility for their own hour of need. If we do not have the resources to acquire a year's supply, then *we can strive to begin with having one month's supply.* I believe if we are provident and wise in the management of our personal and family affairs and are faithful, God will sustain us through our trials. He has revealed: "For the earth is full, and there is enough and to spare; yea, I prepared all things, and have given unto the children of men to be agents unto themselves" (D&C 104:17) (*Ensign,* May 1986, p. 22).

President *Thomas S. Monson,* in 1988, stressed that the best effort is a family effort:

We should remember that *the best storehouse system would be for every family to have a year's supply* of needed food, clothing, and, where possible, the other necessities of life" (*Ensign,* November 1988, p. 47).

In 1995 Elder *L. Thomas Perry* admonished the saints to not disregard counsel, to prepare:

I believe it is time, and perhaps with some urgency, to review the counsel we have received in dealing with our personal and family preparedness. We want to be found with oil in our lamps sufficient to endure to the end.

The great blessing of being prepared gives us freedom from fear, as guaranteed to us by the Lord in the Doctrine and Covenants: "If ye are prepared ye shall not fear" [38:30]. Just as it is important to prepare ourselves spiritually, we must also prepare ourselves for our temporal needs. Each of us needs to take the time to ask ourselves, What preparation should I make to care for my needs and the needs of my family? *We have been instructed for years to follow at least four requirements in preparing for that which is to come.*

First, *gain an adequate education.* Learn a trade or profession.

Second, *live strictly within your income* and *save something for a rainy day.*

Third, *avoid excessive debt.*

Fourth, *acquire and store a reserve of food and supplies that will sustain life.*

I would guess that the years of plenty have almost universally caused us to set aside this counsel. I believe the time to disregard this counsel is over. With events in the world today, it must be considered with all seriousness. . . . The instability in the world today makes it imperative to take heed of the counsel and prepare for the future (*Ensign,* November 1995, pp. 35-37).

In the end, gathering together sufficient food storage to meet the needs of one's family is little more than an act of faith and obedience. Whether one follows or ignores the Lord's counsel to prepare ultimately has profound repercussions of both a temporal and a spiritual nature. A willingness to follow the Lord's authorized servants is critical, as expressed in the following verses:

Wherefore the voice of the Lord is unto the ends of the earth, that all that will hear may hear:

Prepare ye, prepare ye for that which is to come, for the Lord is nigh:

And the anger of the Lord is kindled, and his sword is bathed in heaven, and it shall fall upon the inhabitants of the earth.

And the arm of the Lord shall be revealed; and the day cometh that they that will not hear the voice of the Lord, neither the voice of his servants, neither give heed to the words of the prophets and apostles, shall be cut off from among the people (D&C 1:11-14).

May Heavenly Father grant us the wisdom to be included in the number who "will hear" and "prepare" obediently.

CHAPTER
6
A PROPHET DISCUSSES CONCERNS FOR THE 21ST CENTURY

President **Gordon B. Hinckley**, in 1995, spoke frankly of the 21st Century in a talk he delivered to a group of LDS businessmen and businesswomen. He told them that the "21st century looks gloomy" if we don't change the corrosion of family and reverse the national debt. He said,

> . . . I also raise a voice of warning that unless we can change the direction of the family, unless we can muster the discipline to pay our debts and live with honesty and integrity with ourselves and future generations, much of the good that science brings [in the 21st century] will be offset by the growing evils that have become so obvious to our own day.

> You ask why a church man would be concerned over a matter of economics. It is because unmanageable debt has such terribly serious consequences for individuals, organizations and nations. Its corrosive effect destroys families, businesses and entire economies.

> While we have made advances. there have been a host of failures—wars, violence and famine.

> From that day in Sarajevo in 1914, when the shot was fired that started the first World War, until this day in Sarajevo where civil war rages, there has been much conflict—the first World War, the second World War, the Korean War, the Vietnam War and literally scores of lesser wars. These conflicts have cost the lives of millions and brought untold suffering to millions more.

> Until human nature changes, I fear the world will experience much of continuing conflict. Until aggressive greed and unholy ambition disappear among men, we can expect wars both small and great, with their tragedies of homeless refugees, of famine, of death.

He then quoted from the Wall Street Journal:

> This year [1995] the White House wants to spend three times as much as America did to win World War I. Adjusted for inflation, the combined cost of defeating the Nazis and the Japanese in World War II and winning World War I was $4.5 trillion. This is what Washington will spend in peace time in just the next three years to continue losing the war on poverty, drugs, illiteracy, homelessness, and so on.

When state and local expenditures are included, total annual government spending now surpasses $2.5 trillion. That is more than $23,000 of government for every household in America.

He then goes on to state: "... I am confident that unless something is done, *there will come a day of reckoning."* He said, "How can we go on using one-third of the government's income just to pay the interest on government debt? Is this a moral issue? I think it is. I think there is a serious element of dishonesty in it. I think there is a very strong element of deceit. We are grossly fooling ourselves. We are breaking faith with the future.

Speaking of the collapse of the family, he noted that millions of families have "been on a moral slide now for a good while." He continued:

Recovery . . . will not come about through legislative mandate. It is not likely to come about through the public schools, which some 40 years ago abandoned the teaching of moral and ethical values. *If it is to happen, it will have to happen in the homes of the people, fortified by the Church.*

We have made wonderful strides in many fields in this 20th century of which we have been a part. But in that field which is most fraught with consequences for the 21st century—the course of the American family—we have lost ground. There has been a perceptible and alarming unraveling.

The only possible long-term solution lies in redoubling our efforts to strengthen the families of America, the seed bed of character formation.

Otherwise, I fear, the future for the 21st century looks gloomy. We may have all of the scientific discovery in the world to make life better. But life will not be better if we are prisoners in our own homes, fearful of walking the streets, afraid of driving our highways.

As we face this new century, it is time we got on our knees and asked for direction, then to stand on our feet and follow it (Sacramento, California: *The Latter-day Messenger,* March 18, 1995, p. 6).

A NEWSPAPER ACCOUNT
OF TYPICAL AMERICAN LIFE TODAY

The following article, written by the editor of a local weekly advertiser in California (the *Fickle Nickel*), seems to be reflective how far our current society has moved away from the basic principles of honesty and integrity. This editorial supports President Hinckley's expressions of what happens when you lose the family as a basic unit in society. Although it speaks about a small town in the California foothills, it could be most any town or city in the United States. The editor gives the following account:

Growing here from my birth in 1946 until I left home in 1965, the thought of theft was very remote. The hay barn was never locked, cars or pickups always had keys in them, saddles, bridles and other equipment hung behind a closed (but never locked) door. The back door of the house was never locked. Friends might need something besides, the key had been missing for years.

Obviously, during the next 25 years things and society changed. More and more homes were built in the area and, as in most neighborhoods, my parents only knew those neighbors who had lived here forever.

After moving back home in early 1993 I noticed the back door key had been found and several copies had been made. "You'd better lock that back door," became a favorite expression of my parents.

After moving our office here four years ago, the Other Half and I have been here every day. We were burglarized in 1994—not only did they steal all tools, they hauled everything away in the wheelbarrow, then kept that too.

The following night, the same burglars attempted to steal a neighbor's car. Bad decision. The neighbor killed one and injured another suspect. The sheriff's office returned our tools, found in the dead suspect's bedroom. We bought bigger, better chains and locks. That episode slowed burglaries in the area for quite a while. But in the last few months we've discovered a slightly different problem.

It seems some newer residents of the area feel if something is here, and they need it, it is therefore theirs. About three nights out of every seven the dogs begin to bark. This usually occurs anywhere from 1 to 4 a.m. Their bark isn't the usual "chase the cat" bark, it starts out vicious and then suddenly stops. That, naturally gets our attention. Five times in the last six weeks I have raced down the driveway and nearly through the back pasture with gun and flashlight in hand. . . . Our office alarm has been set off three times in four weeks. The shop alarm has gone off once. We have now removed Mother's medical alert program from the house alarm system and installed a burglar alarm. We kept the fire alarm.

And what's been taken? Really dumb things—an ice chest, extension cords, a roll of heavy cable we used to attach newspaper racks to posts or walls, a bedliner, lumber rack and a bunch of little stuff.

Occasionally, during daylight hours people just wander in through the back field and remove what they want. One afternoon I counted four people—not related—out back picking blackberries. Do I care? Not particularly, but how nice it might have been if any one of them had first asked. They later climbed over their own fences and went home. Hope they enjoyed the pies.

A couple years ago I bought a two-seat glider at a yard sale and unloaded it in the driveway. It sat there for about 24 hours until I had time to move it into the yard. During that time a new neighbor arrived and asked if the glider was for sale. I explained I had just bought it and planned to keep it. "Why?" she asked. "Because I want it," I answered. "Well, so do I!" she said. "Why can't I have it?" By this time I was getting a little upset. Calmly I explained again. She finally got mad and demanded I sell it to her for whatever price I paid. It was one of the most unbelievable conversations I had ever had with anyone.

Until, the man came to see if he could purchase the forge inside the old barn. "How did you know it was there?," I asked. "I saw it when I was looking through the barn yesterday," he answered without any guilt. No, he didn't get the forge. He was however, allowed to leave unhurt.

One morning I looked out the front window to find a woman, with shovel in hand, digging up some bulbs. She calmly walked to the trunk of her car (already open), selected one plastic bag already filled with dirt and began to load her bulbs.

I opened the front door and asked if perhaps she didn't also want to take the sycamore. (The tree is 70 years old and about 15 feet in diameter.) She looked up at me, closed her trunk, got in her car and proceeded to dignify her departure with an obscene gesture. I would place her age at somewhere between 75 and 85, and her trunk was filled with plants and bulbs she apparently had gathered that morning.

On occasion, as I sit on the little deck with gun and flame thrower in hand, I can see across the road and into a 200-acre field. This spring it was planted in onions. A never-ending stream of vehicles arrived both day and night. Out would jump one, two or seven or eight people, each carrying a large empty bag, and the pillage would begin.

These were not onions left in the field; these were onions just about ready for harvest. The year before, when the farmer tried corn there, he finally had to fence the property temporarily to keep people from stealing his profits.

One evening the Other Half had reached the end. With seven cars lined up beside the road he headed in that direction. Shortly after his arrival, the cars all left. He returned shaking his head. "Everyone of them yelled, screamed and threatened me," he said, "One man said, 'If it's growing in the dirt it belongs to everyone.'"

Are we just getting old and grouchy or has the respect for private property completely diminished? Does this happen in town too or is it mostly confined to the country? Years ago we suffered from dropped off pets. (The old take-the-dog-to-the-country plan.) After the past few months, "pets" don't look too bad.

We've considered putting a traffic light in the backyard to slow the burglars, (we wouldn't want anyone to fall into a gopher hole and sue us) or perhaps they could steal only on odd-numbered days. This would allow us to sleep on those other days.

Our fear is that we're going to have great difficulty explaining to a jury just why we shot someone for stealing a garden hose with sprinkler attached. No jury is going to accept the argument that it just didn't belong to them.

Footnote: I wrote this story Tuesday afternoon. A little after 2 a.m. Wednesday morning the shop alarm again went off. We found viciously barking dogs, terrorized sheep and one more attempt to enter a locked building (*Fickle Nickel*, vol. 7, no. 34, August 20, 1998).

Need more be said???

THE NEED TO SET OUR HOMES IN ORDER

In his October, 1998 Priesthood session conference talk, President **Gordon B. Hinckley** counseled the priesthood members regarding the need to set their homes in order. He said,

Now brethren, I should like to talk to the older men, hoping that there will be some lesson for the younger as well.

I wish to speak to you about temporal matters.

As a backdrop for what I wish to say, I read to you a few verses from the 41st chapter of Genesis. Pharaoh, the ruler of Egypt, dreamed dreams which greatly troubled him. The wise men of his court could not give an interpretation. Joseph was then brought before him:

"Pharaoh said unto Joseph, In my dream, behold, I stood upon the bank of the river:

"And, behold, there came up out of the river seven kine, fatfleshed and well favoured; and they fed in a meadow:

"And, behold, seven other kine came up after them, poor and very ill favoured and leanfleshed. . . .

"And the lean and the ill favoured kine did eat up the first seven fat kine: . . .

"And, I saw in my dream . . . seven ears came up in one stalk, full and good:

"And, behold, seven ears, withered, thin, and blasted with the east wind, sprung up after them:

"And the thin ears devoured the seven good ears: . . .

"And Joseph said unto Pharaoh, . . . God hath shewed Pharaoh what he is about to do.

"The seven good kine are seven years; and the seven good ears are seven years: the dream is one . . .

". . . What God is about to do he sheweth unto Pharaoh.

"Behold, there come seven years of great plenty throughout all the land of Egypt:

"And there shall arise after them seven year of famine;

". . . And God will shortly bring it to pass." [Genesis 41:17-20, 22-26, 28-30, 32]

Now, brethren, *I want to make it very clear that I am not prophesying, that I am not predicting years of famine in the future. But I am suggesting that the time has come to get our houses in order.*

So many of our people are *living on the very edge of their incomes.* In fact, some are living on borrowing.

We have witnessed in recent weeks wide and fearsome swings in the markets of the world. The economy is a fragile thing. A stumble in the economy in Jakarta or Moscow can immediately affect the entire world. It can eventually reach down to each of us as individuals. *There is a portent of stormy weather ahead to which we had better give heed.*

I hope with all my heart that we shall never slip into a depression. I am a child of the Great Depression of the thirties. I finished the university in 1932, when unemployment in this area exceeded 33 percent.

My father was then president of the largest stake in the Church in this valley. It was before our present welfare program was established. *He walked the floor worrying about his people.* He and his associates established a great wood-chopping project designed to keep the home furnaces and stoves going and the people warm in the winter. They had no money with which to buy coal. Men who had been afflu-ent were among those who chopped wood.

I repeat, I hope we will never again see such a depression. But *I am troubled by the huge consumer installment debt which hangs over the people of the nation, including our own people.* In March 1997 that debt totaled $1.2 trillion which repre-sented a 7 percent increase over the previous year.

In December of 1997, *55 to 60 million households carried credit card balances. These balances averaged more than $7,000 and cost $1,000 per year in interest and fees. Consumer debt as a percentage of disposable income rose from 16.3 percent in 1993 to 19.3 percent in 1996.*

Everyone knows that every dollar borrowed carries with it the penalty of paying interest. When money cannot be repaid, then bankruptcy follows. *There were 1,350,118 bankruptcies in the United States last year. This represented a 50 percent increase from 1992. In the second quarter of this year, nearly 362,000 persons filed for bankruptcy, a record number for a three-month period.*

We are beguiled by seductive advertising. Television carries the enticing invitation to borrow up to 125 percent of the value of one's home. But no mention is made of interest.

President J. Reuben Clark Jr., in the priesthood meeting of the conference of 1938, said from this pulpit: *"Once in debt, interest is your companion every minute of the day and night; you cannot shun it or slip away from it; you cannot dismiss it; it yields neither to entreaties, demands, or orders; and whenever you get in its way or cross its course or fail to meet its demands, it crushes you"* [*Conference Report*, April 1938, p. 103].

I recognize that it might be necessary to borrow to get a home, of course. But let us buy a home that we can afford and thus ease the payments which will constantly hang over our heads without mercy or respite for as long as 30 years.

No one knows when emergencies will strike. I am somewhat familiar with the case of a man who was highly successful in his profession. He lived in comfort. He built a large home. Then one day he was suddenly involved in a serious accident. Instant-ly, without warning, he almost lost his life. He was left a cripple. Destroyed was his earning power. He faced huge medical bills. He had other payments to make. He was helpless before his creditors. One moment he was rich, the next he was broke.

Since the beginnings of the Church, the Lord has spoken on this matter of debt. To Martin Harris through revelation He said: "Pay the debt thou hast contracted with the printer. Release thyself from bondage" (D&C 18:35).

President Heber J. Grant spoke repeatedly on this matter from this pulpit. He said: *"If there is any one thing that will bring peace and contentment into the human heart, and into the family, it is to live within our means.* And if there is any one thing that is grinding and discouraging and disheartening, it is to have debts and obligations that one cannot meet" [*Gospel Standards*, comp. G. Homer Durham [1941], p. 111].

We are carrying a message of self-reliance throughout the Church. Self-reliance cannot obtain when there is serious debt hanging over a household. One has neither independence nor freedom from bondage when he is obligated to others. In managing the affairs of the Church, we have tried to set an example. We have, as a matter of policy, stringently followed the practice of *setting aside each year a percentage of the income of the Church against a possible day of need.*

I am grateful to be able to say that the Church in all its operations, in all its undertakings, in all of its departments, is able to function without borrowed money. *If we cannot get along, we will curtail our programs. We will shrink expenditures to fit the income. We will not borrow.*

One of the happiest days in the life of President Joseph F. Smith was the day the Church paid off it longstanding indebtedness.

What a wonderful feeling it is to be free of debt, to have a little money put away where it can be retrieved when necessary.

President Faust would not tell you this himself. Perhaps I can tell it, and he can take it out on me afterward. He had a mortgage on his home drawing 4 percent interest. Many people would have told him he was foolish to pay off that mortgage when it carried so low a rate of interest. But the first opportunity he had to acquire some means, he and his wife determined they would pay off their mortgage. He has been free of debt since that day. That's why he wears a smile on his face, and that's why he whistles while he works.

I urge you, brethren, to look to the condition of your finances. I urge you to be modest in your expenditures; discipline yourselves in your purchases to avoid debt to the extent possible. Pay off debt as quickly as you can, and free yourselves from bondage.

This is a part of the temporal gospel in which we believe. May the Lord bless you, my beloved brethren, to *set your houses in order. If you have paid your debts, if you have a reserve, even though it be small, then should storms howl about your head, you will have shelter for your wives and children and peace in your hearts.* That's all I have to say about it, but I wish to say it with all the emphasis of which I am capable (*Ensign,* November 1998, pp. 52-54).

You will notice President Hinckley began his address by quoting the experience of Joseph in Egypt. Perhaps a brief comment on Egyptian history and the outcome of Pharaoh's dream might broaden our understanding of why the counsel he gave to the priesthood is so very important today.

About 30 years before Joseph was sold by his brothers, the Egyptians had been conquered by a Semite people who, like Jacob, were sheepherders. The Hyksos, as they were known, ruled and were to reign as pharaohs in Egypt for some two hundred years. Had this situation not existed when Joseph arrived in Egypt, but instead a native pharaoh had reigned, Joseph would never have been heard of—because after all Joseph was a shepherd, a Semite, and a slave, all three disdained by the Egyptians. As you can understand the Egyptians hated their Hyksos conquerors, and thus when the Hyksos were eventually overthrown there ". . . arose up a new [native Egyptian] King over Egypt, which knew not Joseph" (Exodus 1:8). Given this background, it is easy to see why the remaining Semites—the children of Israel—were enslaved.

The Egyptians were further angered because the people of Israel lived ". . . in the best of the land, in the land of Rameses" (Genesis 47:11), and also, they feared them because ". . . the people of the children of Israel are more and mightier than we," thus becoming a threat to the Egyptians. In an effort to subjugate them, the Egyptians began to place heavy burdens on the children of Israel, but the Lord blessed the Israelites and ". . . the more they afflicted them the more they multiplied" (Exodus 1:12), with the eventual result, as you will recall, being their exodus from Egypt.

With this Semite reign as a backdrop, one can understand the unique time that allowed Joseph to rise to power, and thereby preserve the Lord's chosen people. For it was during Joseph's time that the Lord provided specific inspiration to him, to interpret the hated Semite Pharaoh's dream which led to the storage of grain in Egypt.

However, this inspired dream apparently did not similarly motivate the conquered Egyptian people. They may have rejected the idea that a famine was in the making, or perhaps they were never even told. In either event, it was Joseph who gathered one-fifth of the corn for Pharaoh, and when the famine came, the Egyptian people were completely unprepared. As the seven years of famine unfolded and the people were starving, they came to this same hated Pharaoh for food, for which they paid the following heavy prices, one by one, over a seven-year period:

> And Joseph gathered up all the money that was found in the land of Egypt and in the land of Canaan, for corn . . .
> And Joseph said, Give your cattle; and I will give you [food] for your cattle, if money fail. . . .
> And Joseph bought all the land of Egypt for Pharaoh; for the Egyptians sold every man his field . . .
> Then Joseph said unto the people, Behold, I have bought you this day . . . lo, here is seed for you, and ye shall sow the land.
> . . . ye shall give the fifth part unto Pharaoh . . . (Genesis 47:14, 16, 20, 23-24).

Initially, the children of Israel were obedient to the revelation received by Joseph; they were gathered to him and were greatly blest. But after ". . . four hundred and thirty years" (Exodus 12:40) in Egypt, they were reluctant to follow the Lord's revelations, such as those received by Moses. The scripture says that "they hearkened not unto Moses for anguish [Heb. shortness] of spirit, and for cruel bondages" (Exodus 6:9). Therefore, they forfeited many of the blessings the Lord had prepared for them.

OTHER PROPHETS ALSO
HAVE CAUTIONED AGAINST DEBT AND EXTRAVAGANCE

Today we face a similar challenge. We, too, have been counseled—like pharaoh of old—to prepare for a day of want, even with our own food storage. Will this generation of Israel obey and live free? May the Lord bless us with determination to "follow our prophets."

Today many people are living in a make-believe world, one that no longer exists. It is as if most Americans have been enjoying a party on one of the decks of an economic Titanic, a party celebrated on borrowed money and borrowed time. Today people are still clustered around laughing and talking—happy people looking forward to more parties, just like first-class passage on the Titanic, but like those oblivious passengers sitting comfortably in the ship's lounge the party is about to end. There are economic icebergs dead ahead, and as the party goers leave the party they will be given a bill far beyond their ability to pay. At first they will be astounded, and then angry, as they state their belief that they had been told, and actually believed, the party was to be free. But, as we all know, there are no free parties, just as there are no free meals. Somewhere, someone has to pay, and now it will be their turn.

President Gordon B. Hinckley does not speak out against debt and the need to have a strong "financial cushion" alone, as you will see from a selection of quotations from other prophets. As mentioned before, "repetitive" prophetic counsel should "rivet" our attention.

Many years ago President *Heber C. Kimball* warned of speculation and extravagance among the Saints:

> After a while the gentiles will gather to this place by the thousands, and *Salt Lake City will be classed among the wicked cities of the world.*
>
> *A spirit of speculation and extravagance will take possession of the Saints, and the results will be financial bondage. Persecution comes next and all true Latter-day Saints will be tested to the limit* (*Deseret News*, May 23, 1931).

President *Spencer W. Kimball* expressed it this way:

> I am not howling calamity, but I fear that a great majority of our young people never have known *calamity, depression, hunger, homelessness, joblessness,* and cannot conceive of such situations ever coming again. *There are thousands of young families in this city who could not stand without suffering a three-month period without the threat of their home being foreclosed, their car repossessed, their electric and home equipment being taken back and themselves being reduced to unbelievable rations in the necessities* (*The Teachings of Spencer W. Kimball*, p. 372).

President *Ezra Taft Benson*, in speeches delivered in 1957 and 1962, cautioned that many saints foolishly view themselves as exempt from serious economic problems:

Many people do not believe that serious recession will ever come again. Feeling secure in their expectation of continuing employment and a steady flow of wages and salaries, *they obligate their future income without thought of what they would do if they should lose their jobs or if their income stopped* for some other reason. But *the best authorities have repeatedly said that we are not yet smart enough to control our economy without downward adjustments. Sooner or later these adjustments will come* (*The Improvement Era*, June 1957, p. 414).

President Benson later stated:

Too often we bask in our comfortable complacency and rationalize that the ravages of war, economic disaster, famine, and earthquake cannot happen here. Those who believe this are either not acquainted with the revelations of the Lord, or they do not believe them. *Those who smugly think these calamities will not happen, that they somehow will be set aside because of the righteousness of the Saints, are deceived and will rue the day they harbored such a delusion. The Lord has warned and forewarned us against a day of great tribulation and given us counsel, through His servants, on how we can be prepared for these difficult times.* Have we heeded His counsel? (*Teachings of Ezra Taft Benson*, p. 706).

President *J. Reuben Clark* said,

"*Let us avoid debt as we would the plague;* where we are now in debt, let us get out of debt; if not today, then tomorrow.

"*You of small means put your money in foodstuff and wearing apparel, not in stocks and bonds;* you of large means will think you know how to care for yourselves, but I may venture to *suggest that you do not speculate. Let every head of household aim to own his own home, free from mortgage.* Let every man who has a garden spot, *garden it;* every man who owns a farm, farm it." (*Ensign*, November 1980, p. 33).

Bishop *John H. Vandenberg* in 1966, also taught that the Saints need to avoid the dangers of debt:

Perhaps many of us need to take a good look at our own financial situation and philosophy, because *I fear that many Latter-day Saints are being swept into the rising tide of financial insolvency.* The virtues of thrift and saving need to be taught in our families. In accordance with the teachings of the Church, *let us try to be free of debt and have an adequate reserve of food, clothing, and money to meet an emergency.* Remember the adage: "*A family out of debt is out of danger*" (*Conference Report*, October 1966, pp. 68-69).

President *Ezra Taft Benson*, in 1973, expressed these observations regarding economic concerns:

The Saints have been advised to pay their own way and maintain a cash reserve. Recent history has demonstrated that in difficult days it is reserves with intrinsic values that are of most worth, rather than reserves, the value of which may be destroyed through inflation. It is well to remember that *continued government deficits cause inflation; inflation is used as an excuse for ineffective price controls; price controls lead to shortages; artificial shortages inevitably are used as an excuse to implement rationing.* When will we learn these basic economic principles? (*Conference Report,* October 1973, p. 92).

And he also made the following insightful observation:

A nation can hang itself on the gallows of excessive public debt—and the United States is no exception.

Some people would have us believe that the federal treasury is a bottomless grab-bag which never needs to be conserved or replenished (*The Red Carpet*, p. 165).

A wise person said "Greed and fear makes fools of us all."

CHAPTER

7

PROPHETIC STATEMENTS ABOUT EVENTS PRECEDING THE SECOND COMING OF CHRIST

AN OVERVIEW OF GENERAL SIGNS OF THE TIMES

Perhaps it will be helpful to provide a quick review of what the future holds, through events that we have been counseled to be prepared for. In truth, the Lord, through scripture and modern prophets, has not spared even graphic illustrations in his efforts to clearly communicate to each of us the nature of those events which will have to be reckoned with in the not too distant future. Today is the day of preparation, for when the final scenes began to unwind it will be everlastingly too late, for the Lord has said,

> . . . I will take vengeance upon the wicked, *for they will not repent;* for the cup of mine indignation is full; for behold, *my blood shall not cleanse them if they hear me not.*
>
> Wherefore, I the Lord God will send forth flies upon the face of the earth, which shall take hold of the inhabitants thereof, and shall eat their flesh, and shall cause maggots to come in upon them;
>
> And their tongues shall be stayed that they shall not utter against me; and their flesh shall fall from off their bones, and their eyes from their sockets.
>
> And it shall come to pass that the beasts of the forest and the fowls of the air shall devour them up (D&C 29:17-20).

In the prayer offered at the dedication of the Kirkland Temple, the Prophet *Joseph Smith* commented on what is to take place with these words:

> O Lord, *we delight not in the destruction of our fellow men;* their souls are precious before thee;
>
> But thy word must be fulfilled. Help thy servants to say, with thy grace assisting them: *Thy will be done, O Lord, and not ours.*
>
> We know that thou hast spoken by the mouth of thy prophets terrible things concerning the wicked, in the last days—that *thou wilt pour out thy judgments, without measure;*

Therefore, O Lord, *deliver thy people from the calamity of the wicked;* enable thy servants to seal up the law, and bind up the testimony, that they may be prepared against the day of burning (D&C 109:43-46).

President **Brigham Young** reported seeing the beginning of the end with this description of events that will eventually unfold:

When the testimony of the Elders ceases to be given, and the Lord says to them, "Come home; I will now preach my own sermons to the nations of the earth," all you now know can scarcely be called a preface *to the sermon that will be preached with fire and sword, tempests, earthquakes, hail, rain, thunders and lightnings, and fearful destruction.* . . .

You will hear of magnificent cities, now idolized by the people, sinking in the earth, *entombing the inhabitants.* The sea will heave itself beyond its bounds, *engulfing mighty cities. Famine will spread over the nations* and *nation will rise up against nation,* kingdom against kingdom and *states against states, in our own country and in foreign lands; and they will destroy each other, caring not for the blood and lives of their neighbors, of their families, or for their own lives (Discourses of Brigham Young,* pp. 111-12).

A frequently expressed statement regarding the Last Days was originally made by President **Wilford Woodruff** in 1894, given by President Woodruff again in 1896, reiterated by President Joseph Fielding Smith, and which was again referred to by President Benson in general conference—October, 1973.

President Woodruff's statement was as follows:

In one of the revelations the Lord told Joseph Smith: "Behold, verily, I say unto you, the angels are crying unto the Lord day and night, who are ready and waiting to be sent forth to reap the fields." [D&C 86:5]

God has held the angels of destruction for many years lest they should reap down the wheat with the tares. But I want to tell you now, those angels have left the portals of heaven, and they stand over this people and this nation now, and *are hovering over the earth waiting to pour out the judgments. And from this very day they shall be poured out. Calamities and troubles are increasing in the earth,* and there is a meaning to these things. Remember this, and reflect upon these matters. *If you do your duty, and I do my duty, we shall have protection, and shall pass through the afflictions in peace and safety (The Signs of the Times,* pp. 113, 115).

President **Joseph Fielding Smith** outlines what is to come as follows:

The *distress* and *perplexity, bloodshed* and *terror, selfish ambition of despotic rulers,* such as the world has never before seen, all indicate that the great and dreadful day of the Lord is very near, even at our doors. We have been warned by the prophets from the beginning of time. They have declared, by revelation from the Lord, that in this present day, *confusion, bloodshed, misery, plague, famine, earthquake, and other calamities, would cover the face of the earth.* The Lord told his disciples of these dreadful scenes and said *men's hearts would fail them because of these things coming upon the earth* . . . Only the unbelieving and rebellious against the teachings of our Lord and his prophets have failed to comprehend these momentous events (*Doctrines of Salvation*, vol. III, p. 19).

Elder *Neal A. Maxwell*, in 1988, discussed prophecies currently in the process of being fulfilled:

Our times already reflects yet another prophecy: *"Distress of nations, with perplexity"* (Luke 21:25). Before modern times, global perplexity simply was not possible. Now, there is a quick transmission of some crises and problems from one nation to others—*the consequences of debt-ridden economies, the spreading of diseases, the abuse of narcotics, and, perhaps most of all, a shared sense of near helplessness in the face of such perplexities* (*Ensign*, May 1988, p. 8).

Elder **Bruce R. McConkie** summarized the revelations regarding this millennial event, listing a number of "significant moments in time:"

The time for the beginning of the millennium is fixed. It has been definitely set and is known to the Father. It cannot be advanced . . . *Nor can it be postponed* . . . It will commence when Christ comes, and His coming is set by revelation (*Mormon Doctrine*, p. 494).

Elder McConkie later continued:

Many revelations summarized the signs and world conditions, the wars, perils, and commotions of the last days. Preceding our Lord's return, the prophetic word tells of *plagues, pestilence, famine, and disease such as the world has never before seen; . . . of scourges, tribulation, calamities, and disasters without parallel; . . . of strife, wars, rumors of wars, blood, carnage, and desolation which overshadow anything of past ages; of the elements being in commotion with resultant floods, storms, fires, whirlwinds, earthquakes—all of a proportion and intensity unknown to men in former days; of evil, iniquity, wickedness, turmoil, rapine, murder, crime and commotion among men almost beyond comprehension* (*Mormon Doctrine*, p. 691).

Elder McConkie continued on another occasion:

Be it remembered that *tribulations lie ahead. There will be wars in one nation and kingdom after another until war is poured out upon all nations and two hundred million men of war mass their armaments at Armageddon.*

Peace has been taken from the earth, the angels of destruction have begun their work, and their swords shall not be sheathed until the Prince of Peace comes to destroy the wicked and usher in the great Millennium.

There will be *earthquakes and floods and famines.* The waves of the sea shall heave themselves beyond their bounds, *the clouds shall withhold their rain,* and the *crops of the earth shall wither and die.*

There shall be *plagues and pestilence and disease and death. An overflowing scourge shall cover the earth and a desolating sickness shall sweep the land. Flies* shall take hold of the inhabitants of the earth, and *maggots* shall come in upon them. (see D&C 29:14-20.) "Their flesh shall fall from off their bones, and their eyes from their sockets" (D&C 29:19).

Bands of Gadianton robbers will infest every nation, immorality and murder and crime will increase, and it will seem as though every man's hand is against his brother (Ensign, May 1979, p. 93).

The 20th century has the ignoble distinction of being the most violent period in man's history. In this century some 200 million people have died from political violence, either by war between governments or at the hands of their own government.

President *Joseph Fielding Smith*, in 1942, said this century has been one of great turmoil, but this is only the beginning of sorrow:

The greater part of the first half of the twentieth century has been one of war, bloodshed, calamity and destruction, such as the world has never witnessed before, but *these are but the beginning of sorrow and tribulation* which have been predicted to come upon the world for its wickedness and rebellion (*The Signs of the Times*, p. 201).

When we think of the leaders in this slaughter of humanity, the name that most readily comes to mind is Hitler, but in terms of total lives lost, his legacy was actually inconsequential when compared to those killed by Stalin, Lenin and Mao. Others who shared a part in this "carnage century" of violence are Pol Pot, Idi Amin, Mengistu Haile Mariam, Saddam Hussein and a multitude of other smaller players. Add to the above the millions who have acted out their own violence and murder in the streets of otherwise peaceful towns and cities, as well as those perpetrated within own their homes and among families, and you have an era without precedence in recorded history of the human race's escalating destruction of his fellow man.

Satan is very much alive and aware of the fact that the time of his influence and reign is limited. Therefore his focus will become even more violent as these last days dwindle toward their close. He is fully aware that he will be bound for a thousand years, and he is not about to go quietly. Thus, because his days are now truly numbered, the intensity of his efforts will be correspondingly magnified. It would appear that this growth in intensity accounts for the many prophetic utterances of phrases such as "as never before had been seen," "without parallel," "overshadowing anything of past ages," "unknown to men in former days," and "beyond comprehension," which apparently must be used to meaningfully describe this particular era.

THE SAINTS NEED TO BE RIGHTEOUS AND READY

President *Joseph Fielding Smith* voiced his concern of the often-lackadaisical attitude of the Latter-day Saints regarding the second coming of the Savior:

In our own day messengers have come from the presence of the Lord declaring that it is even at our doors, and yet many, even among the Latter-day Saints, go about their affairs as though this coming of the Lord Jesus Christ and the ushering in of this reign of peace had been indefinitely postponed for many generations. *I say to you that it is at our doors. I say this with all confidence because the Lord has said it.*

Is it not time for us to take notice? Should not the members of The Church of Jesus Christ of Latter-day Saints be sober-minded, have the spirit of humility, and faith, and prayers in their hearts, *endeavoring to know the purposes of the Lord and to stand before him in righteousness and thus be prepared should that day come while we are living? Is it not a fatal mistake for us to feel that this day is yet a long time off, that it is not to come in our generation?* (*Doctrines of Salvation*, vol. III, pp. 55-56).

President **Brigham Young**, in 1854, gave these reassuring observations for those who feel that they may not be able to endure the events that will be forthcoming:

[Some of] you that have not passed thro' the trials and persecutions, and drivings with this people from the beginning, but have only read them, or heard some of them related, may think how awful they were to endure, and wonder that the Saints survived them at all. The thought of it makes your heart sink within you, your brain reel, and your body tremble, and you are ready to exclaim, "I could not have endured it." [Yet] I have been in the heat of it, and never felt better in all my life; *I never felt the peace and power of the Almighty more copiously poured upon me than in the keenest part of our trials. They appeared nothing to me* (*Deseret News Weekly*, 24 August 1854, p. 83).

Elder **Bruce R. McConkie** also proclaimed that in the end the righteous will not only be able to endure what will be required of them, but they will prevail:

We see evil forces everywhere uniting to destroy the family, to ridicule morality and decency, to glorify all that is lewd and base. We see wars and plagues and pestilence. Nations rise and fall. Blood and carnage and death are everywhere. Gadianton robbers fill the judgment seats in many nations. An evil power seeks to overthrow the freedom of all nations and countries. *Satan reigns in the hearts of men; it is the great day of his power.*

But amid it all, the work of the Lord rolls on.

Truly the world is and will be in commotion, but *the Zion of God will be unmoved. The wicked and ungodly shall be swept from the Church*, the little stone will continue to grow until it fills the whole earth.

There will yet be martyrs; the doors in Carthage shall again enclose the innocent. *We have not been promised that the trials and evils of the world will entirely pass us by.*

If we, as a people, keep the commandments of God; if we take the side of the Church on all issues, both religious and political; if we take the Holy Spirit for our guide; if we give heed to the words of the apostles and prophets who minister among us—then, from an eternal standpoint, all things will work together for our good (*Ensign*, May 1980, pp. 71-73).

Because Heavenly Father is all-knowing, he is fully aware of Satan's activities. Therefore he is able to instruct his children regarding the measures to be taken to protect them as Satan's fury is unleashed upon the world. From what is outlined above, it would seem that no family should neglect their food storage. Simple reasoning would tell us it will be a critical factor in our temporal salvation in these last days. Note the following:

Please don't casually pass off what you have read; make it a matter of earnest prayer. Life is not designed to be lived without some substantive challenges, but some of them can be either avoided, or substantially tempered, with proper preparation.

PREPARE FOR AN
ACCELERATION OF CALAMITIES WORLD-WIDE

When scripturally looking ahead, we became aware that there is a unique timeline rapidly concluding either at, or very near our day. Just think: as near as we can calculate, in a very short time we will experience the ending of six thousand calendar years of mankind's probationary history, and the beginning of the Millennial seventh thousand year. This particular period has been the subject of numerous prophetic utterances, as both the Savior and the prophets looked forward to our day. And yet, very soon it will no longer be something we "look forward" to, for shortly the prophesied events of those days will be upon us.

Elder *Bruce R. McConkie* made this comment on the Lord's time table and our calendar:

Our revelations speak of "this earth during the seven thousand years of it's continuance, or its temporal existence," and also specifies that Christ will come "in the beginning of the seventh thousand years" (D&C 77). This in no way names the day nor the hour of our Lord's return, and it does not put a stamp of divine approval upon our calendars as they now exist. It simply lets us know that the Biblical account of the chronology relative to Adam and his posterity is either correct or substantially so. The number of years there recited is either accurate or so nearly so that it does not make any real difference for our purpose (*The Promised Messiah*, p. 606).

We are living in a most unusual time in the history of the world. It is a time when profound events either will be, or are now unfolding—events that are extremely difficult for us to fully comprehend. This transactional move from one time period to another will have a monumental effect on all those who experience it. Thus, it seems most appropriate for us to reflect even more deeply on those gifts received through Christ's birth, death, resurrection and atonement, that by so doing we can come to a greater understanding of this millennial gift in our own lives, as well as its relationship to the Savior's second coming.

In doing this, however, let us be careful that we do not confuse the actual coming or physical appearance of Jesus Christ to the world with those events which are to precede his actual appearance. It is not uncommon for some people to lump these two very different experiences together. There is also a natural tendency to draw parallels between events attending His ancient resurrection with those yet to be manifested before, and at the time, of his second coming.

The events surrounding his second coming are very different in context and circumstance from those of his first glorified appearances to the earth shortly after his resurrection. For example, His appearance to those in Book of Mormon times was accompanied singularly by rather immediate events—largely limited to the space of some three hours of destruction. This will not be the case with his second coming, since there are a multitude of comparatively extensive events that must take place before the Messiah can actually take his place as King of Kings.

Through the Book of Mormon, however, we learn more how we might feel when the Savior does come to assume his rightful place. The Book of Mormon describes the relief of those who survived the destructive events brought upon them prior to witnessing Christ's appearance to them here in the Americas. In like manner, those of us in this dispensation are likely to feel at least as much, if not much greater relief and joy by virtue of having survived the multitude of preparatory tribulations that will necessarily have to be completed prior to his arrival and millennial reign upon the earth.

What we, in our day, have individually been warned to prepare for are a multitude of overwhelming events; incidents that are even at our doors wherein *all* the wicked will be destroyed in order for this earth to be properly—even physically—moved into a terrestrial existence. Such a transformational process intimates, in contrast with his first coming, a more global and intensive preparatory period. This transformation cannot be wrought overnight. When someone states they don't believe he will be coming right away, it should nevertheless be noted that this does not eliminate them from their responsibility to be spiritually and temporally prepared, should they wish to withstand the terrible events that must precede his actual appearance.

There are many reasons for the Lord's counsel to be ready at all times, but of paramount importance (and a thing which often escapes the understanding of the Saints) is the simple fact that the Lord requires His people to live, daily, in a constant state of "readiness," a testimony of their obedience, devotion and righteousness. His instructions have been, even from the meridian of times, very clear and pointed on this matter. He began instructing his followers, even then, in many and varied ways that all must "watch and be ready." If the Savior did not want his Saints to daily live by this precept, he would not have began telling them nearly two millennia ago to be in this state of constant preparation. Thus, we must not be lulled into false security by looking "beyond the mark."

In the October, 1972 General Conference, President *Harold B. Lee* gave the following guide on how to approach the important study of Christ's second coming, saying that we should be searching out and understanding the signs:

Are you priesthood bearers aware of the fact that *we need no [sensational] publications to be forewarned*, if we were only conversant with what the scriptures have already spoken to us in plainness?

Let me give you the sure word of prophecy on which you should rely for your guide.

Read the 24th chapter of Matthew—particularly that inspired version as contained in the Pearl of Great Price. (Joseph Smith 1.)

Then *read the 45th section of the Doctrine and Covenants* where the Lord, not man, has documented the signs of the times.

Now turn to *section 101 and section 133 of the Doctrine and Covenants* and hear the step-by-step recounting of events leading up to the coming of the Savior.

Finally, turn to the promises the Lord makes to those who keep the commandments when these judgments descend upon the wicked, as set forth in the *Doctrine and Covenants, section 38 (Ensign*, January 1973, p. 106).

After you have reviewed in detail President Lee's suggested readings, I believe you will be impressed that the events which are now beginning to unfold are going to challenge even the best that is in each of us. Preparation, therefore, continues to be our watchword.

President *Ezra Taft Benson* referred to the events surrounding the Second Coming in these words:

In section 1 of the great Doctrine and Covenants, a volume of modern scripture, we read these words: "*Prepare ye, prepare ye for that which is to come . . .*" (D&C 1:12) Further in this same revelation are these warning words: "*. . . I the Lord, knowing the calamity which should come upon the inhabitants of the earth. . . .*" (D&C 1:17).

What are some of the calamities for which we are to prepare? In section 29 the Lord warns us of "*a great hailstorm sent forth to destroy the crops of the earth.*" (D&C 29:16.) In section 45 we read of "*an overflowing scourge; for a desolating sickness* shall cover the land." (D&C 45:31.) In section 63 the Lord declares he has "decreed *wars upon the face of the earth . . .*" (D&C 63:33).

In Matthew, chapter 24, we learn of "*famines, and pestilences, and earthquakes . . .*" (Matt. 24:7). The Lord declared that these and other calamities shall occur. These particular prophecies seem not to be conditional. The Lord, with his foreknowledge, knows that they will happen. Some will come about through man's manipulations; others through the forces of nature and nature's God, but that they will come seems certain. *Prophecy is but history in reverse—divine disclosure of future events.*

Yet, through all of this, the Lord Jesus Christ has said: "... if ye are prepared ye shall not fear" (D&C 38:30) (*Ensign*, January 1974, pp. 68, 69).

Again, "no man knows the day or the hour" when the Savior will come, but we do know that it is not likely to occur before the end of the first six thousand years of the earth's temporal existence, as we know them. These years are rapidly concluding. Again, are we prepared?

Elder *M. Russell Ballard*, in 1992, discussed some of the current signs of the times:

These are difficult times, when the forces of nature seem to be unleashing a flood of "*famines, and pestilence, and earthquakes, in divers places.*"

Recently, I read a newspaper article that cited statistics from the U.S. Geological Survey indicating that *earthquakes around the world are increasing in frequency and intensity.* According to the article, only two major earthquakes, earthquakes measuring at least six on the Richter scale, occurred during the 1920s. In the 1930s the number increased to five, and then decreased to four during the 1940s. But in the 1950s, nine major earthquakes occurred. followed by fifteen during the 1960s, forty-six during the 1970s, and fifty-two during the 1980s. Already almost as many major earthquakes have occurred during the 1990s as during the entire decade of the 1980s.

Although the prophecies tell us that these things are to take place, more and more people are expressing great alarm at what appears to *be an acceleration of worldwide calamity....* These are difficult times, when the forces of nature seem to be unleashing a flood of "famines, and pestilence, and earthquakes, in divers places." ... But regardless of this dark picture, which will ultimately get worse, *we must never allow ourselves to give up hope! ...* (*Ensign*, November 1992, p. 31).

A YEAR OF DISASTERS—1998

The year 1998 brought with it approximately 700 catastrophic natural disasters, which killed some 50,000 people—making 1998 the most calamitous year on record, according to Munich Reinsurance, a German company that monitors natural disasters. Last year's total measures three times greater than the annual average for natural catastrophes during the 1960's.

Some of the worst recorded in this worst year: 240 windstorms, 170 floods and nine hurricanes (with Mitch killing nearly 10,000 people). There was also a typhoon in Japan, an earthquake in Afghanistan, a cyclone in India, mud slides in Italy, winter storms and a cold wave in Europe, heat waves and forest fires in the U.S., Greece and Brazil. It appears that 1999 is closing with a series of disasters that far exceed those of 1998 in their intensity.

It may be of interest to some that of the 10 largest earthquakes known in American history, surprisingly, only one of them occurred in California. On a peaceful night of December 11, 1811 the small town of New Madrid, Missouri, was shaken awake at 2 a.m. by a quake that literally tore the town apart. Unbelievably, the Mississippi River flowed upstream, pushed by a gigantic wave that was reported to be higher than trees standing 30-feet tall, destroying everything in its path. Earthquake fissures opened and the in-rushing water created a 40-mile-long lake in eastern Arkansas and a ten-mile lake in Tennessee. The quake was so powerful that it was felt 1100 miles away in Boston. One is reminded of the Lord's referral in D&C 121:33 regarding the Missouri river as it relates to man's "puny arm" and the power of the Lord.

Because of the number of prophecies that must be fulfilled, some may assume that there is considerable time left before we fully experience the events that will precede Christ's second coming. On the other hand, it may come as a great surprise to all of us how rapidly these events could unfold, with many events overlapping each other and culminating simultaneously. As wars, famine and natural disasters engulf the world's population, a number of the prophesied events may be or have been quietly fulfilled, with little awareness on our part. Indeed, the world at large may likely become so tumultuous and caught up in efforts to merely survive the days of tribulation, that significant events may come and go, often completely unnoticed by them, as well as by many of the Saints.

Joseph Smith listed several prophecies that must be fulfilled before the coming of Christ:

> *Judah must return, Jerusalem must be rebuilt, and the temple,* and *water come out* from under the temple, and the *waters of the dead Sea be healed.* It will take some time to rebuild the walls of the city and the temple, &c.; and all this must be done before the Son of Man will make His appearance (*Teachings of the Prophet Joseph Smith*, p. 286).

Elder *Neal A. Maxwell,* in 1988 gave this review of the time frame for fulfilling prophecies:

> Some prophecies, such as the return of the Jewish people to Israel, were decades in their fulfillment . . . Other prophecies can be fulfilled in a compressed period of time. Taking the restored gospel "for a witness" to all the nations of the world involves generations but a "desolating scourge" can cover the land quickly. Sadly, more than one qualifying possibility already exists for such scourges (*Ensign,* May 1988, p. 7).

The Lord tells us that the history of this world will again come full circle, as it has on other occasions. Thus, careful consideration will disclose that as we are involved in the closing chapters of the earth's history we will face a repeat performance like unto the "days of Noe." The Lord expresses it this way:

> And as it was in the days of Noe, so shall it be also in the days of the Son of man.
>
> They did eat, they drank, they married wives, they were given in marriage, until the day that Noe entered into the ark, and the flood came, and destroyed them all.
>
> Likewise also as it was in the days of Lot; they did eat, they drank, they bought, they sold, they planted, they builded;
>
> But the same day that Lot went out of Sodom it rained fire and brimstone from heaven, and destroyed them all.
>
> Even thus shall it be in the day when the Son of man is revealed (Luke 17: 26-30).

As we can see, the Lord has indicated that the wickedness of man in the days of Noah would be replicated in our day. How wicked were they in Noah's day?

> And God saw that the wickedness of men had become great in the earth; and every man was lifted up in the imagination of the thoughts of his heart, being only evil continually (Moses 8:22).

From the above, it is easy to see why we should not be casual nor passive about being both temporally and spiritually prepared for what lies ahead. The Lord has indicated there will be great turmoil and tribulation as the wicked are destroyed before and at His coming:

> For behold, and lo, vengeance cometh speedily upon the ungodly as the whirlwind; and who shall escape it?
>
> The Lord's scourge shall pass over by night and by day, and *the report thereof shall vex all people;* yea, it shall not be stayed until the Lord come (D&C 97:22-23).

In order to survive this pre-millennial period we should maintain our lives in a constant state of readiness before the Lord. We should continually seek to hear his word, learn his word, and actively live it on a daily basis—which includes keeping the counsel of his prophets in both spiritual and temporal matters. For those who wish to be prepared, one of those counsels which has been consistently encouraged has been food storage and preparations.

.

CHAPTER
8
THE PREPAREDNESS RESPONSIBILITIES OF LOCAL CHURCH LEADERS

THE NEED TO PREPARE BEFORE THE DAYS OF TRIBULATION

When times of great distress come, those holding the keys of leadership may well spend many sleepless nights as they attempt to feed, clothe, and shelter the people over whom they preside. No doubt many may will feel a heavy burden and a grave sadness if they haven't done all they could to motivate their people to be personally prepared. For example, President *Gordon B. Hinckley* related the following:

[During the Great Depression], my father was . . . president of the largest stake in this valley. It was before our present welfare program was established. *He walked the floor worrying about his people* (*Ensign*, November 1998, p. 53).

Hopefully, priesthood leaders will not delude themselves into thinking that many of today's "self-absorbed," ill-prepared generation will not petition them for food in time of crisis. Their excuses and justifications for having failed to prepare will be unique, creative and endless. When this happens, how will stake presidents and bishops respond to the hungry wide eyes of children looking pleadingly at them as they seek to be fed, clothed and sheltered? Will they tell them they are sorry their parents failed to prepare when they had the opportunity to do so, then remind their parents that they had been sufficiently warned and therefore cannot receive assistance?

Or, will priesthood leaders ignore the depth of the problem and treat everyone's request in an equal fashion, all the while knowing, as they have previously been taught, that there is not going to be enough to help everyone? It is true that priesthood leaders can currently ignore this issue with an "I'll let other priesthood leaders worry about it" attitude—but the reality that their people are unprepared still exists, and while they are pretending it is not going to be their problem to face, this serious problem may very well become theirs.

Factually, the only way to avoid this inevitable difficulty is for all leaders to have their members constantly prepared to handle difficult times whenever they do occur. It is not a problem that will go away simply because it is ignored, nor because some members are unresponsive to council. If church leaders are truly interested in avoiding what has the potential to become a monumental tragedy, they need to start laboring with their membership now.

PRIESTHOOD LEADERSHIP IS ESSENTIAL

Priesthood leaders in the Church today face a serious challenge in helping the Saints understand the necessity of food storage and preparation, an awareness many members have yet to grasp. It is not enough for leaders to lay all of the responsibility at the feet of the individual member unless they have also done their part, because there is more to "teaching" than just telling members to prepare. Leaders need to set the example by being obedient to this principle in their own homes, and then actively encourage the members to do the same—a process of learning, living and then teaching.

THE CHURCH HAS CONSISTENTLY SET THE EXAMPLE

It is obvious that the Church intends to set the example for the membership at large; having encouraged members to store grain and other essentials, they have followed their own counsel. The following statement is indicative of how serious the Church is about being generally prepared:

> *A year's supply of fuel for all these trucks* is stored in Salt Lake City and throughout the country at welfare facilities. *A year's supply of tires and maintenance parts* is also kept on hand. These reserves enable the Church to properly respond in nearly every emergency. *The Church practices what it teaches its members to do—be prepared to remain independent for at least a year in case of an emergency* (Pure Religion, p. 227).

Considering construction of Regional Store Houses back in 1977, President **Spencer W. Kimball** emphasized the need for grain storage:

> 'What are you brethren doing about grain storage?" The room was silent for a moment. They had not thought of granaries as part of the expansion program. President Kimball then said that the *Church could not build storehouses and canneries without granaries* (Pure Religion, p. 187).

INSTRUCTIONS TO PRIESTHOOD LEADERS: THEY ARE ALSO TO SET AN EXAMPLE

The requirement to prepare is as much, if not more, a responsibility of priesthood leaders as it is for those over whom they preside. Back as early as 1867, President **Brigham Young** insisted that bishops were not only to see that members were prepared but were also to set the example:

> I wish now to say a few words to the Bishops . . . We have said much to the people *with regard to laying up provisions to last them a few years*. This is our duty now;

it has been our duty for years. *How many of our bishops have provisions laid up for one year, two years, or seven years?* There may be a few bishops who have got their grain laid away to last their families a year, but the great majority of them have not. *The people do, or should look to their bishop for example.* Each bishop should be an example to his ward. *If the bishop of a ward lays up wheat to last his family a year, two years, or seven years, as the case may be, his neighbors on the right and on the left will be very apt to do the same (Journal of Discourses,* vol. 12, p. 106).

That same year, Elder *George A. Smith* noted that leadership responsibility to be prepared extends even beyond immediate members:

> *Terrible destruction awaits the wicked. They will come to us by thousands by-and-by, saying, "Can you not feed us? Can you not do something for us?"* It is said by the prophets they shall come bending and shall say you are the priests of the Lord. What priest could administer greater earthly blessings than *food to the hungry, who have fled from a country where the sword, famine, and pestilence were sweeping away their thousands?* I look upon the subject of storing grain and other kinds of food as a very religious matter (*Journal of Discourses,* vol. 12, p. 141).

In 1942, instructions were given by President *Harold B. Lee* similar to that expressed by President Young in 1867. The question is just as pertinent today:

> We renew our counsel, said the leaders of the Church, and repeat our instructions: "Let every Latter-day Saint that has land, produce some valuable essential foodstuff thereon and then preserve it." . . . *Let me ask you leaders who are here today: In 1937 did you store in your own basements and in your own private storehouses and granaries sufficient for a year's supply?* (*Conference Report,* April 1943, p. 127).

President *Ezra Taft Benson*, in 1965, taught that priesthood leaders are not exempt from famine; if they are not prepared they will suffer the same consequences as the unprepared over whom they preside:

> *Should the Lord decide at this time to cleanse the Church*—and *the need for that cleansing seems to be increasing*—a famine of one year's duration could wipe out a large percentage of slothful members, including some ward and stake officers. Yet we cannot say we have not been warned (*Conference Report,* April 1965, p. 12).

HOW SHOULD PRIESTHOOD LEADERS PROCEED?

President *Henry D. Moyle*, in 1956, repeated the counsel given by President David O. McKay in 1936: begin with the "circle of light," allowing it to illuminate the way:

> I can say this to you: The first circle of light we have seen is October 1st, 1936, when *by that date we shall see to it that we have sufficient food, fuel, clothing, etc., to see every needy family through this coming winter,* and by the time we get to October 1st, *the light will have extended sufficiently far to permit us to see the next move we*

should make. I can promise you one thing, that we'll be running in the light all the way through this dark night (*Conference Report*, April 1956, p. 60).

President **Spencer W. Kimball**, in 1976, discussed how priesthood leaders must lead the way, noting that they could make a difference:

> The Lord said also, "Not every one that saith unto me, Lord, Lord, shall enter into the kingdom of heaven: but he that doeth the will of my Father which is in heaven." (Matt.7:21.) And I was thinking that there are as many wards and branches in the Church as there are people in this room, one for one. And *what great accomplishment there would be if every bishop and every branch president in all the world*, wherever it's possible . . . *had a storage such as has been suggested here this morning—and took to their three or four or five hundred members the same message, quoting scripture and insisting that the people of their wards and branches do the things the Lord has requested*, for we know that there are many who are failing. "Why call ye me, Lord, Lord, and do not the things which I say?"
>
> Think of the number of people represented here this day by the stake presidents, mission presidents, and others who are directors, who have many people under them. Our 750 stakes—all of them including hundreds, sometimes thousands, of members—could show *the power that we have, if we go to work and actually push this matter until it is done. We talk about it, we listen to it, but sometimes we do not do the things which the Lord says* (*Ensign*, May 1976, p. 124).

President **Spencer W. Kimball** reviewed what he would do pertaining to welfare services if he still were a stake president:

> From these experiences [as a stake president], coupled with observations of the needs of our people at this time, I should like to share with you what I would do today in welfare services if I were now serving as a stake president.
>
> First, *I would learn the program.* I would study the scriptures, handbooks, and materials relating to welfare. I would come to understand that Welfare Services is nothing more nor less than "gospel in action" . . .
>
> Most of us learn best what we apply in our own lives. I hope I would not be found wanting in applying basic gospel principles in my life, in my own home, with my own family. *I would live the precepts of personal and family preparedness.* That means *having a garden*, wisely *managing family resources*, and *expanding my educational horizons*. It means *staying fit, replenishing the family year's supply, fixing up our property*, and all the rest we have been asked of the Lord to do . . .
>
> Second, having learned everything I could, *I would teach my ward and stake officers the principles and practices of Welfare Services.* This includes *instructing them in gospel principles, duties, and specific assignments*. With my counselors, I would teach bishops to "(search) after the poor to administer to their wants by humbling the rich and the proud" as the scriptures teach (D&C 84:112) . . .
>
> Third, *I would implement welfare services as best my stake could.* It is in the doing that the real blessing comes. Do it! (*Ensign*, May 1979, pp. 99-100).

President *Ezra Taft Benson* indicated that all levels of church government should be concerned about the implementation of the food storage program in the lives of the Saints:

> *We must do more to get our people prepared for the difficult days we face in the future.* Our major concern should be their *spiritual preparation* so they will *respond with faith and not fear.* "If ye are prepared, ye shall not fear"(D&C 38:30). Our next concern should be for their *temporal preparation. When the economies of nations fail, when famine and other disasters prevent people from buying food in stores, the Saints must be prepared to handle these emergencies.* This is a matter of concern for area, region and stake councils (*Teachings of Ezra Taft Benson*, p. 264).

FAMILY PREPAREDNESS: CORNERSTONE OF THE CHURCH WELFARE PROGRAM

Some church members have failed to catch the vision of how essential personal preparedness is because they view the vast resources and welfare services of the Church as being somehow endless, and their bishops always able and willing to meet their every need, especially in times of personal crisis or emergency. However, the Brethren have gone to great lengths to clarify that the principles by which we are saved in these matters are taught by the Church, but must be implemented individually; eventually it is "we" who must save "ourselves."

In April, 1983 Presidents *Spencer W. Kimball*, *Marion G. Romney*, and *Gordon B. Hinckley*, The First Presidency, announced a major change in church production projects:

> Many stakes would no longer [even] have a welfare production project. The Brethren emphasized that they were not doing away with production projects, but *they were changing the emphasis to family preparedness and self-reliance* (*Pure Religion*, p. 238).

Elder *Russell M. Nelson*, in 1986, taught that the Lord's storehouse is within the homes of the Latter-day Saints. He said that

> "An important part of *the Lord's storehouse is maintained as a year's supply*, stored, where possible, *in the homes of faithful families* of the Church" (*Ensign*, May 1986, p. 27).

President *Thomas S. Monson*, in 1986, followed President Faust's earlier admonition with the following:

> As has been said so often, the best storehouse system that the Church could devise would be for *every family to store a year's supply of food, clothing, and, where possible, the other necessities of life.* It is our sacred duty to care for our families, including our extended families (*Ensign*, September 1986, p. 4).

Again, the First Presidency issued a statement to all priesthood leaders in a letter to be read in Sacrament meeting titled "Preparing for Emergencies." The Presidency reinforced previous counsel and encouraged members to become broadly prepared for times of crisis. This letter was issued June 24, 1988 by Presidents *Ezra Taft Benson, Gordon B. Hinckley*, and *Thomas S. Monson*:

> *We continue to encourage members to store sufficient food, clothing, and where possible fuel for at least one year.* We have not laid down an exact formula for what should be stored. However, we suggest that members **concentrate on essential foods that sustain life, such as grains, legumes, cooking oil, powdered milk, salt, sugar or honey, and water.** Most families can achieve and maintain this basic level of preparedness. The decision to do more than this rests with the individual.

But there is an additional purpose and need for the members to be prepared: President *Ezra Taft Benson* wrote that the Saints must be independent for the Church to be independent.

> The strength of the Church Welfare Program lies in every family following the inspired direction of the Church leaders to be self-sustaining through adequate preparation. *God intends for His Saints to so prepare themselves "that the Church may stand independent above all other creatures beneath the celestial world"* (D&C 78:14) (*Teachings of Ezra Taft Benson*, p. 265).

Elder *J. Thomas Fyans* noted that family preparedness is an essential to church preparedness:

> I feel a greater sense of pride and gratitude in the Church's welfare system, including the sweep and scope of the *Storehouse Resource System*. However, I think it important to note, brothers and sisters, that the real welfare strength of this church does not reside in the food stored in our storehouses, nor in the production capacity of our welfare farms, nor even in the important power our employment system has in helping to find jobs for members seeking employment.
>
> *The real strength of the Church lies in the savings accounts, the gardens, the income-producing skill, the home storage, the resiliency, the talents, and the testimonies of each individual member of the Church and in the family of which each of us is a part . . .*
>
> Stated in plainness, *each family unit's personal and family preparedness activity is every bit as important as this vast and marvelous welfare system.* The real strength of the Church does not ultimately lie in the financial and commodity reserves of the Church; rather, *it rests in the reserves and strength of every household* (*Ensign,* November 1979, p. 86).

PRIESTHOOD LEADERS ASSIGNED THE TASK OF TEACHING PREPARATION

Teaching the principle of food storage should not be neglected. Inspiring, motivating and converting today's "entitlement generation" will be no small challenge.

In 1863, bishops were instructed to personally look into the preparation of each ward member by President **Brigham Young:**

> Again *I request of the Bishops to be certain that the members of their Wards have their supply of breadstuffs in reserve to last them until another harvest,* and we will trust in God for the coming year. Be not so unwise as to sell the bread that you and your children need. ". . . and remember that you cannot buy any from me, unless you pay a fair price for it." (*Journal of Discourses,* vol. 10, p. 256).

This performance obligation of the bishops was reiterated by President **Brigham Young** in 1864 at the next General Conference:

> At our Semi-Annual conference last fall *the Bishops were instructed to go to each house and see what breadstuffs were on hand.* Why? "Because the time is coming when they will want breadstuffs." It comes to my ear every day that this one and that one is in want. "Such a one has had no bread for three days" (*Journal of Discourses,* vol. 10, p. 292).

In the 1911 October Conference Stake Presidents and Bishops were instructed by Elder **Reed Smoot** to encourage their people to prepare:

> It would not surprise me to see the time come when the people will suffer for want of sufficient breadstuff. *I hope the people will have at least a year's wheat supply on hand, rather than, as many are today, being in debt for the wheat consumed during the past year.* So presidents of stakes, bishops of wards, leading brethren, wherever you give advice, *encourage the people to take care of all the bounties that God is bestowing upon them,* and I know if you will do it, it will be better for every man, and every family. (*Conference Report,* October 1911, p. 28).

Bishop **Victor L. Brown**, in 1976, noted that it is "critical" for church leaders and members to be prepared, and that conversion to the principle of preparedness must be brought about through their teaching efforts:

> We look to you stake presidents, bishops, and Relief Society Presidents to *teach the people the basic principles of self-reliance and independence. It is of critical importance that the members of the Church be converted to this principle.* If the Church as a whole would practice these teachings we would have no need to fear regardless of problems that will undoubtedly arise.
>
> The Lord has said: *"For if you will that I give unto you a place in the celestial world, you must prepare yourselves by doing the things which I have commanded you and required of you . . .*

"Behold, this is the preparation wherewith I prepare you, and the foundation, and the ensample which I give unto you, whereby you may accomplish the commandments which are given you;

"That through my providence, notwithstanding the tribulation which shall descend upon you, that the Church may stand independent above all other creatures beneath the celestial world." (D&C 78: 7, 13-14.)

Family preparedness is the key to meeting the needs of family members and is the foundation upon which church preparedness is based (Ensign, May 1976, pp. 110, 112).

Also in 1976, Bishop **Vaughn J. Featherstone** challenged priesthood leaders to set a goal to have their people prepared by April 1977:

Brothers and sisters, what have we *done in our stakes and wards* to see that every Latter-day Saint has a year's reserve of food to sustain life? *Let's not only keep teaching the principle, but let's also teach our people how . . .*

The Lord will make it possible, if we make a firm commitment for every Latter-day Saint family to have a year's supply of food reserves.

Bishops and stake presidents, let us accept the challenge on behalf of the Saints in our wards and stakes. It will prove to be a very Christlike deed on your part. Follow through and *check up one year from now and make certain we achieve results* (Ensign, May 1976, pp. 116-118).

In 1977 President **Ezra Taft Benson** taught that every officer in the Church should be trained and then teach each member to be prepared:

The times require that every officer of the Church be uniformly trained in principles of welfare, and that *each one in turn train the rank and file until every individual is prepared for the calamities which are to come.* I think it not extreme for me to say at this point that when all is written about the events to come, we may have hardly enough time to prepare, even if all our resources, spiritual and temporal, are taxed to the limit (*The Training Challenge,* General Welfare Services Committee meeting, Salt Lake City, February, 1977).

Also in 1977, President **Gordon B. Hinckley** stressed that it was the quorums' responsibility to teach family preparedness to the Saints:

Each quorum must be a working brotherhood for every member if its purpose is to be realized. *There must be instruction in principles of personal and family preparedness.* If effectively taught, *such instruction will become preventative welfare,* because the quorum member and his family, equipped with such knowledge, will be the better prepared to handle many difficulties that might arise. *The teaching of financial and resource management, home production and storage, the fostering of such activities as will promote physical, emotional, and spiritual health might all be the proper and legitimate concerns of the presidency of the quorum in behalf of its members* (Ensign, November 1977, p. 86).

In 1980 Church leaders were again asked to teach and convert members to food storage, this time by Bishop *Victor L. Brown*:

I implore you stake leaders to *see that the messages of this Welfare Services Meeting get to the bishops, the quorum leaders and the ward Relief Society presidents so that the members of the Church can be taught and converted sufficiently to live the basic principles of which we speak and thus put their houses in order.*

Our concern and the thrust of my message, which has been repeated from this pulpit many times, is that *the welfare program rests on the basic principle of personal and family, not on Church preparedness.*

May I again implore you priesthood and Relief Society leaders to *see that all members of the Church everywhere understand the responsibility they have for their own welfare,* that our people will be blessed to live provident and righteous lives (*Ensign*, November 1980, p. 80).

Elder *L. Tom Perry*, in 1981, counseled leaders to teach "prevention" and to set family preparedness as a priority:

It is time to ask ourselves, What has created the problem of placing such a heavy burden on the Church to supply our welfare needs? My analysis of this problem would lead me to believe that, as leaders, *we have spent far too much time in administering relief and far too little in prevention by having our families prepared to administer to their own needs.*

It is time to teach the basics—again. *It is time to make the number one priority of our welfare efforts personal and family preparedness.* We must prepare now so that in time of need more of our members will be able to draw upon their own preparedness and not have to seek assistance from the Church. . . .

The home must be the heart of the welfare program. *We must focus our training of personal and family preparedness to reach the family organization.* We must teach that *every family should be headed by an executive committee comprised of a husband and wife who will set aside sufficient time to plan for their family needs* (*Ensign*, May 1981, p. 88).

Again, in 1988 Elder *Joseph B. Wirthlin* taught that

"*Members should be taught to provide for themselves and their families.* That is the Lord's way. When they are caring for their own they are in a better position to help others as the gospel requires" (*Pure Religion*, p. 386).

THE CHURCH'S CAPACITY TO FEED MEMBERS IS LIMITED

Priesthood leaders should consistently stress something many members often do not understand: the Church is to provide only for those genuinely unable to care for themselves, not for those who had an opportunity to prepare but elected to ignore the counsel. Note the following statements:

President *Brigham Young:*

My warfare is, and has been for years, to get the people to understand that *if they do not take care of themselves they will not be taken care of;* that if we do not lay the foundation to feed and clothe and shelter ourselves we shall perish with hunger and with cold; we might also suffer in the summer season from the direct rays of the sun upon our naked and unprotected bodies (*Discourses of Brigham Young,* pp. 16-17).

President *J. Reuben Clark, Jr.:*

There is no church dole; that is one reason why we must make the care of the needy a local problem, and why we should continue to make it local. *The Church cannot give a dole; it cannot provide a great reservoir to which bishops could send and get all they need for their poor* just as if the Church were a United States Treasury that could be dipped into. It cannot be done (*Ensign,* May 1976, p. 110).

President *Ezra Taft Benson:*

Our Bishops storehouses are not intended to stock enough commodities to care for all the members of the Church. Storehouses are only established to care for the poor and the needy. For this reason, *members of the Church have been instructed to personally store a year's supply of food, clothing, and, where possible, fuel.* By following this counsel, most members will be prepared and able to *care for themselves and their family members, and be able to share with others as may be needed* (*Ensign,* May 1977, p. 82).

Bishop *Victor L. Brown:*

We are concerned that because the Church program includes production projects, canneries, bishops' storehouses, Deseret Industries, and other visible activities, *our people are mistakenly led to believe these things replace the need for them to provide for themselves. This is simply not so.* The evidence that this illusion exists, is seen in the experience of the last few months as the draw on fast offerings and storehouse commodities has spiraled. (*Ensign,* November 1980, p. 81).

President *James E. Faust:*

The Church cannot be expected to provide for every one of its millions of members in case of public or personal disaster. It is therefore necessary that each home and ·family do what they can do to assume the responsibility for their own hour of need (*Ensign,* May 1986, p. 22).

PRIESTHOOD LEADERS TO TEACH INDIVIDUAL RESPONSIBILITY

For reasons that are not yet fully understood, the majority of the Saints remain essentially unprepared to meet a long-term family, community or national crisis. It is as though the Saints feel if they listen to, understand, teach or discuss food storage they have in some way completed the assignment; living the instructions seems to have somehow escaped them! It is amazing how many unprepared Saints will proudly discuss the Church's food storage program with non-members and yet put forth no effort in their own behalf. Priesthood leaders need to make sure this topic has been clearly communicated. It will not totally cure the problem, but it will certainly reduce the impact of such statements as, "Well, no one ever told me," or "Had I known I would have certainly done something!"

President *Spencer W. Kimball* taught the difference between "give me" and "self help":

> Let me say that as a stake president long ago, we had a flood in the Duncan Valley in Arizona. As soon as we overcame the excitement of the first report of it, my counselors and I formulated a telegram and sent it to Salt Lake City and said, "Please send us $10,000 by return mail." I found that I was learning about welfare programs when no $10,000 came. When President Lee, President Romney and President Moyle came down and took me back in my little office in my business place we sat down around the table and they said, *"This isn't a program of "give me." This is a program of "self-help."* And so we learned much from those brethren . . .
>
> Now it would have been an easy thing, I think, for the Brethren to have sent us that $10,000 and it wouldn't have been too hard to sit in my office and distribute it; but *what a lot of good came to us as we had hundreds of men go to Duncan and build fences and haul the hay and level the ground and do all the things that needed doing. That is self-help (Conference Report,* April 1974, pp. 183-84).

Bishop *Victor L. Brown* explained that church welfare and family preparedness are one and the same:

> We need to address ourselves constantly to the following question: What is the responsibility of the individual, family, and the Church in seeing to the needs of our people? There is much evidence that there are those who still do not understand or at least do not take seriously the counsel that has been given for many years. It appears that some have the notion that the Church will care for them regardless of what they have done for themselves.
>
> *We simply must recognize that the foundation of the Welfare Services program of the Church rests on the degree of preparedness of the individual and the family to take care of themselves.* If our people could but understand that *these teachings come because the Lord loves them and in his infinite wisdom desires that his people be blessed particularly in troublesome times.* As has often been quoted, however, this "must needs be done in mine own way" (D&C 104:16) (*Ensign,* May 1976, p. 110).

If we, as a people, become prayerfully and "anxiously engaged," the Lord may yet grant us sufficient harvest, and time, to assemble a year's supply. However, should the Saints not rise to this opportunity, it appears that this generation will have decided—either by default or intent—to enter the prophesied millennial period of tribulation with the majority of them completely unprepared to care for themselves, let alone their families. If this current situation remains unchanged, priesthood leaders will very likely be overwhelmed during the times of the up-coming crisis.

Someone once reported that a Chinese general had wisely taught the following:

> If the world is to be brought to order, my nation must first be changed. If my nation is to be changed, my hometown must be made over. If my hometown is to be reordered, my family must first be set right. If my family is to be regenerated, I myself must be first.

Since food storage is a matter of considerable importance, perhaps priesthood leaders should ask themselves, "Have I obeyed the counsel to prepare, and have I diligently pursued this responsibility with those over whom I preside?" At the very least, if food storage is to play the part which the prophets have told us it must play, it certainly deserves serious discussion and action at leadership levels.

In making food storage a matter of serious consideration, priesthood leaders perhaps need to become more responsive to President Benson's admonition wherein he stated, *"This is a matter of concern for area, region and stake councils."* Hopefully, in pursuing this course of action, the membership of the Church will exhibit a positive response and eventually lay claim to the Lord's promise, "If ye are prepared ye shall not fear."

RELIEF SOCIETY LEADERS' RESPONSIBILITIES

With the establishment of the Saints in Utah, the needs of the poor continued to weigh so heavily upon President Brigham Young that he turned to the Relief Society for assistance in meeting those needs. It is significant to note that the Relief Society and its members have always filled a very important place in the ward in meeting the needs of individual families.

In the later part of 1867, *Brigham Young* reestablished the Relief Society that the Prophet Joseph Smith had organized in Nauvoo, doing so with the following observations:

> Now, Bishops, *you have smart women for wives* . . . let them organize Female Relief Societies in the various wards. We have many talented women among us, and we wish their help in this matter. Some may think this is a trifling thing, but it is not; and *you will find that the sisters will be the mainspring of the movement.* Give them the benefit of your wisdom and experience, give them your influence, guide and direct them wisely and well, and they will find rooms for the poor, and obtain the means for supporting them ten times quicker than even the Bishop could (*Deseret Evening News*, December 14, 1867, p. 2).

To this day nothing has changed. The Relief Society continues the assignment of working under the direction of priesthood leaders in caring for the needy. However,

Priesthood leaders should not feel exempt from the responsibility to teach family preparedness, but they can accomplish the task, in part by encouraging the sisters over whom they preside, including those who are single, to obtain food supplies sufficient to feed themselves and their children during times of distress. Often a family's food storage is assembled because of the faithful efforts of a wife and/or mother in the home. Women are more likely to see and feel the essential need for it because they daily face the responsibility of seeing that their family is properly fed.

When President Brigham Young determined that priesthood leaders and heads of family's were either unable or unwilling to adhere to the counsel of the First Presidency to put up seven years of wheat, as counseled in 1857, in 1864 and renewed in 1868, President Young found himself again turning to the Relief Society. The background for this additional assignment given to the Relief Society by President Young was shared in a 1940 General Conference by *Amy Brown Lyman*, the president of the Relief Society, as follows:

> *The storing of grain in the LDS Church was inaugurated by President Brigham Young in 1876. It was given as a special mission to the women of the Church.*
>
> For a number of years the brethren had been advised to save and store grain against a day of need. They had been told that in this isolated region grain was of more consequence even than gold or silver. But each year they had put the matter off, no doubt feeling the need in this new developing country for any cash they were able to raise by selling surplus grain and other produce.
>
> *In late September of 1876, President Young sent for Mrs. Emmeline B. Wells to come to his office as he had something of importance to discuss with her.* When she arrived *he told her he wanted the women of Zion to gather and store grain against a time of need or famine*, and that he desired her to lead out in the movement. He spoke of drought, crop failure, and the tolls often taken by grasshoppers, and emphasized the fact that *the wheat would be held as a reserve and constant protection (Deseret News,* September 7, 1940, p. 1).

The sisters were asked to go out in the fields after the wheat had been harvested and glean what they could for storage. By 1877 (only one year later), this industrious, dedicated group of women had gathered 10,465 bushels of wheat and by the end of 1878 they had gathered for storage 25,000 bushels. Interestingly, the United States government came up short of wheat during World War I and purchased some 200,000 bushels from the Relief Society at some period around 1914. By 1978 the Relief Society had again accumulated in storage some 266,291 bushels, and at the general October conference Barbara Smith, general Relief Society President at that time, proposed, and it was sustained by the sisters, that the Relief Society wheat become a part of the Church welfare program, and further, that the wheat fund would continue to be used for the purchase of grain. This successful completion of an assignment reflects the faithful efforts of thousands of dedicated Relief Society sisters over a 102-year period.

Because of the remarkable efforts of the sisters, the Church decided to erect a grain elevator on Welfare Square in 1940 in order to adequately store the grain the sisters gathered. Further, the value of the preparatory standard set by these marvelous sisters became more profound when, in concert with this first grain elevator's construction, the president of the Church spoke of a time in the future when the Saints would want for food.

Just prior to the dedication of the huge grain elevator on Welfare Square, President *Harold B. Lee* made the following comment:

> Why should the Grain Elevator be built? To me there is only one answer. *The elevator stands as a prophecy of a time when we will need wheat; of a time when, perhaps, money cannot buy food.* Thank the Lord for the wisdom and the foresight of the men who guide this Church! (Minutes of Salt Lake Regional Welfare Council meeting, August 21, 1940, see *Pure Religion*, p. 82).

It is important to further note that the responsibility of the Relief Society sisters to teach the families of the Church to prepare and store at least a year's supply continues to this day. President *Barbara B. Smith*, in 1976, gave this challenge to Relief Society leaders to teach the principles of food storage and preparation:

> Relief Society can help give direction to women by *providing them with expert instruction and learning experiences.* The best place for this teaching is in the ward homemaking meeting, in lessons and in mini-classes. Instruction could also be given in homemaking fairs, seminars, and workshops sponsored by stake and district Relief Societies. Home storage could be a topic for summer visiting teaching messages and could be a suggested theme for talks in ward and stake meetings. Stake and district Relief Society teachers could make this matter a subject of active planning and enlist the cooperation of ward Relief Societies in implementing it.
>
> *Each ward or branch Relief Society presidency should make an assessment of the general circumstances of the sisters living within their area and prepare a one-year plan for homemaking meeting instruction to be given on subjects relating to home production and storage, according to the needs and conditions of the women.*
>
> These classes could include the following guidelines to provident living:
>
> 1. How to save systematically for emergencies and home storage.
> 2. How to, what to, and where to store.
> 3. How to store seeds, prepare soil, acquire proper tools for gardening.
> 4. How to grow your own vegetables.
> 5. How to can and dry foods.
> 6. How to teach and help your family eat foods needed for physical health.
> 7. How to do basic machine and hand sewing, mending, and clothing remodeling.

8. How to plan and prepare nutritious, appetizing meals using the resources available, and foods from home storage shelves.

May I suggest that *when approving such plans, each Relief Society presidency use the following checklist:*

1. Are we as Relief Society officers motivating and actually training the sisters in the necessary skills of family preparedness, and then helping them to put these into practice?

2. Are we counseling among ourselves and with our priesthood leaders so that adequate and realistic plans for home storage and production are being developed and carried out?

3. Do our homemaking mini-class plans respond to the various needs of the women in our ward?

4. Are we helping the sisters know how to estimate needs and replenish their home production and storage program?

I consider the woman described in the thirty-first chapter of Proverbs a provident woman. . . . The guidelines for Relief Society sisters now are the same as they were in biblical days: *Obey, Plan, Organize, Teach,* and *Do. Obedience is training and doing (Ensign, May,* 1976, pp. 118-119).

In the past, sisters have found creative ways to express their desire to be obedient to the counsel to be prepared. The following story reflects the creative efforts of one such sister:

Sewing became a way for me to keep busy when I wasn't playing with the children [in the park] and also to deal with my uncertainties about living in the city. . . .

Lynda tried to incorporate the values of the people she admired into her new life in creative ways. *Preserving food became for her a symbol of self-sufficiency,* so when she couldn't get fresh fruits and vegetable in the city to preserve, she made a list of all the things she remembered her mother and grandmothers putting into bottles and made quilt blocks representing many of those things. As she stitched, Lynda created a tribute to her pioneer ancestors and a family history for her children to enjoy. *She also taught her family hard work, the law of the harvest, and self-confidence in a new environment (Ensign,* August, 1998, p. 37).

President *Spencer W. Kimball*, in 1977, encouraged the use of the Relief Society's program for preparation and provident Living:

I like the way the Relief Society teaches personal and family preparedness as "provident living." This implies the *husbanding of our resources,* the *wise planning of financial matters, full provision for personal health,* and *adequate preparation for education and career development,* giving appropriate *attention to home production and storage* as well as the *development of emotional resilience.*

Yes, we are laying up resources in store, but perhaps the greater good is contained in the lessens of life we learn as we live providently and extend to our children their pioneer heritage.

Let's do these things because they are right, because they are satisfying and because we are obedient to the counsels of the Lord. In this spirit we will be prepared for most eventualities, and the Lord will prosper and comfort us. *It is true that difficult times will come—for the Lord has foretold them—and,* yes, *stakes of Zion are "for a defense, and for a refuge from the storm"* (D&C 115:6). But *if we live wisely and providently, we will be as safe as in the palm of His hand* (*Ensign,* November 1977, p. 78).

And Elder *L. Tom Perry*, in 1981, suggested that emergency preparedness is a part of living the Gospel:

. . . *[The] Priesthood and Relief Society, working together, bring the family to a realization that personal and family preparedness is living the gospel . . .*

The foundation of the Church Welfare program is personal and family preparedness. The organizational support is in place to train and prepare the membership in this basic responsibility. *What is needed is for each priesthood and Relief Society leader to place the proper priority on this important work* (*Ensign,* May 1981, pp. 88-89).

It may be necessary again to give a "Special Mission" to the sisters in the Church to see that their families have food in the home sufficient to meet family needs for at least a year. Such an assignment may become necessary, in part, due to our historical tendency to look to the adult female in the home to confide our hunger, or ask openly, "What can we eat?" Thus, children and perhaps even husbands look to their wives and mothers to somehow bring food to the family table, especially during times of distress—even when no preparation effort by the family has ever been made.

If an assignment similar to President Brigham Young's were renewed, perhaps the women of the Church would rise to the challenge and see that food is quickly gathered, sufficient to meet family needs in times of tribulation. Maybe the time has come to see if the women of this generation are made of the same mettle as those of previous generations—frankly, I believe they are.

President *Brigham Young* said,

Brethren, learn. You have learned a good deal, it is true; but learn more; learn to sustain yourselves; lay up grain and flour, and save it against a day of scarcity. Sisters, do not ask your husbands to sell the last bushel of grain you have to buy something for you our of the stores, but aid your husbands in storing it up against a day of want, and *always have a year's, or two, provision on hand* (*Discourses of Brigham Young,* p. 293).

May the Lord richly bless those who preside over us as they seek to seriously lead out in this grave and essential principle, and help us as Latter-day Saints to become a "prepared people."

CHAPTER
9
THE SAINTS ARE NOT PREPARED

Although it obviously should not be so, it appears that relatively few members are motivated to place food storage high on their priority lists if it is not consistently stressed as a priority by general, stake and ward leaders. As we have seen, the Saints have been warned and fore-warned, time and again, regarding the importance of food storage, but it appears that every new generation must be specifically reminded.

If the program is not reemphasized, it is easy for many to take the position that the seriousness of past warnings applied only to some other generation but not necessarily to their own. This is especially apparent today, as we have seen many of the older, depression-era generation put forth an extended effort to be prepared in their day, while today's younger generation often remains almost completely unprepared.

THE MESSAGE OF SURVEYS AND STUDIES

Various studies during the past four decades show that the majority of the Latter-day Saints are without adequate food-storage supplies on hand. For instance, a sampling taken in 1959, as reported in *The Improvement Era*, showed:

Temporal enemies can attack in the form of an accident, sickness, famine, unemployment, or war. Let us again emphasize this counsel because *a recent survey in a ward revealed that approximately 80% of our active Melchizedek Priesthood holders do not have on hand the essentials that will preserve life for one year* (*The Improvement Era*, September 1959, p. 702).

In 1975 Bishop **H. Burke Peterson** reported on a study made by the Utah State University regarding the Saints' response to storing food as counseled:

The study revealed that *only about 5 percent of our church members had a year's supply of meat products, 3 percent had a year's supply of dried or canned fruits or vegetables, approximately 18 percent had a year's supply of grains*. In the milk group, *only three families in a hundred had a year's supply of canned or powdered milk*.

On the average, *about 30 percent of the Church had a two-month supply of food*; the remainder had little or none.

These survey statistics indicate that most church members are not prepared to meet month-to-month problems and future economic trials. Clearly, in this area of home production and storage, it is extremely important that priesthood and Relief Society leaders and all Latter-day Saints place greater emphasis on home storage—

on obtaining and carefully storing a year's supply of food, clothing, and where possible, fuel (*Ensign*, November 1975, p. 116).

Bishop *Victor L. Brown*, in 1980, said,

A recent church survey . . . indicates that in emergency circumstances—such as job loss, illness, or natural disaster—*the average family had the following supplies: food, twenty-six weeks; clothes, fifty-two weeks; water, two weeks; and fuel, four days.* This is not even close to a year's supply.

The survey also indicated that financial reserves are low. *Only 17 percent could live for more than one year on their financial reserves if income were cut off; 45 percent reported they could only live for three months* (*Ensign*, May, 1980, p. 89).

President *Thomas S. Monson*, in 1986, while commenting on the status of the food storage programs within the Church, indicated that surveys have shown a serious erosion in the number of families who have a year's supply of life's necessities. He observed that "Most members plan to do it—too few have begun" (*Ensign*, September 1986, p. 4).

A poll taken December 14-18, 1998 in Utah County, Utah, revealed these results in answer to the question "Do you have any food storage in your home?" 84% said Yes, 15% said No, 1% said Don't know. Of the 84% that answered the question *Yes* they were asked: "How long could you and your household live on that food storage?" They responded as follows:

Didn't know: 5%

Less than one week: 5%

One to two weeks: 10%

Two weeks to one month: 16%

One to three months: 20%

The above question could give the impression that one or two weeks, or even a couple of months, represented some sort of food storage, which is obviously not the case. Most every household maintains a certain amount of food on their shelves that has nothing to do with "food storage," it's just there for day-to-day living. But the questions did reveal that some 56% (way over one-half of the 84% of those that answered *Yes*) would be lucky to make it through a week or at the very best, 90 days, without going to the grocery store; 16% could go without shopping for three to six months; 19% could function without shopping for food six months to one year. From this we see that of the 84% who responded in the poll that they have some food storage only 31% felt they could survive for a period of six to twelve months duration. Only eight percent said they could survive without shopping for more than one year. (*Deseret News*, January 24, 1999).

If we assume that most of these figures are even somewhat accurate, they would indicate that the Saints have been extremely irresponsible in the area of food storage. Yet we also must consider the possibility that their responses are seriously inaccurate. The exception would most likely be the eight percent responding they had enough for "more than one year." In answering the questions, families were not asked to make an inventory of what they had, but merely to pick a generalized answer. The likelihood is that most families would be in trouble far sooner than they would ever guess. Though sad to say, Utah County probably mirrors the rest of the families in the Church quite accurately, at least those living in the United States. From the results of this study, one could surmise that the response to priesthood counsel to obtain a year's supply of food has certainly been "underwhelming."

The 1999 Y2K scare caused some panic buying. One food storage distributor observed that some people "are spending their life's saving on food. It's absolutely insane." Generally speaking, the Latter-day Saints have missed the whole point of the Lord's admonition to prepare. Panic buying represents "foolishness," not a testimony of obedient preparedness. It's even worse yet if you are using a credit card to purchase the food storage on a pay-later basis. The Prophet *Gordon B. Hinckley* has said very simply, "I'm suggesting that the time has come to get our houses in order . . . Pay off debt as quickly as you can and free yourselves from bondage." Those who are belatedly trying to obey historical counsel by going into debt for food storage or are panic buying are desperately trying to correct one failure to obey by not following the current counsel of the Prophet. Those in a state of panic over Y2K have really missed the whole point of having a prophet.

ECONOMIC DOWNTURNS SHOW TOO-HEAVY RELIANCE ON FAST OFFERINGS FUNDS

Statements by Church leaders indicate the serious lack of emergency readiness of many of Latter-day Saints. For instance, difficult economic times in the United States in the late 1971's brought forth comments such as the statement by Bishop *Victor L. Brown* that members are too dependent on the Church and refuse to assume responsibility for their own welfare:

In recent months, it has been increasingly evident that *there are many who are not prepared. Within the last twelve months, the distribution of fast offerings and commodities by the bishops has been alarming.* At the present rate of demand, the *Church resources will be almost expended in a short time.* As a matter of fact, *some commodities have already been depleted, and this when the evidence is that the recession will be of a short duration.*

It would appear that in altogether too many cases the teachings about preparedness have been either misunderstood or knowingly rejected. *Many of our members appear to feel that when difficulty comes, the Church will come to their aid, even when they could have prepared themselves had their priorities been appropriate (Ensign,* May 1980, p. 79).

Elder *L. Tom Perry* observed that fast offering assistance jumps markedly in a slow economy, indicating members cannot handle even minor economic slumps without turning to Church Welfare:

Let us, for a minute, examine our leadership report card to see how well we have fulfilled our assignment to teach the principles of personal and family preparedness.

Our rate of annual increase for the period from 1970 to 1978 in total fast-offering assistance was 15 percent. Then we had a little upset in our economy, and the rate last year jumped to 32 percent.

We look even worse when we examine total commodity assistance. *For the period 1970-78, the annual rate of increase in commodity assistance was 11.3 percent. Last year, the rate was a disastrous 53.5 percent. A little dip in the economy found the membership without oil for their lamps.* Immediately it was necessary for those not adequately prepared to turn to the Church for assistance.

The results indicate that training of families in basic principles of self-reliance and independence over the past years has not been as effective as it should have been.

With such alarming results we must remind ourselves that *the Church welfare system was never designed or intended to care for the healthy member who, as a result of his poor management or lack of preparation, has found himself in difficulty (Ensign,* May 1981, p. 87).

What do you think the membership of the Church will do in the future if there is a major downward adjustment in the economy? What would the current priesthood "leadership report card" look like regarding how well they had trained their families to be prepared?

Even when personal finances, health, and reserves have failed and Church assistance has become necessary, members and leaders often still do not follow the counsel of the Brethren to help the Saints be self sufficient. Studies also revealed how few worked for assistance given to them by their bishop. Bishop *H. Burke Peterson* said in 1975,

The statistics show that *only about 25 percent of those families receiving assistance are working for what they receive. We feel that at least 75 percent of the families who receive assistance should be working in some measure for what they receive,* in order to maintain their spiritual strength and earn the welfare assistance received. About 25 percent of those receiving help are not in a position to work, although perhaps even they could do something if priesthood leaders made creative and spirited efforts to find the service that could be done. The spiritual strength of God's children is destroyed when the program is not followed as the Lord has outlined it. *Our people need to work for what they receive (Ensign,* November 1975, pp. 117, 118).

Even non-members are aware that some of our members are unprepared. In a May 1, 1998 newsletter, Dr. Gary North, a non-Mormon financial advisor, was discussing the effects of a potential breakdown in our fragile world economy and the potential for subsequent panic food-buying in such situations. At that time he made this interesting observation about LDS Church members, and sadly, it appears that he is all too accurate:

> There may even be a [problem obtaining food when, as] . . . Mormons . . . remember[ing] the official position of the LDS on food storage . . . start buying up their year's supply of food. But, given how most people apply their churches' official theology to real life, probably not.

In December of 1998 he added the following observation:

> Even most Mormons, who have been told for a generation to have a year's supply of food in reserve, have not done it. They have trusted the food-delivery system.

It is certainly a puzzle why something like the food storage program, that is of such common knowledge among members, has had such a low response rate, even among the very active. This author sold food-storage items in the early 1960's and, surprisingly, the most dedicated buyers were frequently not LDS but rather Catholics, who took our church's counsel very seriously.

That this continues today was evident in a 1999 conversation the author had with an employee at a local Church cannery. He indicated that there had recently been a large increase in home canning at that facility, but as kind of an after-thought he added, "Half of the home canning here has been done by non-members."

This failure to act has not always been the case. For example, when the first major Church canning facility was opened in May of 1953, we witnessed the following:

> . . . during the first twenty-two months of operations, 2,135,000 cans were processed. *Eighty-five percent of the canning was done by church members for their family food storage programs.* During this time, 869 different groups, made up of 18,000 people, participated in the canning.
>
> Among the participants during the first year was a group of sisters from Anaheim, California. They came a day before the general Relief Society conference so they could use the cannery. After the conference they took their commodities home with them. . . .
>
> The cannery proved to be a great blessing to families who wanted to accumulate a year's supply of food for storage. In addition to family storage, the cannery provided fruits and vegetables for the storehouse distribution system (*Pure Religion*, pp. 109-111).

Recently, the Y2K (Year 2000) computer glitch is reported to have motivated some additional members to work on their food storage. However, these numbers fall far short of even a small portion of the active membership of the Church. Again, one wonders what it will take to motivate even the active members—a group you would suppose would be at least engaged, if not already prepared. And, the puzzlement increases when it appears that the counsel of the Lord through His prophets to prepare seems less motivating to many members than a Y2K scare.

History has clearly shown that fear has never been a healthy motivator because as time passes, families most frequently return to their previous attitudes and their hurriedly assembled food storage gradually disappears. In truth, a meaningful food storage program will not be maintained unless those involved gain a greater testimony of this principle, not just a transient feeling of fear.

As Latter-day Saints, we should awaken to know that when the Lord gives His people direction, that direction stands until He rescinds it. The food storage and preparedness counsel has not been withdrawn, and so we, no matter the generation, are required to live by it or suffer the consequences.

If we listen to the Brethren and consider their instructions with care, we will see that they have always spoken with concern regarding this very important issue. It has been explained to the Saints from every conceivable direction, yet many still hurry through their days doing their own thing, almost mindlessly oblivious to how it relates to their precariousness. Will we only *see* when it is too late?

CHAPTER
10
WHERE SHOULD LATTER-DAY SAINTS LIVE DURING TIMES OF TRIBULATION?

It is not uncommon to hear families within the Church discussing whether or not they should move closer to traditional "Mormon country." This is especially true during times of crisis. Yet times have changed, the Church is no longer just an American institution. The Kingdom of God is worldwide and includes all of our Heavenly Father's children wherever they may live. The restoration of the gospel brought with it the organization of local Stakes of Zion wherein the Saints were to reside in safety. Obviously, not every Stake in the world will be safe from turmoil in the last days but, by revelation, the Lord has made known that He will direct his people to Stakes of "refuge" where the Saints will find peace and safety from the storm when the need arises. The Lord has clearly indicated that Stakes appointed for gathering will be designated by revelation, and members of the Church will be directed by the First Presidency where and when they are to gather.

THE STAKES ARE TO BE PLACES OF REFUGE

The Prophet *Joseph Smith* was clear regarding where peace and safety would be found in the last days:

> There will be here and there a Stake [of Zion] for the gathering of the Saints. Some may have cried peace, but the Saints and the world will have little peace from henceforth. *Let this not hinder us from going to the Stakes; for God has told us to flee, not dallying, or we shall be scattered, one here, and another there. . . .*
>
> I prophesy, that man who tarries after he has an opportunity of going, will be afflicted by the devil. . . .
>
> . . . the time is soon coming when no man will have any peace *but in Zion and her stakes* (*History of the Church*, vol. 3, p. 390).

President *Ezra Taft Benson* also said that the Stakes are a place of defense for the Saints:

> Stakes are to be a defense (see D&C 115:6). *They do this as they unify under their local priesthood officers and dedicate themselves to do their duty and keep their covenants. Those covenants, if kept, become a protection from error, evil, or calamity.*

Stakes are a defense for the Saints from enemies both seen and unseen. The defense is provided through priesthood channels that strengthen testimony and promote family solidarity and individual righteousness (*Teachings of Ezra Taft Benson*, p. 150).

President *Harold B. Lee*, in 1943, gave instructions based on the Doctrine and Covenants to the oft-asked question, "Where shall we live?" He first cited D&C 115:5-6:

Verily I say unto you all: Arise and shine forth, that thy light may be a standard for the nations:

And that the gathering together *upon the land of Zion, and upon her stakes, may be for a defense, and for a refuge from the storm, and from wrath* when it shall be poured out without mixture upon the whole earth" (D&C 115:5-6).

He continued:

I was down in Kelsey, Texas, last November, and I heard a group of anxious people asking, "Is now the day for us to come up to Zion, where we can come to the mountain of the Lord, where we can be protected from our enemies?" I pondered that question, I prayed about it. What should we say to those people who were in their anxiety? I have studied it a bit, *I have learned something of what the Spirit has taught, and I know now that the place of safety in this world is not in any given place;* it doesn't make so much difference where we live; but *the all-important thing is how we live, and I have found that the security can come to Israel only when they keep the commandments*, when they live so that they can *enjoy the companionship, the direction, the comfort, and the guidance of the Holy Spirit* of the Lord, when they are willing *to listen to these men whom God has set* here to preside as His mouthpieces, and when *we obey the counsels of the Church* (*Conference Report*, April 1943, p. 129).

Five years later, President *Harold B. Lee* made this further observation:

After designating certain places in that day where the Saints were to gather, the Lord said this: "Until the day cometh when there is found no more room for them; and then I have other places which I will appoint unto them" (D&C 101:21).

Thus, clearly, *the Lord has placed the responsibility for directing the work of gathering in the hands of the leaders of the Church to whom he will reveal his will where and when such gatherings would take place in the future.* It would be well before the frightening events concerning the fulfillment of all God's promises and predictions are upon us, that *the Saints in every land prepare themselves and look forward to the instruction that shall come to them from the First Presidency of this Church as to where they shall be gathered* and not be disturbed in their feelings until such instruction is given to them as it is revealed by the Lord to the proper authority (*Improvement Era*, June, 1948, p. 320).

Again, in 1969, President *Harold B. Lee* emphasized that it is not where you live but how you live:

I was in California, where we had some anxious parents . . . [who] wondered if they should move . . . to the Salt Lake Valley to get away from the influences that seem to be crowding in upon them. And so that question. I suppose that I had it asked by no less than a dozen or twenty people during the course of the conference there. And I said, "*Now the all-important thing for you folks is not where you live, because you cannot escape the power of evil; but the all-important thing is how you live.* If you folks want to be protected during this time of stress, you have given you in the gospel of Jesus Christ the fundamental principles by which you can be saved. If you will have your family home evening and teach your children in the home, the promise has been made that there won't be one in a hundred that will ever go astray. . . . you will have a strength in the raising of your family that will be far beyond any pulling power in the opposite (*Conference Report*, October 1969).

President Lee commented further:

One of our brethren was reported to have said that the people of California should move up to the tops of the Rocky Mountains, that only there would be safety. Contrary to that, *we are constantly saying to our people that safety is where the pure in heart are, and that there is just as much safety wherever you are, if you are living and keeping the commandments of God* (*Conference Report*, April 1970, p. 56).

EVERY NATION
IS THE GATHERING PLACE FOR ITS PEOPLE

President *James E. Faust*, speaking in a priesthood leadership meeting held in 1994 in Sacramento, California, said that "The answer isn't for everyone here to move to the Rocky Mountains." Referring to the many California Latter-day Saints who had packed up for Utah, he cautioned about future last days events in California and the rest of the nation, saying that governmental authority will diminish and

Fault lines will be built among ethnic diversity and broken families. . . . Where does this leave us? *We've got to become a unified people. We must draw strength from each other.* We need to take the sacrament together. . . . Our young people need to interact. *It appears that society is splitting into more fractions and groups,* all doing their own thing. *We need to do our own thing. That means caring for each other* (Priesthood Leaders' Meeting, Sacramento, California, October 15, 1994).

In an area conference held in Mexico City in 1972, Elder *Bruce R. McConkie* gave this insight into where Latter-day Saints should reside as the last days unfold:

[The] revealed words speak of . . . there being congregations of . . . covenant people of the Lord in every nation, speaking every tongue, and among every people when the Lord comes again. . . .

The place of gathering for the Mexican Saints is in Mexico; the place of gathering for the Guatemalan Saints is in Guatemala; the place of gathering for the Brazilian Saints is in Brazil; and so it goes throughout the length and breadth of the whole earth. . . . *Every nation is the gathering place for its own people (Ensign,* November 1992, p. 71).

LIVE WHERE YOU'RE DIRECTED TO GO BY PERSONAL PROMPTINGS

Faithful Latter-day Saints know that they can receive personal guidance concerning where they should live and what actions they should take to meet the economic and safety needs of their families. For those who feel impressed to move, and there are circumstances that might necessitate a relocation of their family, the following true accounts from World War II may give some insight into things to prayerfully consider:

A German gentleman, witnessing Hitler's take-over of the government and fearing another world war, took very specific preventive measures for himself and his family. He was a philosophy teacher in a high school. Knowing that philosophy was a controversial subject in a tyrannical regime, he switched to teaching math. Secondly, he found a job in a rural school away from large cities, moving to a small town in southern Germany prior to the breaking out of WWII. Next, he purchased a home with some land that could be used to raise a few farm animals and a place to raise a garden sufficient to meet his family's needs. In his effort to be independent he also acquired tools essential to his new way of life. Because of his precautionary measures, he emerged from the war with the bulk of his capital intact. It is true that he took a moderate reduction in income and status, but in acting with some foresight his family was able to survive. The city he had moved from was reduced to a pile of rubble.

Another story is told of a family with concerns. Seeing the potential for disaster in their homeland, they decided to find another place to live in an effort to avoid the anticipated war, a war that seemed inevitable. They studied night after night, searching maps and completing an extensive reading list regarding other lands in an effort to find a place they felt no other people could possibly want. They were searching for a place that would be so remote and of such little value that no one could possibly have a need to fight over it. After considerable research and evaluation, the family selected a little-known island in the South Pacific—the name of that island was Guadalcanal. As you may recall, this remote, tiny island saw some of the heaviest fighting in the Pacific during WWII.

The point of these two stories, both of which are true, is that with careful planning we might be able to avoid a disaster, but on the other hand, we may instead dive headlong into one. Man, with his limited foresight cannot, even with his best efforts, anticipate all of the unknowns. Our guidance, then, needs to come from three sources: (1) from the scriptures, (2) from the inspired prophets who are called to receive and speak God's will to the entire Church and to mankind, and (3) from the

Holy Ghost, whose calling is to convey to us God's word and will on an individual basis. Thus the answer for each of us is the Lord's counsel to prayerfully seek and listen for the whisperings of the Holy Ghost as we "follow the prophets" and their counsel. *Joseph Smith* expressed it this way:

> *You must make yourselves acquainted with those men who like Daniel pray three times a day toward the House of the Lord. Look to the Presidency and receive instruction.* Every man who is afraid, covetous, will be taken in a snare. *The time is soon coming when no man will have any peace but in Zion and her stakes* (*The Signs of the Times*, p. 126).

Hopefully, as you continue reading the words of the Lord compiled in this book and elsewhere, it will help you solidify your desires to be prepared and to follow the direction of the scriptures, of the Presidency of the Church to all the Saints, and the promptings of the Holy Spirit to and for you and your family. May your desires grow and break forth into prompt and consistent action.

CHAPTER

11

SHOULD WE SHARE OUR FOOD STORAGE WITH OTHERS?

Perhaps the best way to respond to this question is to relate an incident that occurred in the Mexico flood of 1998:

Hector Trejo, his wife and several of their small grandchildren climbed on the roof in the evening and spent the night and half the next day there until a boat came to take them off. Their food, newly purchased in anticipation of the storm, floated away on the water in bags, along with [the] sacks of clothing Sister Trejo couldn't hold against the surging current.

However, they managed to drag a large water container to the roof. Another woman on a nearby roof had food, and made a small fire and cooked tortillas for the Trejos, then put the food in a plastic bag and dropped it into the swirling waters that carried it to the Trejos' rooftop where it was eagerly and thankfully retrieved (*Church News*, September 19, 1998).

The question is often put forth by some who have gathered together a year's supply of food (and sometimes by those trying to find an excuse not to do so), "Should we assist those who have failed to put forth any effort to prepare?"

When a time of great need does come, what will be your response? Or, more importantly, what will be your situation? Will you be someone who seeks out another to obtain life-giving sustenance for your family, or will you, through your obedience, have sufficient for yourself and also some available to share?

While considering the possibility of sharing with others, it is important for those who have prepared to keep in mind that their first obligation is to their immediate family. Husbands have promised to care for their wives, and both have assumed the responsibility of caring for their children and their parents where necessary.

PLAN IN FAMILY COUNCIL MEETINGS

Not only can poor personal and family preparations limit our capacity to care for ourselves, but poor planning within and between families can compound our problems and further limit the help we can offer others. Thus, it could be a great blessing to your family and your extended family if all of you came together to discuss what should be done by each individual family, and by the extended family at large, in times of serious economic or societal problems or natural disasters. Planning of this nature could well be the means of saving lives, and would surely do no harm, even if little of serious consequence should happen for many years.

Nothing could be worse than for a family to be scattered in times of trouble, having no idea where to gather, nor what their means of meeting basic needs for themselves and each other would be when a crisis is upon them.

CARE FOR THE NEEDS OF YOUR OWN FAMILY

Few people in this nation have the slightest idea how they would survive in a local, let alone a national, crisis. Those who fail to put away food storage live in a "fantasy world" where grocery stores will always be filled with an unending supply of food. It is difficult for most to comprehend the possibility that weather or disease could decimate major food crops in the United States, or that our national economy could be seriously disrupted by depression, wars, strikes, etc. Most individuals have never experienced the panic that quickly unfolds as desperate people rush to find food in stores with empty shelves, or attempt to withdraw money from a mutual fund or from their bank in a time of crisis.

It is a marvel that so many of us assume that because nothing serious of this nature has yet happened to us, it could never happen. Yet, even today television reveals an unending drama of individuals and families caught up in horrendous situations worldwide; it is therefore a very naive soul which would conclude that nothing similar could ever happen to him, or to his family or community, or to this nation. Thus, one would think that individuals desiring to be responsible adults would put forth at least a minimal effort to prepare for circumstances (of whatever nature) which would be beyond their control, especially a people who have been so thoroughly warned by the Savior and His prophets.

As a parent, where do you think your children will go when tumultuous, latter-day scenes begin to unfold? Will you, and they, be prepared to meet their essential life-sustaining needs? Will you have helped them prepare to care for themselves, or will you be as empty handed as they may well be? If you smugly believe that it can't happen to you, you may be in the company of a great many who will yet live to regret having entertained such an irrational belief.

Remember, it is our basic responsibility as parents, and especially as Latter-day Saint parents, to provide for both the present and future needs and well-being of our families.

After having prepared our own selves and family, it would be good if we could put aside something extra to bless others—perhaps for our extended family, our friends, or our neighbors who may become destitute.

However, when extending assistance, this basic principle should not be overlooked: remember to let others do something, where possible, for what they receive.

It will more fully bless their lives. Someone once said, "at zero price there is greater demand than supply." Working for what one receives blesses all those concerned in many ways. President *Heber J. Grant* suggested this approach:

My experience has taught me, and it has become a principle with me, that *it is never any benefit to give out and out, to man or woman, money, food, clothing, or anything else, if they are able-bodied and can work and earn what they need,* when there is anything on earth for them to do. This is my principle and I try to act upon it. To pursue a contrary course would ruin any community in the world and make them idlers.

And what would ruin a community would ruin a state, and I might incidentally remark, a nation also (*Conference Report*, October 1936, pp. 2-6).

This is following the counsel set forth by the *Apostle Paul*: "For even when we were with you, this we commanded you, *that if any would not work, neither should he eat*" (2 Thess. 3:10).

This is still good advice, for these were not compassionless men, or words. Rather, they serve to carefully remind us of our individual responsibility. When others come to us for supplies and are able-bodied individuals, we can give them the opportunity of doing something for supplies received. This allows them to preserve their own integrity. This was the case with even the hobos our family fed during the depression. Everyone knew there was a major difference between a hobo and a bum, someone who would receive something for nothing. A true hobo would never take food if not allowed to work for it. I can still remember coming home from school on a number of occasions and seeing a large pile of chopped wood, and I instantly knew that a hobo had called at our home and received a meal.

BE WILLING TO SHARE WITH OTHERS

The Brethren have continually counseled, and demonstrated their counsel by example—that help should always be given to others in time of need, where we are able. Note the following excerpts:

The Twelve were low on provisions, and other leaders were without teams. President Young had started the journey with a year's supply of provisions for his family. This supply was gone. *He used this food to feed many in the camp who did not come prepared* (*Church News*, May 25, 1996, p. 12).

President *Brigham Young* set the example for the Church back in 1848 when he committed his family and himself to feed anyone who came and asked him for food. He recognized that if he provided for others, God would, in turn, provide for him:

The first year that I came into this valley *I had not flour enough to last my family until harvest, . . . and persons were coming to my house every day for bread.* I had the blues about [it] one day; I went down to the old fort, and by the time I got back to my house I was completely cured. I said to my wife, "Do not let a person come here for food and go *away empty handed, for if you do we shall suffer before harvest; but if you give to every individual that comes we shall have enough to last us through.*"

I intend to keep doing so, that my bread may hold out, for if I do not I shall come short.

Do you believe that principle? I know it is true, because I have proven it so many times. . . .

You who have flour and meat, deal it out, and do not be afraid that you will be too much straightened, for if you will give, you will have plenty, for it is God who sustains us and we have got to learn this lesson (*Journal of Discourses*, vol. 3, pp. 332, 333).

His counselor, President *Heber C. Kimball* had the same perspective:

I will prove to you that I will *put my faith with my works and lay up stores for my family and for my friends* . . . and I will be to them as Joseph was to the people in the land of Egypt. *Every man and woman will be a savior if they will do as I say* (*Journal of Discourses*, vol. 5, p. 10).

In September, 1875, President *Wilford Woodruff* looked ahead to the time when the saints will need to be prepared to feed others, not of our faith, on a large scale:

We shall want bread, and the Gentiles will want bread, and if we are wise we shall have something to feed them and ourselves when famine comes. We have fed thousand of them in days past, who would have laid their bones on the plains if it had not been for the counsel of President Young to us to cultivate the earth and have wheat on hand to feed them. And *the day will come again when corn will be wanted in Zion, and it will be sought for.* I hope the Latter-day Saints will take heed to these things and be wise (*Journal of Discourses*, vol. 18, p. 121).

In more recent times, the counsel that we should be willing to share our food storage with others in times of emergency has been repeatedly given. For instance, Bishop *Vaughn J. Featherstone* said,

I should like to address a few remarks to those who ask, "Do I share with my neighbors who have not followed the counsel? And what about nonmembers who do not have a year's supply? Do we have to share with them?" No, we don't *have* to share—we *get* to share! Let us not be concerned about silly thoughts of whether we would share or not. *Of course we would share!* What would Jesus do? *I could not possibly eat food and see my neighbors starving.* And if you starve to death after sharing, "greater love hath no man than this . . . (John 15:13) (*Ensign*, May 1976, p. 117).

President *Marion G. Romney* stressed that if we trust in the Lord while sharing with others, He will bless us:

I don't know how things will work out. People say to me, "What will we do? If we have a year's supply and others do not, it will be gone in a day." Well, it will last as long as it lasts, but I'm not worried about that. *If we will do what the Lord tells us to do, he will take care of us all right. Let us do what he has told us to do and then put our trust in him.* He can take care of us, and in the day of need he will do so (*Ensign,* May 1979, p. 95).

President *Spencer W. Kimball* also spoke of the need for us to help each other during times of disaster:

Do all of you people have a year's supply of the basic commodities? Be sure that you consider it very seriously. We realize that there may be some situations where it may be difficult, but we want you to keep it in mind. *When distress or disaster comes to any of our people, we must be ready to help each other* (*Teachings of Spencer W. Kimball,* p. 375).

Bishop *Vaughn J. Featherstone* gave this counsel to those who believe that food may be taken from them:

Now what about those who would plunder and break in and take that which we have stored for our families' needs? *Don't give this one more idle thought. There is a God in heaven whom we have obeyed. Do you suppose he would abandon those who have kept his commandment?* He said, "If ye are prepared, ye need not fear." (D&C 38:30.) Prepare, O men of Zion, and fear not. Let Zion put on her beautiful garments. Let us put on the full armor of God. Let us be pure in heart, love mercy, be just, and stand in holy places. *Commit to have a year's supply of food* (*Ensign,* May 1976, p. 117).

SHARING IN TIMES OF NEED BRINGS UNITY AND STRENGTH

Elder *Enzio Busche* explained that tribulation brings a sense of unity, closeness and meaningful memories to those involved:

The true nature of people becomes obvious in times of real need. Good people become better; they get close to one another; they learn to share and become united. The strength that develops out of unity of the many good people becomes a real survival factor. On the other hand, people who lack emotional stability become cruel and ruthless under trying circumstances; however, they do not seem to become an overbearing threat because of the closeness and unity of the majority of the people.

Therefore, strangely enough, those who have survived hardships look back with fond memories to the awful period of pain and destruction because they recall the closeness that developed as *they united themselves to survive by sharing whatever they had* (*Conference Report,* June 1982, p. 19).

President *Spencer W. Kimball* explained how sharing with others develops in each of us a genuine concern for them:

How well I remember my boyhood years in Arizona. Our living came from the soil. There was little money and seldom enough to go around. Going without and making do was our way of life. *We learned to share: we shared the work; we shared joys and sorrows; we shared our food and our means. We had genuine concern for one another.* Our daily prayers reminded us how dependent we are upon the Lord. We prayed and worked continually for our daily bread (*Ensign,* May 1981, p. 79).

President *Harold B. Lee* noted how in times of serious distress we might choose to give aid to one another, in a family-to-family assistance program:

I found, however, *in one mission something that was ingenious.* In one of these areas *they had worked out a two weeks' suggested food list for an average-size family. They had two varieties in case the tastes were different.* They had an "A" variety for two weeks' supply and a "B" variety. Whenever the branch president would find a needy family, he would call upon the John Doe family to give up their two weeks' supply of the "A" variety and maybe the Bill Smith family to give up their two weeks' supply of the "B" variety and put them together, and there was provided a month's supply for the needy family. That was their contribution to the welfare program, and *they of course replenished their own stock. . . .*

The next time the branch president had a needy family he called upon another family in the "A" group, and another in the "B" group, or maybe two in each, if the need was greater. Then they would replenish their supplies, and if there were still another need, he would go down the list until everybody in the branch had the privilege of contributing from his own private stock. In a sense, don't you see, *it was home storage welfare distribution to the needy families.* Now again *I am not instructing you,* I am merely telling you what some of you have already done (*Stand Ye in Holy Places,* p. 265).

President *John Taylor*, speaking in 1878, cautioned that prayer should not be regarded as taking the place of actively assisting the poor:

If a man were poor or hungry, [some] would say, let us pray for him. I would suggest a little different regiment for a person in this condition: rather *take him a bag of flour and a little beef or pork, and a little sugar and butter.* A few such comforts will do him more good than your prayers. And *I would be ashamed to ask the Lord to do something that I would not do myself.* Then go to work and help the poor among yourselves first, and *do all you can for them, and then call upon God to do the balance* (*Journal of Discourses,* vol. 19, p. 340).

LESSONS FROM HOLLAND ABOUT SHARING

A striking example of helping others can be found in the following account taken from the *Church News,* December 6, 1947:

In the first week of November, 1947, ten huge trucks moved across Holland. They headed towards the East and contained a costly cargo—seventy-five tons of potatoes, a gift from the Dutch Church members to the Saints in Germany. Why? Here is this most unique story surrounding a gift of potatoes:

In 1945 when Holland was liberated from five years of German occupation, it was completely exhausted of nearly all of it resources. What a joy it was when the mission's first welfare goods were received. *No words can describe the thankfulness of the members when they were supplied with food and clothing from Zion.*

For eighteen months a group of missionaries and local members worked day after day in the central welfare house in The Hague to supply the members with necessary clothing and to distribute cans of vegetables and fruit to them regularly.

Special meetings were called for this purpose in order to convey to the members the depth and beauty of the Welfare Plan.

In the spring of 1947, the members within the Dutch mission were asked to begin a welfare project of their own. The proposal was welcomed with enthusiasm. *There was nothing the Saints would rather do than show their willingness to give as well as receive.* The priesthood went to work and within a short time every quorum had found a suitable piece of land for the project. It was recommended that potatoes and green vegetable such as beans, peas and cabbage be grown. Potatoes are the basic food of Holland since they yield an abundant harvest. The women as well as the men worked the entire summer on the land.

In many branches the planting of potatoes was made a special occasion, and the branch members turned out in masse. There was singing, speaking and praying, at the end of which the potatoes were entrusted to the soil. Soon there came news of good prospects for the harvest and cautious estimates were made as to how large the yield would be.

News of the hardships being suffered in Germany eventually came to Walter Stover, president of the East Germany Mission, while he was visiting with Cornelius Zappey of the Dutch Mission. The suffering had become very serious in Germany because supplies had been slow in reaching the members there. President Zappey had the following feelings:

If we—if we could only give our potatoes to the members of our Church in Germany. What a beautiful lesson could be learned from this; but what would they say if we should ask them for food for which they had worked so hard to give to the people who had caused them such suffering and depredation—the people who had ruthlessly confiscated the last bit of their food and exposed their little children to starvation. And if they should approve of the idea, how would we be able to export the potatoes, for the exportation of food to Germany is strictly forbidden by the Dutch government, because the Dutch people don't possess sufficient food for their own use.

When President Zappey began to inquire regarding the feelings of the Dutch members, The results was startling. The Saints thought it a wonderful plan. The word "enemy" was not heard. The progress of the potato project was now watched with double interest and proudly came the reports, "We have so many potatoes for Germany," and "We have so much."

When the various potato welfare projects were completed, they were shipped to The Hague where the Saints there unloaded them in preparation for delivery to Germany. From the potatoes reserved to assist the needy Dutch Saints, one older Dutch widow recipient returned the sack of potatoes she had received when informed the Saints in Germany were to receive the others, saying, "My potatoes must be with them."

The persistent question was how to get permission to move the potatoes into Germany. As President Zappey was being turned down time and again by the Dutch government, other parts of the puzzles were moving into place. Elder Alma Sonne was visiting in Holland and as the Lord would have it, he came in contact with Dr. Vincent Cardon, a friend of many years. Dr Cardon was representing the U.S. Department of Agriculture and had been attending a conference in Geneva, Switzerland at which time he had been asked to go to the Hague to attend a conference on animal feed.

Dr. Cardon, a friend, was asked by Elder Sonne to write a letter of introduction to the Holland Minister of Food Supply, a letter which immediately began to open doors. Although all other relief agencies had been turned down, an exception was made in this case for Dutch food to be shipped to Germany. In the beginning the anticipated crop to be sent had been 15 tons but because the Lord blessed the Dutch Saint's efforts, 75 tons were eventually shipped. This shipment of potatoes was to make the difference between life or starvation for many Saints in Germany.

A year later there was another chapter to the story:

. . . of a still greater gesture of unselfishness and love on the part of these same Dutch Saints. This year [1948] the welfare harvest of potatoes in this land yielded over 90 tons, all of which were shipped in seven carloads across the border to be received by the German Saints. . . .

Then to add to their generous gesture, the Dutch members contributed enough money from their own funds with which to purchase one full carload of herring, consisting of nine tons of the finest fish that money could buy.

According to President Cornelius Zappey of the Netherlands Mission, whose energy and enthusiasm directed this year's welfare accomplishment as well as last year's, the Lord certainly blessed their efforts in the potato crop. When the men were loading the last car, they found they had many more sacks than they had figured on. As they had only six cars, they put all possible in the last car.

The weight broke the springs of the car, but luckily it broke in Dutch territory and that one car was taken out, repaired and the contents put into two cars, following the rest into Germany by a few days (*Church News*, December 15, 1948).

This account should serve as an excellent example to each of us as it adds insight into how the Lord would have us treat one another. The Dutch Saints had lived through the horrors of war, and it took a strong spirit of caring to feed their brothers and sisters in Germany after this war. During the time of occupation, many Dutch people had been killed for resisting the German presence. When the German soldiers had left Holland they had taken everything they could carry, leaving the Dutch people and their children literally in a state of starvation. Yet, when they heard of the hunger of their German brothers and sisters, the Dutch Saints took it upon themselves to provide food for them, while experiencing scanty personal stores themselves. This was an act of great Christ-like love by these humble Dutch Saints.

The story of a Dutch family during WWII provides another valuable lesson.

An article appeared in the *Los Angeles Times* on April 27, 1980, written by Lola Gillebaard, regarding events that took place in Germany during World War II. Mrs. Gillebaard's husband's parents had a wedding gift from his mother to his father which was a family "legacy." It was a gold watch made in 1790, sprinkled with diamonds and rubies, and it had a chime inside. During the war the Gillebaards lived in Amsterdam where the Germans required food to be rationed because the Allied air force had cut off the industrial west from the most densely populated portion of Holland.

The Gillebaard's received the following allotment for their family of seven: *two pounds of sugar beets, two pounds of potatoes, and one loaf of bread per person per week.* The Dutch guilders (money) bought rationed food and paid rent for some families. For other purchases, inflation had made money nearly worthless. The results they narrated were as follows:

Mama's sugar beet potato soup was mostly water by the middle of the week.

One night after sending the children to bed hungry, Mama slipped something into Papa's pocket. Papa protested. Mama insisted. The next morning Papa swapped Mama's diamond bracelet on the black market for a goat that was supposedly a milk goat.

The goat actually turned out to be a billy goat and wound up being slaughtered by the local butcher for half the goat. By early 1945, food rations had dwindled to *half a loaf of bread and two potatoes per person per week.* The family survived on tulip bulbs whenever Mama could find them. The weather was freezing and the family was without wood or coal to burn; the Gillebaards, with many other Dutch people, were freezing and slowly starving to death. Their story continued:

One Sunday afternoon, Papa and one of his employees bicycled to the farmland outside the city of Amsterdam. They pedaled on bicycle rims. All rubber had been confiscated many months before. Those two knocked on the door of every farm house. They asked each farmer if he had any food to sell. Papa revealed his antique gold watch, he now must trade for nourishment. Each farmer examined the watch and listened to the chimes. Then he shook his head, gave the watch back, and said, "I've got gold coming out of my ears." With that he slammed the door.

Papa and his employee turned up their coat collars against the wind and continued to cycle. And then they found a farmer who looked at the watch not at all. "What can you do?" The employee said, "I'm a carpenter." The farmer smiled and said, "There's work here for you." The farmer was also without heat. He ordered the employee to fill every crack in the house to insulate against the cold. Papa helped as best he could.

Upon completion of the work, the farmer gave the two men four sacks of beans. As the two loaded the beans onto bicycles, the light of the wintry day was disappearing. The farmer said, "Let me see that watch again." Papa's heart pounded. He displayed the watch in the palm of his hand. He pressed for the chime. The farmer listened. He propped his hands against his hips. He said, "I've got enough diamonds and gold to open a jewelry store of my own. I'll give you a sack of beans for the watch."

Papa said, "Make it two." The farmer said, "One sack of beans. That's it." Papa thought about the seven stomachs he needed to fill. He said, "I'll take the beans."

The Gillebaard family survived and Papa told the story many times. He always ended by saying, *"The skills of labor are worth more than precious gold."*

It would seem that the key words in all of this are the words "prepare" and "share." Sharing with others and enjoying that which they share in return has the capacity to bond people together, whether they be family, friends, neighbors, or the stranger in need. Sometimes sharing occurs when the recipient is not able bodied and has little more to give than appreciation, but if accepted for its true value, all parties to the transaction are genuinely blest.

If in times of turmoil we desire our prayers to be heard and answered upon our heads, we should remember the following counsel from the Book of Mormon:

> . . . If ye turn away the needy, and the naked, and visit not the sick and afflicted, and *impart of your substance, if ye have, to those who stand in need*—I say unto you, if ye do not any of these things, behold, *your prayer is vain, and availeth you nothing*, and ye are as hypocrites who do deny the faith (Alma 34:28).

CHAPTER
12
TO DISBELIEVERS AND THOSE WHO "ALMOST" BELIEVE

The history of the world is filled with stories of those who did not accept inspired counsel from the Lord through His prophets. A review of the scriptures reveals that, in the end, those who ignored the counsel never fared very well. In fact, as a group, they consistently lived to regret their disobedience. For those reluctant to believe, or who have merely ignored the counsel to prepare for a time of need, this chapter is offered with the hope that they may decide to reconsider their position.

THE POSSIBILITIES OF MAN-MADE AND NATURAL DISASTERS ARE ENDLESS

If only from a temporal point of view, one should be readily willing to concede that family food storage is essential when one witnesses recent large-scale disasters which have devastated whole nations, such as the huge 1999 earthquakes in Turkey and Greece and the economic sufferings experienced by Asian and Russian peoples who have been reduced to weathering shortage and wants of every kind. All too often we hear such "weather reports," so to speak, and yet dismiss their application to our own lives because we have come to believe those events in "other nations" certainly could never happen here in America—and especially not "to me." As we sit contentedly in our easy chairs, watching the ever-widening turmoil in the world about us, what would we do if our own skies were suddenly to darken, and, without notice, the full fury of similar storms came upon us, obliterating our opportunity to prepare or escape?

When a major crisis comes upon us suddenly, one by one our critical linkages to the machine/computer age have the potential to disintegrate. In one simple worse-case scenario, our electrical systems may begin to flicker and then instant darkness drape itself over our neighborhoods, as we find our lights, TV, and even telephone and emergency response systems eliminated. Then batteries fade and the radio grows silent. Our houses grow cold and unbelievably dark. Roads become impassable, crowded with cars out of gas—because electricity pumps our fuel. Food supplies dwindle, and store shelves become empty. Day-to-day reminders of our modern civilization—banks, machines, mass transit, retailers, computers, satellites, airplanes, speculative stock interests and governments—all quickly recede into irrelevance.

Should the above chaos seem too far-fetched, we should ask ourselves several possible probing questions. What is to keep electrical power failure, such as happened in New York City and more recently in San Francisco, from accelerating and affecting many other parts of this nation? What is there to keep another 1930's type of dust bowl from affecting the mid-west, or the possibility of excessive wet years that could keep farmers out of their fields? Why should we believe that no disease or early or late frosts could ever decimate major, essential crops in the United States? Where is it recorded that earthquakes, hurricanes, fires, and other natural disasters cannot occur where we live?

The Lord warns of one devastating event that is to occur: "There shall be a great hailstorm sent forth to destroy the crops of the earth" (D&C 29:16).

President *Joseph F. Smith*, on July 16, 1893, taught the Saints that the Lord can, and will, teach them a lesson when He wills to do so:

> The world today will laugh at you if you talk about a famine in this land. Why, they say, such a thing is absolutely impossible. We are so connected and bound together with the iron rails, and by navigation, that it is utterly impossible for any section of the country to be left destitute, because there will be abundance of food somewhere, and the railroads can speedily take from the lands that teem with plenty to the lands that are impoverished. But notwithstanding this, we hear very frequently of famine in the land.
>
> A few days ago we read of the farmers in the western portion of Kansas famishing for the necessaries of life, and this in our own land! But *I am not here to try to scare anybody with famine, although the Lord has revealed through His servants that famine is one of the scourges that He will send upon the inhabitants of the earth in the last days, and as the Lord lives, He will send it in His time.* As the Lord blessed the earth in the beginning, and caused it to be fruitful and bring forth food for man, *so sure can He put His curse upon it, as He did upon the land of Canaan and caused it to be barren and unfruitful:* and so sure can He *send the devouring insect, to sweep the earth of the crops that are upon it,* and He can *scourge the nations* that boast of their wealth, and of their power to resist the providences of God. *He can teach them a lesson when He wills; and when the time comes, as God lives, He will teach them a lesson, however little they may believe it possible for Him to do it. It is as easy for Him to send famine in this bountiful land of ours as it is for Him to send the cyclone* (*Collected Discourses*, vol. 3, p. 313).

Let us consider further, what it is that prevents wars, political and economic chaos, or terrorism from touching our soil. More will be discussed concerning this possibility later. The intended point, for now, is that the possibilities of man-made or natural disasters are endless.

In any event, the world you and I have known could quickly be left bare for any number of reasons, leaving us reduced to survival elements of our own devices and ownership, coupled with whatever help we can obtain from family and neighbors.

CAN FOOD STORAGE SERVE AS A PROTECTIVE SHIELD?

Have you considered the possibility that the very act of having your food storage on hand actually might be serving as a protective shield, causing the Lord to turn away events and situations which might be harmful to you and your family? Consider this observation made by President *James E. Faust*:

> Some have said, "We have followed this counsel in the past and have never had need to use our year's supply, so we have difficulty keeping this in mind as a major priority." *Perhaps following this counsel could be the reason why they have not needed to use their reserve (Ensign, May, 1986, p. 22).*

We must never lose sight of the fact that Heavenly Father rewards obedience in various ways, and and do not think that the unraveling of the world we live in—as pre-millennial events unfold—will not affect you. I would declare that thought to be pure fantasy. Prophecy from the mouth of the Lord clearly warns each of us that there is coming an end of much that is old and familiar, and birth of a completely new millennial social order which will eventually emerge from this era of tumultuous chaos. At times that change may involve episodes of personal dislocation or even forced migration, family and national mobilization, economic breakdown, communication blackouts and social disintegration, along with times of great hunger and exposure.

History demonstrates that we must never take today's circumstances as an absolute indicator of future activities and events, whether they be good or bad. Contemplate for a moment and picture yourself and your loved ones caught in the midst of nature's unbelievable power, or in the downward twist of the laws of economics or of an unthinkable war churning its way across this nation or the world. Then think about what you would need, where you would turn to find help, and what other resources would be available to you. Then consider, are they really available?

As these pre-millennial storms impact on our lives, there may be unprepared individuals who will become bitter and disillusioned, who will turn against others in very cruel and destructive ways. And yet among others, we will witness greater manifestations of virtue, character, and sacrifice emerging—such as trust, reliability, patience, perseverance, thrift, and selflessness. These people will become a source of dependable "currency" in these times of crisis.

OUR ATTITUDES AND ACTIONS WILL SHAPE OUR FATE

Each of us must eventually determine how we will respond to these trying situations, and whether or not we will use both appropriate preparation and a positive attitude, as we encounter the worst while laboring and hoping for the best. What better way to develop and enhance our future attitude than by diligently and physically preparing now—living each day obediently "ready" to meet our Lord should we be called home, thereby making ourselves more worthy and confident of the Lord's blessings later, whether in this life or in the life to come.

As with any major crisis, personal dealings will become enhanced and flourish; direct and positive contact with friends, neighbors, employers, employees, customers, suppliers, creditors, debtors, public officials and Church members will become essential. All these can be made more positive and Spirit-evoking with forethought and preparation. Since we will also feel concern for the welfare of others, we can see why our leaders have suggested that we put away "extra"—it is our opportunity to share our resources.

As cumulative crises unfold, there will be a sharp distinction drawn between those who are seen as dependable and those who are not. Thus, another way to prepare is by building a reputation of being someone with honor and integrity; someone who values self-restraint, keeps family commitments, possesses cultural decency, and offers mutual trust—in short, someone who can be counted on. To do this, one needs to be a good neighbor and worker, mannerly, adhering to the best that the Church and community represents.

Those individuals who are perceived as predatory, parasitical, or corrupting will generally be at serious risk because they will necessarily be "going it alone" or involved with those of similar destructive inclinations. As always, provident and right-living will be valued in a multitude of ways. During a major, long term economic crisis, unlike short-term problems of the past, generous government supplies of benefits such as cash, health, housing, and social services will likely disappear and do so very rapidly. In times of profound crisis traditional employment will likely become scarce if not unavailable. Thus, you should plan and prepare accordingly.

Something we can do to cushion the potential impact of a crisis is to get out, and stay out, of debt, and begin saving sufficient money for essential needs even if we have to cut back on our current lifestyle. Avoid leveraged investments and long-term debt, because a crisis generally brings massive inflation or deflation. We should be aware of where our money is; and be especially careful regarding over-investment in stocks, mutual funds, and other speculative entities, since in a panic they are the first to collapse. We should be certain to have at least a years supply of food—even more if we are able, since nothing will quiet fears better than a good, dependable food supply and some extra to share. If we haven't already, let us start practicing good health habits by exercising, reducing junk food in our diets, and in other ways preparing for optimum health.

Finally, we should become aware that our family will become our ultimate safety net! Accordingly, we will be glad if we have developed and maintained relationships of trust with our extended family, (not just knowing who they are but where and how they live, and don't leave out cousins). A time of crisis is not the time to be unprepared, or to manifest an "I can handle it all by myself" attitude. It is not a time to be, or feel, socially stranded. Of course, these are principles by which we should always be living anyway.

Now, at this juncture I wish to reemphasize our need for a positive, obedient attitude in all of our preparations for such is essential if we are to find ourselves appropriately hearing and following the Lord's instructions to us through His servants, the prophets.

WARNINGS OF APPROACHING WARS AND TRIBULATIONS

The prophets, throughout the seasons of the restoration, have specifically discussed various future events for which we should become prepared, especially in the area of wars and national turmoil. In response to one of the questions posed at the beginning of this chapter, the following quote should be given serious consideration. In the world man will continue to make great efforts to halt wars that will engulf many nations, but to no avail. The League of Nations (1918) and the United Nations of today are reflected in the following prophecy. It was spoken by Elder *Jedediah M. Grant*, on April 2, 1854:

> We see it in the preparations of war, and the framing of treaties of peace among nations. The world is in commotion and the hearts of men shall fail them for fear of the impending storm that threatens to enshroud all nations in its black mantle. Treaties of peace may be made, and war will stop for a season, but there are certain decrees of God, and certain bounds fixed, and laws and edicts passed by the high courts of heaven beyond which the nations cannot pass; and *when the Almighty decrees the wicked shall slay the wicked, strong nations may interfere, peace conventions may become rife in the world and exert their influences to sheathe the sword of war, and make treaties of peace, calm the troubled surface of all Europe, to no effect; the war cloud is still booming o'er the heavens, darkening the earth, and threatening the world with desolation* (The Signs of the Times, pp. 129-130).

On November 1, 1831 the Lord clearly stated that "The hour is not yet, but is nigh at hand, when *peace is taken from the earth, and the devil shall have power over his own dominion*" (D&C 1:35).

Elder *George A. Smith* added this observation to what the Lord had said:

Peace is taken from the earth, and wrath and indignation among the people is the result; they care not for anything but to quarrel and destroy each other. *The same spirit that dwelt in the breasts of the Nephites during the last battles that were fought by them on this continent, when they continued to fight until they were exterminated, is again on earth and is increasing* (*Journal History,* September 23, 1855).

Elder *Bruce R. McConkie,* in 1979, said the Lord's injunction to watch and be ready seems to indicate that the Saints be forewarned:

It is *one of the sad heresies of our time* that peace will be gained by weary diplomats as they prepare treaties of compromise, or that the Millennium will be ushered in because men will learn to live in peace and to keep the commandments, or *that the predicted plagues and promised desolations of latter days can in some way be avoided.*

We must do all we can to proclaim peace, to avoid war, to heal disease, to prepare for natural disaster—but with it all, that which is to be shall be.

We do not know when the calamities and troubles of the last days will fall upon any of us as individuals or upon bodies of the Saints. The Lord deliberately withholds from us the day and hour of his coming and of the tribulations which shall precede it—all as part of the testing and probationary experiences of mortality. He simply tells us to watch and be ready (*Ensign,* May 1979, p. 93).

Today peacekeeping forces are struggling throughout the world, trying to keep wars from erupting, but if they succeed it will obviously be only for an interim period. Even this great nation of America will not be able to escape the turmoil of future wars. With the above in mind, the following prophecies become more understandable and sobering: Elder *Bruce R. McConkie,* in 1979, said the promise of security only comes with preparation:

We do not say that all of the Saints will be spared and saved from the coming day of desolation. But we do say there is no promise of safety and no promise of security except for those who love the Lord and who are seeking to do all that he commands.

It may be, for instance, that nothing except the power of faith and authority of the priesthood can save individuals and congregations from *the atomic holocausts that surely shall be.*

And so we raise the warning voice and say: *Take heed; prepare; watch and be ready. There is no security in any course except the course of obedience and conformity and righteousness* (*Ensign,* May 1979, p. 93).

In 1946, President *George Albert Smith* told of a vision he had been given of future war and its terrible after-effects:

> *I have had a troublesome vision of another great and terrible war* that made the war that just ended [World Ward II] look like a training exercise, and people died like flies. . . .
>
> The aftermath was dreadful. Think of the worst, most difficult times of the depression . . . *that worse time of the depression will seem like a sunday school picnic when compared with how conditions will be after that great war* (George Albert Smith, *Conference Report*, April 1950, p. 169).

Clearly, this nation is not immune from political and civil turmoil. But in addition to prophesied international conflict, there have been repeated prophetic warnings of future internal conflict within the perimeters of the United States. Consider these prophetic statements: Elder *Orson Pratt*, in 1877, prophesied that the United States will be caught up in another civil war.

> It has been revealed that *the time will come in the history our nation, that one state will rise against another, one city against another, even every man's hand shall be against his neighbor, until the whole Republic will be in general commotion and warfare.* How and when this will take place, the Lord, in his wisdom, had not told us; but it is sufficient for us to say, that he has told us of the facts that such and such will be the case (*Journal of Discourses*, vol. 18, p. 341).

President *John Taylor*, in 1879, also saw this great nation of America caught in another terrible civil war:

> *Were we surprised when the last terrible [civil] war took place here in the United States.? No; . . . You will see worse things than that, for God will lay his hand upon this nation, and they will feel it more terribly than ever they have done before; there will be more bloodshed, more ruin, more devastation than ever they have seen before.* Write it down! You will see it come to pass; it is only just starting in. . . . there is yet to come a sound of war, trouble and distress, in which brother will be arrayed against brother, father against son, son against father, *a scene of desolation and destruction that will permeate our land* until it will be a vexation to hear the report thereof (*Journal of Discourses*, vol. 20, p. 318).

Elder *Orson Pratt* spoke again, in 1879, concerning a future American Civil War:

> *What then will be the condition of that people, when this great and terrible war shall come?* It will be very different from the war between the North and the South. Do you wish me to describe it? I will do so. It will be *a war of neighbor against neighborhood, city against city, town against town, county against county, state against state*, and they will go forth destroying and being destroyed and *manufacturing will, in a great measure, cease*, for a time, among the American nation. Why? Because in these terrible wars, they will not be privileged to manufacture; *there will be too much bloodshed—too much mobocracy—too much going forth in bands and destroying*

and pillaging the land to suffer people to pursue any local vocation with any degree of safety. What will become of millions of the farmers upon that land? *They will leave their farms and they will remain uncultivated, they will flee before the ravaging armies from place to place;* and thus will they go forth *burning and pillaging the whole country;* and *that great and powerful nation, . . . will be wasted away*, unless they repent. Now these are prediction you may record. You may let them sink down into your hearts. . . . you will see my words fulfilled to the very letter. *They are not my words, but the words of inspiration—the words of the everlasting God, who has sent his servants with this message to warn the nations of the earth* (*Journal of Discourses*, vol. 20, p. 151).

Elder *George Q. Cannon*, in 1884, also bore testimony of a future civil war in America:

The day will come when our own nation will be convulsed with intestine strife. *The civil war that is past is not the only war that will take place in this land.* It is a matter of regret to think it should be otherwise. But *God has spoken. There will be intestine strife in our own nation.* Already we can see, as it were, the seeds of this germinating and sprouting in the midst of neighborhoods and of communities, and it will break out after a while, and *men will flee to Zion* (*Journal of Discourses*, vol. 25, p. 243).

Elder *Moses Thatcher*, in 1885, also commented on a future civil war:

I will say *when this nation, having sown to the wind, reaps the whirlwind;* when brother takes up sword against brother; when father contends against son, and son against father; *when he who will not take up his sword against his neighbor must needs flee to Zion for safety . . .* (*Journal of Discourses*, vol. 26, p. 333).

On December 25, 1832 the Lord gave the revelation indicating that a civil war would begin in South Carolina and ultimately go from this nation to the whole world. The Lord's counsel to the Saints at that time would seem to apply just a readily to our day as it did when it was originally given: "*Stand ye in holy places, and be not moved,* until the day of the Lord come; for behold, it cometh quickly, saith the Lord." (D&C 87:8).

It should be noted that the North and South, during the 1860's Civil War, lost nearly three-quarters of a million men, more than those killed in all the other wars fought before and since by this nation combined. And this number does not take into account the civilian population that was killed during that terrible civil war.

In 1972, President *Ezra Taft Benson* said this nation is headed for serious problems:

We live in difficult days—very difficult days. They are not improving. However, I do feel that there is some increase in awakening to the dangers that face us. *I am not sure that the awakening is going to be fast enough to avoid the disaster which could very seriously result in bloodshed, hardship, and much sorrow in this beloved country* (*Teachings of Ezra Taft Benson*, p. 106).

President *J. Reuben Clark* also addressed his concern in this prophetic statement:

Brethren, let us think about that, because I say unto you with all the soberness I can, that *we stand in danger of losing our liberties, and that once lost, only blood will bring them back;* and *once lost, we of this church will, in order to keep the Church going forward, have more sacrifices to make and more persecutions to endure than we have yet known, heavy as our sacrifices and grievous as our persecutions of the past have been* (*The Improvement Era*, May 1944, p. 337).

Those who believe that this great democratic nation can never be reduced to anarchy need to consider the following statement by Elder *Neal A. Maxwell*:

The vulnerability of democratic government in the United States thus comes not primarily from external threats, though such threats are real . . . but rather from the internal dynamics of democracy itself in a highly educated, mobilized, and participant society. "Democracy never lasts long," John Adams observed. "It soon wastes, exhausts, and murders itself. There never was a democracy yet that did not commit suicide." That suicide is more likely to be the product of overindulgence than of any other cause (*Wherefore Ye Must Press Forward*, p. 13).

WE MUST CHOOSE TO EITHER ACCEPT OR REJECT PROPHETIC COUNCIL

In all of this world and national turmoil, each of us must determine where we personally stand. We now find ourselves back to the same questions posed by Elder Henry B. Eyring at the beginning: Are we a member of "strong faith," of "little faith," are we amongst those "without faith," or do we find ourselves living "another fallacy" believing that we are at liberty to make a "choice" without consequences regarding prophetic counsel?

In 1997 Elder *Henry Eyring* said,

We are blessed to live in a time when the priesthood keys are on the earth. We are blessed to know where to look and how to listen for the voice that will fulfill the promise of the Lord that He will gather us to safety (*Ensign*, May 1997, p. 26).

The Lord speaks to those who disbelieve, but perhaps even more so to those who are never quite willing to seriously consider His instructions: "*In the day of their peace they esteemed lightly my counsel; but, in the day of their trouble, of necessity they feel after me*" (D&C 101:8).

Never before has there been such a need for the spiritual resurgence President *Spencer W. Kimball* called for:

We speak not by way of alarm but by way of gentle counsel. *Let us go back to the basics and follow the fundamentals.* Thus we will experience *a spiritual resurgence in our lives* which will help us through these tempestuous times (*Ensign,* May 1981, p. 80).

It has always been a source of puzzlement that any discussion of future events, given to us prophetically, seems to be received by so many Saints as information which they need not be overly concerned about; that somehow it applies to others, even to another generation. As a group, we seem willing to speak up in church classes and clearly discuss how Heavenly Father's people have stumbled in the past, and we often expound on what his children may experience in the future. We confess feeling perplexed that Israel could be instructed so clearly by the Lord, and yet be so unwilling to modify their behavior in order to obtain the blessings.

However, in so many ways we are really no different than ancient Israel. As with ancient Israel, time and time again, some of "present Israel" knowingly ignores the warnings and counsel of the prophets of their day. If prophecy comes uncomfortably close to our personal lives or pocketbooks, it seems to be tuned out or responded to with an attitude similar to that of Scarlet O'Hara in *Gone With The Wind:* "I'll think about that tomorrow!"

For those who would like to believe, but struggle to obtain the required hope and faith to move forward, perhaps the following letter to the president of the British Mission will serve as a first step in sustaining the prophets. This letter was written by Willard Richards and John Taylor twelve days after the martyrdom of Joseph and Hyrum Smith:

> It is in this period of time that we are permitted to live. *It is at the dawning of that day of days in which our [H]eavenly Father is about to usher in that glorious period when times and seasons shall be changed and earth renewed,* when after rumors and commotions, turmoils, strife, confusion, blood and slaughter, the sword shall be beaten into ploughshares, and *peace and truth triumphantly prevail o'er all the footstool of Jehovah. The day of these events has dawned,* although to human view a cloud has o'erspread the horizon (*History of the Church,* vol. 7, p. 172).

In the end it is not going to be so much a question of what any one of us elects to believe or how much we know, but more a question of what we have or haven't done with what we have been taught. Look around. Ask yourself, what is the status of your food storage? What do you see when you open the doors to your cupboard? Perhaps there is not a more tangible way to establish where you are, since what you have clearly reflects your level of obedience. Only a true inventory of what you have assembled will give you the information of what is yet to be done.

Remember, an inventory will also reveal to each of us the most accurate measure of our level of obedience, sacrifice, and commitment to follow the Lord's directives, whatever they may be. But be aware that you will have the memory whispering in your ear: "You were told this was going to happen."

THE STUMBLING BLOCK OF PRIDE

Many of the Saints are unaware how pride may become a factor in whether or not we choose to observe the directions of the Lord to be a prepared people. Mormon, in chapter nine of his writings, directs his comments to ". . . those who do not believe in Christ," and in chapter eight he speaks to churches who claim to be followers of Christ but are caught up in "pride" and "envying." He then goes on to make an extensive prophetic statement concerning pride in a last-days context, saying: "Behold, look ye unto the revelations of God; for behold, the time cometh *at that day* when all these things must be fulfilled" (Mormon 8:33; 9:1). For those who doubt that someone nearly 1,600 years ago could possibly see and understand our day, Mormon clarifies his awareness when he states:

> Behold, I speak unto you as if ye were present, and yet ye are not. But behold, Jesus Christ hath shown you unto me, and I know your doing. . . .
>
> And I know that *ye do walk in the pride of your hearts;* and there are none save a few only who do not lift themselves up in the pride of their hearts."

Moroni then outlines aspects of pride which are areas of concern—problems such as: "fine apparel," "envying," "strifes," "malice," and love of "money" (Mormon 8:33-37).

Pride is an affliction which distorts our perception of ourselves and the world around us. It is a filter that refuses to allow external feedback and counsel to be accurately integrated into our lives.

Let us ponder pride's negative influence on some within the Church, the result of which, in part, is their failure to obtain a meaningful year's supply of food and other necessities. That is why the subject of pride is being considered in this context.

President *Ezra Taft Benson*, in the spring of 1989, focused his entire General Conference talk on the subject of pride. With the above thoughts in mind, let's review some excerpts from President Benson's memorable address. He said:

> • The Doctrine and Covenants tells us that the Book of Mormon is the "record of a fallen people" (D&C 20:9). Why did they fall? This is one of the major messages of the Book of Mormon. Mormon gives the answer in the closing chapters of the book in these words: *"Behold, the pride of this nation, or the people of the Nephites, hath proven their destruction"* (Moro. 8:27). And then, lest we miss that momentous Book of Mormon message from that fallen people, the Lord warns us in the Doctrine and Covenants, *"Beware of pride, lest ye become as the Nephites of old"* (D&C 38:39).
>
> In the premortal council, it was pride that felled Lucifer, "a son of the morning" (2 Ne. 24:12-15).

Three times in the Doctrine and Covenants the Lord uses the phrase "Beware of pride."

Pride is a very misunderstood sin, and *many are sinning in ignorance* (See Mosiah 3:11; 3 Ne. 6:18). In the scriptures there is no such thing as righteous pride—it is always considered a sin . . .

Most of us think of pride as self-centeredness, conceit, boastful, arrogance, or haughtiness. All of these are elements of the sin, but the heart, or core, is still missing . . .

Pride is essentially competitive in nature. We pit our will against God's. When we direct our pride toward God, it is in the spirit of "my will and not thine be done." . . .

The proud cannot accept the authority of God giving direction to their lives. (See Hel. 12:6.) *They pit their perceptions of truth against God's great knowledge, their abilities versus God's priesthood power, their accomplishments against His mighty works.*

Our enmity toward God takes on many labels, such as rebellion, hard-heartedness, stiff-neckedness, unrepentant, puffed up, easily offended, and sign seekers. The proud wish God would agree with them. They aren't interested in changing their opinions to agree with God's . . .

The proud make every man their adversary by pitting their intellects, opinions, works, wealth, talents, or any other worldly measuring device against others. In the words of C.S. Lewis: "Pride gets no pleasure out of having something, only out of having more of it than the next man . . . It is the comparison that makes you proud: the pleasure of being above the rest." Once the element of competition has gone, pride has gone.

Pride is a sin that can readily be seen in others but is rarely admitted in ourselves. Most of us consider pride to be a sin of those on the top, such as the rich and the learned, looking down at the rest of us. (See 2 Ne. 9:42.) There is, however, a far more common ailment among us—and that is pride from the bottom looking up. *It is manifest in so many ways, such as faultfinding, gossiping, backbiting, murmuring, living beyond our means, envying, coveting, withholding gratitude and praise that might lift another, and being unforgiving and jealous.*

Disobedience is essentially a prideful power struggle against someone in authority over us. It can be a parent, a priesthood leader, a teacher, or ultimately God. A proud person hates the fact that someone is above him. He thinks this lowers his position.

Selfishness is one of the more common faces of pride. "How everything affects me" is the center of all that matters—self-conceit, self-pity, worldly self-fulfillment, self-gratification, and self-seeking . . .

The proud do not receive counsel or correction easily. (See Prov. 15:10; Amos 5:10.) Defensiveness is used by them to justify and rationalize their frailties and failures. (See Matt. 3:9; John 6:30-59.)

The proud depend upon the world to tell them whether they have value or not. Their self-esteem is determined by where they are judged to be on the ladders of worldly success . . .

Pride fades our feeling of son-ship to God and brotherhood to man. It separates and divides us by "ranks," according to our "riches" and our "chances for learning." (3 Ne. 6:12.) Unity is impossible for a proud people, and unless we are one we are not the Lord's. (See Mosiah 18:21; D&C 38:27; 105:2–4; Moses 7:18.) . . .

Pride affects all of us at various times and in various degrees. Now you can see why the building in Lehi's dream that represents the pride of the world was large and spacious, and great was the multitude that did enter into it. (See 1 Ne. 8:26, 33; 11:35-36.)

Pride is the universal sin, the great vice. Yes, pride is the universal sin, the great vice.

The antidote for pride is humility—meekness, submissiveness. (See Alma 7:32.) It is the broken heart and contrite spirit (See 3 Ne. 9:20, 12:19).

God *will* have a humble people. *Either we can choose to be humble or we can be compelled to be humble . . .*

Pride is the great stumbling block to Zion. I repeat: Pride is the great stumbling block to Zion.

We must cleanse the inner vessel by conquering pride. (See Alma 6:2-4; Matt.23:25-26.)

We must yield "to the enticings of the Holy Spirit," put off the prideful "natural man," become "a saint through the atonement of Christ the Lord," and become "as a child, submissive, meek, humble." (Mosiah 3:19; see also Alma 13:28.) (*Ensign,* May 1989, pp. 4-7).

President Benson began his address with an observation that should "rivet" our attention. "This message [on pride] has been weighing heavily on my soul for some time. I know the Lord wants this message delivered now."

It would seem that the message is of no less importance today. Perhaps it is even of greater importance since we are now closer to the beginning chapters of the millennium.

President Benson's address has been included because I'm of the opinion that the Adversary effectively uses pride as a tool to keep us from assembling our food storage. Let me explain. As I understand it, the kind of pride the prophet was speaking of limits or restricts our willingness to accept the Lord's counsel and directly apply it to ourselves. It is not that we don't understand the counsel to be prepared, nor do we see it as unimportant; we who are a prideful people "take great pride" in knowing just such things! Rather, it appears that the problem is we see ourselves as so self-sufficient, or find it so important to maintain our social appearances or status, that we never get around to obediently preparing ourselves and our food storage.

Further, we prideful people do not like to be told what to do; like a two-year-old we insist, "I can do it myself!" Prideful people like to see themselves as exceptions to the rule, thinking of course others should have a year's supply of food, while maintaining an "I can take care of myself" attitude. If pressed to look at the Lord's counsel to be prepared we may become defensive—exhibiting great skill in self-justification. Then, if pressed too hard, we can become angry and self-righteous. When our pride has been stepped on hard enough we often become stubbornly determined not to give in—to neglect obedience no matter how much it hurts us.

Mormon did indeed see our day and the pride he witnessed in us is no less destructive for us than it was in his day. Some of latter-day Israel needs a change of heart, an obedient spirit that motivates them to prepare and maintain a year's supply. This is as good as any place to begin the process of our repentance.

Of course, many of those with food storage will continue to struggle with pride, but it is a great humbling, obedient step in the right direction. Remember President Benson's prophetic warning and voice of encouragement: *"God will have a humble people. Either we can choose to be humble or we can be compelled to be humble . . .* Let us choose to be humble. We can do it. I know we can."

CHAPTER
13
FOOD STORAGE—
AN ACT OF FAITH,
OBEDIENCE AND DEVOTION

Perhaps it would be helpful if we reviewed the subject of food storage preparation as the principle it truly is—a reflection of our faith and devotion, or lack of it. Although at some level each of us naturally seeks to move out of harm's way in order to find safety for ourselves and our families, the greater question which we face is: are we willing to exercise faith and devotion to the Lord sufficient to allow prophetic counsel to become part of that effort?

As Heavenly Father's children, we often fail to understand how obedience to seemingly insignificant counsel can have such everlasting impact in our lives. Certainly, in the beginning, no one knows the ultimate blessings that will come from a thing as simple as maintaining a year's supply of food for their family.

Alma, speaking to his son Helaman, declared:

> Now ye may suppose that this is foolishness in me; but behold I say unto you, that *by small and simple things are great things brought to pass;* and small means in many instances doth confound the wise (Alma 37:6).

BY SIMPLE ACTS
GREAT THINGS ARE BROUGHT TO PASS

Perhaps we, as a people, see food storage as too simple an act to have tremendous overall significance in our lives and miss the greater purpose that the Lord may have in mind. What if the greatest purpose which the Lord had in mind in blessing our lives with food storage and preparation instructions is not *physical safety*, but *spiritual safety?* The kind of spiritual "rod of iron" that would help us stay constantly focused on our purpose for coming to this earth life. Maybe the simpleness of it confuses the issue of its importance, such as in Moses's era when the Lord sent

> . . . fiery flying serpents among them [Israel]; and after they were bitten he prepared a way that they might be healed; and *the labor which they had to perform was*

to look; and *because of the simpleness of the way, or the easiness of it, there were many who perished* (1 Nephi 17:41).

Perhaps we can find meaning for ourselves by looking at Abraham's struggle concerning the city of Sodom and Gomorrah (see Genesis 18:23-33). In his situation, as you may recall, Abraham was laboring with the Lord to save the city if sufficient righteous men could be found. In our day the story might go something like this:

"Peradventure" Lord, wilt thou save the Saints if we can find sufficient with seven years supply of food storage?" (as the Lord instructed the Saints through the prophet Brigham Young). And the Lord responds, "If you find those with seven years supply, I will save them." Then our doubt begins to set in, because we know it is very unlikely that there is hardly anyone with a seven-year food supply, so we quickly ask the Lord to consider another possibility:

"Peradventure" that some shall have but one year less, wilt thou save them if we can find those with six years of food storage? And the Lord answering says, "If you can find those with six years of food storage I will save the Saints."

And so it goes; and as with Abraham we continue to press the Lord, trying to reduce our anxiety and cover our doubts. Thus, we have has gone from 7 years of food storage to 6, to 5, to 4, to 3, to 2, and eventually to a minimum of a year's supply as the Lord, sadly, acquiesces before us—a people unwilling to extend themselves to meet the greater requirement, but one none the less in our best interest. You will also note that the Lord has reduced the amount to be stored to a minimum, from the food we regularly eat to that which would "keep us from starving." And so it is with us today, as the history of the food storage program has unfolded.

DID THE LORD REDUCE THE REQUIREMENT TO ACCOMMODATE OUR RELUCTANCE?

As with Abraham, so it has been with our generation—the Lord has been willing to work patiently with us, his children. But are we, for whatever reasons, like Lot's sons-in-law who heard but would not listen and obey, or are we like his wife who looked or turned back contrary to the Lord's counsel? We must bear in mind that the Lord never did go to zero with his servant Abraham—in the end only three individuals obeyed and were righteous enough to be saved from that city's destruction (Gen. 19:14-30). Since there is naturally a year between harvests, it would seem highly unlikely that the Lord will ever further shorten the time nor reduce the amount He requires for us to prepare and store.

There is no certain way to determine it, but it would seem doubtful that many additional Saints completed their food storage when the time to prepare was shortened to 6 years over the number who had completed it for seven years. For that matter, it is also unlikely that the counsel given us to only store supplies for one year brought about any noticeable increase in consistently prepared Saints over their counsel to have prepared for two years. For the most part, those who are willing to abide the Lord's counsel will remain consistently obedient, regardless of the length of time the Lord sets forth. Should the Lord reduce the requirement to a mere six months, it is not likely that there would be a greater surge amongst the Saints to prepare, because this counsel to prepare is really a matter of obedience and sacrifice, rather than being dependent upon the length of time that we are requested to be prepared for. Perhaps the Lord's willingness to reduce the number of years is merely His way of countering the Saints' excuses that if He had reduced the number of years required they would have more willingly complied.

Intellectually, those of us with a testimony of the gospel know that there will be difficult, even terrible times endured prior to Christ's second coming. But human nature being what it is, we emotionally feel that it won't happen tomorrow, next month or next year, and especially not "to me" or "on my watch." Yet, we should not assume just because the Lord reduced His requirement from seven years to one year to accommodate our reluctance to be obedient, that there will not be seven years of need at some period of time. It may be of interest to note that not only did the midwest suffer extended drought in the 1930's, but California was also affected with a drought which lasted nearly 7 years, with only a 1-year break in the middle of which was an abnormally wet year.

It appears that what the Lord has done is to show us at what minimal level of requirement necessary to save our bodies and our souls we are willing to be obedient. Yet sadly, only a very small fraction of the Saints have actually prepared as counseled, even to that meager amount.

ARE WE WILLING TO BE "MINIMAL SAINTS"?

Why have the Saints seemingly forgotten that "sacrifice brings forth the blessings of heaven."? Does our refusal or avoidance in storing supplies come about simply because this instruction to us is not given by way of "commandment?" Have we forgotten that the Lord requires a willing heart and does not want a people that must be "commanded in all things," but rather a people who are "anxiously engaged" of their own free will and choice? Do we not realize that if we only obey commandments, then we are unexampled "minimal Saints" (reluctant followers) who are only willing to be as devoted as we must in order to barely be allowed through the doors of the kingdom? Is that really the kind of Saint we want to be? And what kind of love and devotion does a heart that must be "commanded in all things" show for the Lord?

Who would want a wife who only cooked for her family those meals which we specifically demanded her to cook, or a husband who only provided for his family whatever food and provisions a court ordered him to provide? Where would be the care, the cherishing, the love and devotion in that kind of a relationship? Is there any difference when we are unwilling to do what the Lord has asked of us? What love and care are we showing Him? What faith and devotion?

ONLY HURTING OURSELVES?

Then too, I am reminded of the individual who said, "I don't know why Church leaders place so much focus on food and personal preparedness. When, and if, I put away a food storage is, after all, nobody's business but mine. If I don't do it at all, I won't be hurting anyone but myself!"

This comment brings to mind how often, through the years of my youth, I heard that same statement from smokers who saw no reason to quit smoking: "It is nobody's business but my own! After all, I'm only hurting myself." Well, now these many years later, it is common knowledge that this is not a true belief—secondhand smoke is just as serious, if not more so.

In like manner, the people who don't put up their food storage are willingly placing themselves and their families in a circumstance to take from the scanty stores of another, unless in the unlikely event they choose to go hungry rather than ask for assistance. It is indeed everyone's business, even though it does remain each individual's personal choice of agency.

BEING SLOW TO HEARKEN, AND BEGUILED BY THE TEMPTER

It would seem that a people who were forewarned, blessed with sufficient means, and given an extraordinary amount of time to prepare—but who, none-the-less, elected to respond with a deaf ear to the Lord's counsel for preparation—may well find their prayerful pleas in a time of need, receiving the following responses from the Lord,

> They were slow to hearken unto the voice of the Lord their God; *therefore, the Lord their God is slow to hearken unto their prayers, to answer them in the day of their trouble.*
>
> . . . In the day of their peace they esteemed lightly my counsel; but, in the day of their trouble, of necessity they feel after me (D&C 101:7-8).

The adversary is aware of the Lord's counsel. If we are not extremely careful, Satan will take us by the hand and lead us "carefully down to hell" (1 Nephi 28:21). He enthusiastically whispers "sweet nothings" in our ears, convincing us that we needn't worry, and reassuring us that the Lord will take care of us regardless of what we do—or fail to do. Sometimes, with nothing more than a little nudge from the Adversary, we become determined that what we really need, much more than food storage, is a new computer, TV, VCR, cable, or a better home, car, clothes, etc.

As enjoyable as the above things are, they will make a most undigestible meal in a time of need, and they most certainly have nothing to do with our love and devotion for the Lord nor our living in a manner in which we are prepared to meet Him. Thus, as the days and months drag on, we experience ever more "cumulative disobedience" as we live in a constant state of "procrastination." This must bring great pleasure to the adversary, for he knows that one of the main reasons for food storage and preparedness is to keep our hearts focused on our obedience to the Lord—the reward of which is our safety.

Elder *Orson Hyde*, in 1857, discussed the concept of being beguiled by the tempter:

> *Now, all this is in the midst of this counsel to store up your grain, and to hold on to it. It is the counterpart, or tempter to beguile.* How many will there be who will go and exchange one for the other? Say one and another, I must have a little of this, a little of that, and a little of the other; and thus, little by little, goes the grain that we were commencing to store up, until it has leaked away and our granaries are empty. . . .

> *If this grain be stored up and properly taken care of, we may go destitute of many comforts that we desire;* but, *after the Lord has proven us,* in this respect, to see *if we will resist the temptations of the adversary*—to see *if we will resist the shining gold and the fine apparel, and to see if we will abide the law,* and lock up and *preserve our grain, is it not as easy for Him to provide us with those things that we really need for clothing as it was to increase our limited stores, or to give us now a plentiful harvest?* . . .

> *Brethren, the test is right before us.* It is not an imaginary thing, but it is actually coming to test us, *to see whether we will, under these circumstances, abide the counsel that has been given to us.*

> *There is hardly ever a commandment given to any person or persons before whom a temptation is not placed to decoy them, if possible, from obedience to that commandment.* . . .

> Well, if counsel has been given unto us to store up our grain, I should not wonder if there were temptations placed before us, to induce us to noncompliance. . . .

> We should like the comforts of life, and would no doubt like to purchase them; but the counsel of the servants of the Lord would lead us to do differently. . . .

> Remember it, brethren and sisters; for I want to impress it upon your minds. *Keep your grain for yourselves and for strangers who, in times of famine abroad, seek at your hands bread from heaven and earth.* When the servants of God set good counsel before you, and these temptations follow, they will not command, perhaps, when the temptation is present; and these will be trying to you: they will be so, *to see if you will stand by your integrity, or fall by your instability.* . . .

Now, we have the gift of God, and that is the gift of wise counsel—of good counsel given unto us for the purpose of self-preservation. Will we, by any reason, by any craft, by any devise, by any machinations, by any swerving from our purpose, lose that gift?

Remember the counsel that is given, "Store up all your grain," and take care of it! Prize it above gold and silver, above rich clothing and fine apparel, and above everything else except the bread of life! (Journal of Discourses, vol. 5, pp. 15-17).

THE GREATEST TEST MAY BE PROSPERITY, NOT POVERTY

It seems that the more affluent the Saints become, the less likely they are to use their economic increase to be consistently obedient in maintaining their food storage. Does this remind you of the foolishness of the people in the Book of Mormon who could never seem to "stand prosperity?" Well, no matter who the people are, or which dispensation of time, it seems that human nature consistently has to be bridled and tempered or we will thoughtlessly drift into losing ourselves and our souls.

It was Elder *Daniel H. Wells* who, in 1878, cautioned that the Saints' greatest test may be not poverty, but prosperity:

The Lord never had a people who were received with open arms by the world, admired, cherished and respected; on the contrary *they have been persecuted or totally destroyed* from off the earth. . . . The Latter-day Saints have had the same experience to pass through. . . . *There will come a time, however, in the history of the Saints, when they will be tried with peace, prosperity, popularity and riches (Journal of Discourses,* vol. 19, p. 367).

WE'RE ASKED TO LIVE IN A STATE OF OBEDIENT PREPARATION

The Lord has always required, since the days when He walked upon the earth, a people who were to "watch and be ready," who were asked to live in a constant state of obedient preparation. If any of us should die today, are we ready to stand before Him? Does our obedience to His counsel reflect that we were indeed living in this daily state of being prepared to meet Him now or at His coming? Can we see that obedience to this consistent counsel and our readiness to stand before Him are a reflection of one and the same thing?

It is hoped that as we contemplate what we have read, we will desire to become a people of "strong faith" and experience a sense of appreciation for the gifts of knowledge and awareness with which the Lord and His prophets have blessed us. This fore-knowledge offers each of us an opportunity to prepare our lives and where possible, our families, to meet the challenging "moments in time" that will continue to rapidly unfold in the days that lie ahead. It also offers us the opportunity to set an example before our children and friends of how important it is to keep our hearts and lives ready to greet our Lord.

As stated at the beginning, the Lord has given us a very simple but powerful promise: "If ye are prepared ye shall not fear." Later, the Lord went on to add this challenging thought: "*It is my purpose to provide for my saints, for all things are mine. But it must be done in mine own way*" (D&C 104:15-16).

May the Lord help us truly come to the understanding of the magnificent blessing the food storage and preparedness program really is. Indeed, it is a law of spiritual protection just as much as it is a law of physical protection. What greater way can the Lord help us daily to focus on Him, upon Heavenly Father, and upon how we should obediently live our lives with the aid of the Holy Ghost, than by instructing us regarding things to come, and to "watch and be ready"?

It is important to keep in mind that in many ways Hell is really a state of awareness. And it will never be more real then at the precise moment when one awakens to the fact that his "moment in time" to have obeyed has really past. It is as simple as this: when the time of need comes and you open your cupboard doors, what will you find? In an instant you will come face to face with the reality of your obedience, or with the reality of your disobedience, and with the fact that you must live with your failure to obey. You will immediately know your circumstances, and you will be unable to change where you are; there will be no replays. How sad it would be if we had truly repented, almost in time—but just one day too late! Remember the days of tribulation are set on the Lord's calendar and will not be altered.

We sometimes forget that the food storage and "watch and be ready" injunctions are not just a gift from the Lord to protect us. They also are our opportunity to manifest an obedient heart, by which our compliance becomes symbolic of our gifts back to Him as we become determined to follow His counsel. This may indeed be "the greater purpose" for which these instructions are given.

May Heavenly Father bless us all with the integrity of soul to show our love and devotion to Him by living this great law.

CHAPTER
14
SUMMARY OF FOOD STORAGE
RECOMMENDATIONS—1840'S TO 1990'S

As the Saints were being driven out of Nauvoo, the initial concern for President Brigham Young and the Twelve was how to feed them as they sat destitute in the dead of winter on the west bank of the Mississippi River.

The next major problem for Church leaders was how to provide food for the members as they moved westward across the great plains towards what eventually became known as the Great Salt Lake Valley. During the initial part of the journey, some foodstuff was worked for or purchased from the residents of the areas the Saints were passing through, and in several places crops were planted to provide food for those who were to follow.

After their arrival in the Valley, the Brethren then faced the ultimate challenge of how to assist the Saints to survive in a desert, nearly a thousand miles in any direction away from any alternative food source.

Today, the Brethren face similar challenges as they attempt to feed far too many unprepared Saints during a time of relative prosperity. The difficult times which can be seen on the horizon would surely be tempered if every Latter-day Saint family had their year's supply of food and essentials in place—but currently, such is not the case.

YEAR-BY-YEAR RECOMMENDATIONS

The following is an abbreviated recap covering some 150 years, describing periods of time when the Saints had to fend for themselves.

You will also find some suggestions regarding the kinds of food to be considered for storage. You will observe that over the years, as circumstances have changed, there have also been changes in some products suggested for families to store, and to the number of years for which we may need to prepare. You will also note that early storage recommendations were largely limited to grains (mostly wheat). But as the years and historical events have unfolded, you will notice that more sophisticated recommendations began to be developed, and then they eventually returned to the more simplified foods.

The following is a summary of the detailed counsel that was given to the Saints, with suggested lists of basic foods to store and the recommended amounts of time they were to prepare for:

Year	# Years	By Whom	Recommended Foodstuffs
1856	3 to 5	Pres. Young	Wheat
1857	7	Presidents Young & Heber Kimball	Wheat, Pumpkins, Squash, Currents, Apples, Peaches, Beans, Peas
1864	7	Pres. Young	Wheat
1867	7	Elder Geo. Smith	Wheat
1868		Pres. Young	Wheat,Oats, Barley, Corn, Vegetables, Fruit
1891		Geo. Q. Cannon	Grains & Fruits
1893	1 to 2	Geo. Q. Cannon	
1916	1	Elder Charles Nibley	
1933		An *Improvement Era* suggestion noted below (a one month outline then projected to one year):	

Item	Mo.	Yr.
Cod Liver Oil	12 oz	4.5 qts
Milk.	30 qts	360 qts
Vegetables Greens, Spinach, Beet Greens	1 qt	12 qts
Other canned vegetables; Peas, String Beans, Asparagus	2 qts	24 qts
Dried Corn	1/2 pt	12 qts
Stored Vegetables; Cabbage, Beets, Potatoes, Onions, Carrots . .	24 lbs	288 lbs
Tomatoes	3 qts	36 qts
Fruits:		
Berries: Raspberries, Strawberries, & Goose/dew berries. . . .	2 qts	24 qts
Large Fruits: Peaches, Pears, Apricots, Plums.	3 qts	36 qts
Other Fruits: Cherries, Rhubarb, Fruit Juice.	3 qts	36 qts
Apples (stored)	6 lbs	72 lbs
Flour: whole wheat	8 lbs	96 lbs
Cereals: Rolled Oats, Whole Wheat, Roman Meal	2 lbs	24 lbs
Proteins:		
Meat, dried/cured.	1 1/2 lbs	18 lbs
Meat, beef/chicken	2 1/2 lbs	30 lbs
Salmon	1/2 pt	6 qts
Meat, fresh	1 lb	12 lbs
Beans, dried	1/2 lb	6 lbs
Cheese; American, cottage.	1 1/2 lbs	18 lbs
Eggs: Children	30	360
Adults.	30/60	360/720
Fats: Lard/bacon	1 1/2 lbs	18 lbs
Sweets: Sugar, Honey, Molasses	3 lbs	36 lbs

Total	Mo.	Yr.
Castor oil	12 oz	4 qts
Fruits & Vegetables	52 qts	564 qts
"Foodstuffs".	269 lbs	3,228 lbs
Average Eggs	30/60	540

Year	# Years	By Whom	Recommended Foodstuffs
1936		Pres. McKay	Can Fruits and Vegetables
1942	1	First Presidency	
1954	1	Bishop Buehner	
1958		*The Improvement Era*, "Counsel Regarding Food Storage:"	

The scriptural parable of the wise virgins who filled their lamps with oil in preparation for the coming of the bridegroom portrays vividly the maxim that "Where there is no vision, the people perish!" If there is no foresight, the future of an individual or a society is uncertain. Man may work strenuously for what he can now see, but he can also plan for what he cannot see—if he does so with foresight and vision.

Foresight implies an understanding of events in the future as arising from specific cause. To know the cause is to foresee the results. Food security is achieved through anticipating the causes of food scarcity and food deterioration. Successful storage of food is built upon foresight.

Food storage should be undertaken with two general goals in mind. First is long-life storage, intended to meet the possible need for emergency food as the results of catastrophe. The other goal, economic and recurring in nature, is short-life storage. In each case the principles governing the types of food selected, as well as their maintenance and use, may differ.

Uses for long-life food storage are normally emergency in nature. They may be acute and total or infrequent and indefinite, though perhaps for short periods of time, since they may arise from destructive wars, floods, hurricanes, quakes, pestilences, major industry breakdowns, and other disasters. Foods for such storage should be selected primarily on the basis of maximum stability, with ample nourishment in view.

The uses for shortlife or economic storage are related to the everyday risks of residing in a complex society in which production and marketing are critically interdependent. These risks involve such things as possible unemployment, interruption of transportation systems, and inflation of prices for goods or services. . . . Foods for such storage should be selected on the basis of frequency of uses in the family, consistency with nutritional completeness, and rotational stability (*The Improvement Era*, July 1958, p. 550).

Year	# Years	By Whom	Recommended Foodstuffs
1959	1	*The Improvement Era*, "What this [1959] plan would provide:"	

In summary the following are what seem adequate for the average adult woman for a one year's supply: Wheat, 300 lbs; Powdered Milk (Non-fat); 100 lbs; Sugar; 100 lbs; Salt, 5 lbs; Multiple vit. tabs, 365; Water, ?

This would provide a diet that would supply approximately 2300 calories a day which is the recommended needs of a 25-year-old average American woman. If we use these amounts then we will have more than a child will eat and less than adolescent or adult male will eat. This will balance out roughly since a small child will eat about 1000 calories less and an adult male about 1000 calories more a day than the adult woman about who we are making our calculations. Such a procedure makes our calculations much simpler and yet they are practical.

This would supply approximately 94 grams of protein a day which is well above the recommended minimum of 55 to 65 grams a day for women or men respectively. It is even sufficient for a man in the 16 to 20 years age range who has the greatest requirement of all. It would supply approximately 7.6 grams of fats a day, and it would supply approximately 444 grams of carbohydrates a day (*The Improvement Era*, September 1959, p. 702).

Year	# Years	By Whom	Recommended Foodstuffs
1966	1	Pres. Lee	Think in terms of what would keep us alive.
1973	1	Pres. Benson	Leather, bolts of cloth
1973	1	First Presidency:	
		Grains: wheat, rice or other grass cereals:	300 lbs
		Sugar/honey:	100 lbs
		Salt:	5 lbs

These items, used exclusively, provide a diet that supplies approximately 2,300 calories per day which is recommended for an average woman 25 years old. A small child will use a 1,000 calories less and an adult male 1,000 calories more per day.

First aid items

Fuel

Sewing Material: Fabrics, thread, needles, etc.

Year	# Years	By Whom	Recommended Foodstuffs
1973		Pres. Benson	Clothes, Leather, Bolts of Cloth.
1976	1	Pres. Kimball	
1977**		[See "Bishop Jack West" Story, Below]	
1978	1	Pres. Packer	
1980	1	Pres. Benson	Berry bushes, grapevines, fruit trees & vegetables, food, clothing, water & fuel—wood, coal, gas, oil, kerosene, & candles
1982	1	Elder Busche	Vegetable oil, honey & powered milk
1988	1	First Presidency	Clothing, fuel, grains, legumes, cooking oil, powered milk, sugar/honey & water
1995		Elder Perry	Life sustaining food

BISHOP JACK WEST'S STORY

In the 1950's, 1960's and 1970's there was a concentrated, ongoing effort amongst the Saints to obtain at least a one—and preferably a two years', supply of food, as that was the general counsel then. There was considerable encouragement from the Brethren to prepare, and much discussion and information was shared among the members as they labored towards completing this food storage assignment.

FROM A 1977 FOOD STORAGE FIRESIDE IN SACRAMENTO, CALIFORNIA A BISHOP'S EFFORT TO PREPARE

This is the story of one bishop, amongst many other leaders and members, all who played and important and tireless, behind-the-scene role in the development of the Church's Food Storage Program. Bishop West put forth considerable effort to first set his own house in order, after which he labored helping the members of the ward he presided over to prepare. There were many mistakes and much to be learned, but what was learned has proven to be an asset to many of the Saints today.

In the fall of 1977, Jack H. West was asked to give firesides in the Sacramento, California area on the subject of Food Storage because of the part he played in its on-going development. Some of Bishop West's comments are taken from notes recorded in one of those firesides.

Bishop West indicated that he was "set apart as the first bishop of Glendora Ward" and immediately set about doing surveys to determine who in the ward had adequate food storage. The results indicated that "less than 5% of our people had even a year's supply of food," let alone a two-years supply. In order to set a leadership example, he discussed with his wife that:

> "Maybe we had better set the pace for the rest of the ward." The results were that there shortly appeared "two giant trucks and trailers" turning into his driveway, sufficient to meet the needs of feeding a "family of eight" for two years. And I said, "You're kidding—we can't possibly be eating that much food." Well, she took me to a full length mirror and turned me side-ways and I didn't have any more questions.

What his family found out was that not only did they have a great deal of canned food but a lot of frozen food as well, especially meat. He said they immediately began experiencing a number of problems. A freak loss of power in the Glendora area resulted in the loss of their meat. They then faced the problem of how to organize and rotate cases of food that were "stacked nine feet high." To correct this problem he built shelves and:

> . . . angled the 2 x 4's just exactly one can apart and we'd fill those slanted units with the cans of food. Then when we pulled a can out from the bottom, every can rotated like they had asked us to do.

But with this type of storage, the problem was that he never could tell how many cans were left. Another problem which became apparent was that Sister West could only estimate how much of any given food they would use in two years, and so:

> . . . the first thing we knew, we were using more of one thing than another. . . . Well, it did not work.

As Brother and Sister West checked, they determined that their diet became very unbalanced. Procrastination resulted in a failure to replace used products as they should have, bringing:

> . . . bulging cans everywhere you looked. . . . The first thing you know, the whole thing was completely shot to pieces. . . .
>
> Well, I went back to the [ward] Welfare Committee and said, "Look, one of the things the Word of Wisdom tells us to do (and that's the direct word of the Lord) is to use the food in the season thereof. We are using two-year old food constantly in times

of non-emergency and I just couldn't believe that was the program the Lord had in mind for us." So I said, "Let's fast and pray about this thing—we'll get the whole ward to fast and pray about it and see if we can come up with some better answers for a year's supply of food, or even a two year's supply."

So we did, and then we started to search the scriptures, of course, and we found in some 72 places, as I remember, it mentioned the "land flowing with milk and honey" as the ideal land. So we made note of that—we marked down milk and honey—there might be something to that. And then we went to the Word of Wisdom and we found that the staff of life was "grain" . . . particularly "wheat for man." So we went to the scriptures again and we found if the "salt has lost its savior" . . . We marked down salt as maybe an important thing." [Surprisingly, they didn't include olive oil, which is also in the scriptures.]

Bishop West was acquainted with two well-known dieticians and wrote to them, asking "What would you think about it, if we were to use four basic foods as an emergency supply—wheat, honey, salt and milk?" They wrote back and said: "You've just about hit the jackpot. There is just one thing you'd be low on and that is vitamin C, and that you'd be dangerously low on." So we went to vitamin C tablets.

As it turned out, vitamin C tablets do not have a long shelf life, so Bishop West reviewed various alternatives as they tried to find a suitable source for vitamin C; in relationship to this he related the following incident:

Then I was over in Mesa, Arizona one day and—have you ever seen someone walking toward you on the street that you were just absolutely certain had died two years before? That was a real thrill. I saw this young fellow walking toward me who was all hunched over the last time I had seen him and his bones were knurled and he looked like death itself and he told me that he had less than two months to live. Well here he was walking towards me hail and hardy and straight as an arrow. I said, "Ted, is that really you?" He said "Yes it is me." He was the brother-in law of one of my counselors in the bishopric. I said "What in the world saved your life?" he said, "Wheat greens." I said, "What? Wheat greens—What does wheat greens have in it that would save your life?" He said, "It is the highest known source of vitamin C in assimilable form for the human system." And I said, "Great scott, that's an answer to prayer. We have been looking for something that would give us vitamin C and here we've had the wheat all the time."" "You grow greens as you need it from the wheat you have on hand.

He then went on to relate that he had a friend, Anne Wigmore, Ph.D., MD and DD, who had written a book called *Wheat Grass—God's Manna*, who told him how to grow wheat grass. He then called his two dietician friends who confirmed the value of using wheat grass, especially as it relates to vitamin C.

A cousin of Bishop West, Elder Harold B. Lee, wrote to him several times requesting information on the four basics. Bishop West notes:

When he became President of the Church he twice asked for more literature. Just before he passed away, he completely changed his mind from asking people to get a year's or a two year's supply of their normal food, and rotate it, to reversing his field and coming back to the identical four basics that we had found worked so beautifully.

Out of the prayerful and persistent effort that Bishop West and his ward put forth came an organized, functional food storage plan which became a part of the cornerstone in the Church's current food storage program.

It should be noted that compared to the 1959 *Improvement Era* food list, the 1988 First Presidency outline for a one-year's supply of food is simple, easily stored, comparatively inexpensive and requires only a limited amount of space.

In reviewing what has been suggested for us to store, one item should be added. Some years ago the public panicked and in an instant all canning jars disappeared off store shelves. A good food supply requires 100 or more canning jars and lids (or canning wax to seal canned foods with). These jars do not necessarily need to be immediately filled, but should be available so that a family can personally add to their storage any perishable foods they might grow or obtain which would otherwise become a loss to them.

The previously quoted statement in the 1958 *Improvement Era* and the following 1959 *Improvement Era* statement gives us a very clear and understandable review of some of the purposes for assembling a year's supply of food:

> We are told that in the last days the privation and hardships will be greater than any mankind has been forced to suffer on this earth. "For in those days shall be affliction, such as was not from the beginning of the creation which God created unto this time, neither shall be."
>
> What better insurance could we have than a rotated one year's food supply? This may be much more valuable under emergency conditions than a large bank account if supplies are exhausted. Also, this can serve as a partial health and accident policy in case one has misfortune such as accident or loss of health resulting in loss of employment.
>
> Consider the following good reasons for storage: first, our prophets, seers, and revelators have so counseled us. Second, history has demonstrated repeatedly that prosperity and plenty will not always be with us. There are times of harvest and times between harvest. The wise man saves from the harvest for the lean months. The sluggard pays no attention to this thinking that the status quo of the world will always be. Or he hopes that someone will look out for him. As one season is less productive than another, so go also the years. Surely a one-year's supply is little enough. Third, the head of a household is charged with the scriptural injunction . . . to provide for his family (*The Improvement Era*, September 1959, p. 702).

OBTAIN LAND FOR GARDENS

It would seem that the only meaningful addition to the above detailed list is the need for an adequate piece of land, paid for, meaning deed in hand. Every family, or at the very least every extended family unit, coordinating together, should have land with sufficient water, good soil, and a large-enough space to raise a garden adequate to meet basic family needs. Ownership of usable land could be essential during times of serious need, whether it be an individual family crisis or a disaster facing the extended family. Today Russian families as well as families in a number of other countries survive only because they have access to a piece of land upon which they can grow something as simple as potatoes. It is possible, if families and extended families are willing to plan ahead, for them to obtain such a piece of land, and it may at some time be the only thing they will be able to lay claim to.

Right now would be a great time to either buy a piece of land or make arrangements with a very close friend or family member who owns a farm or large piece of land, to participate in creating a garden. Perhaps it would even be possible to build a storage shed on their property where a year's supply of food could be stored. Should you elect to do either of the above, it is important to keep in mind that nothing is free whether in the city or the country—so be prepared to pay your own way. Ultimately, even in times of great distress, no responsible person, (not even family members or close friends) should assume they could arrive at someone else's farm and be cared for without having and contributing at least their year's supply.

The Church set an example for us during the depression years of the early 1930's, when land was made available as a means of assisting the Saints to raise essential foods. Obviously, the Church now is far too spread out to again make land available to all Saints in time of need, but the necessity of having land during difficult times is certainly a sound principle, as seen from the Church's efforts during the depression years:

> Ward welfare farms began to arise throughout the West as bishops used small parcels of property in their ward areas to grow crops for their people in need. These commodities were given directly to the needy or to a bishops' storehouse for distribution.
>
> The Pioneer Stake allowed members to plant crops on a large piece of property within its boundaries. Members planted sugar beets, potatoes, tomatoes, onions, and other crops.
>
> . . . Many other stakes also developed vacant properties for the raising of vegetable and fruits for their people (*Pure Religion*, pp. 29-30).

A garden is a great way to supplement a year's supply of food. Difficult times will be weathered in a much more positive way by those Saints who have exercised enough foresight to have access to both.

President **Brigham Young** said that "The riches of a kingdom or a nation do not consist so much as the fulness of its treasury as in *the fertility of its soil* and *the industry of its people*" (*Discourses of Brigham Young*, p. 297).

The above comment by President Young is verified in the previously quoted story of the Dutch farmer who, as you may recall, when offered a jeweled watch for beans insisted that at most it was worth only one bag of beans and then commented, "I've got enough diamonds and gold to open a jewelry store of my own" (see p. 131).

CHAPTER
15
SOME OBSERVATIONS
ON FINANCIAL READINESS

THE HUMAN FACTOR IN ECONOMICS

President Hinckley's oft-repeated instruction to get out of debt has been more than clear, but there are a number of human factors that sometimes interfere with our individual response to counsel on financial and economic matters, even when it could dramatically affect our lives.

It is difficult for some of us to respond to a suggested correction regarding the course our economic life when we feel confident about the status of our immediate personal and financial affairs. At present, some seem to be much like the Captain of the Titanic, who received seven warnings to slow down and change course, but to little avail. He felt confident that his ship was unsinkable and therefore could charge full-steam ahead through fields of icebergs, just as many are doing today in the area of economics.

In like manner, the financial world is full of icebergs that should offer a clue to any family that all is not well. Like icebergs, the warnings may be perceived as only small pieces of ice rather than tips of a greater danger that lies silently just under the surface, the larger part being much more deadly than what is readily apparent on the surface.

THE ECONOMIC CYCLE

It is hard to understand how we as a people and a government have gotten ourselves into our current economic fix of being trillions of dollars in debt. Perhaps it can be better understood if we review a little of human psychology and see how it fits into the world of economics. Economic disasters have cycled about every 60 years. They are more than just notes in the history books—they also are tragic in personal ways that few of us can fully appreciate. The following material should give us a clue regarding President Hinckley's admonition to get out of debt, and we shall see how others have struggled with what most likely will eventually be our lot in life, especially if we ignore prophetic counsel and are not prepared.

History tells us that at the end of a depression the generation which was just "burned" becomes extremely conservative. Bloodied lenders retrench, making only totally-safe no-risk loans to individuals that probably don't need the money anyway. Investors who somehow survived the disaster look for the "sure thing," even if it offers only a minuscule return. Others simply hoard what little they have left. Investment and exchange, along with economic stability and the growth they could bring, grinds to a halt. As a result of such ultra-conservative attitudes following the Great Depression, it was the middle of the 1950's before the Dow Jones Industrial Average struggled back to the 1920 boom level, a return which didn't include inflation.

Then, some 30 years later, a new generation takes over, made up of those who can only remember stories about the depression. They have a need to break away from the restraints of the older generation, whom they feel are missing many obviously positive opportunities by being overly cautious. And to some extent they will be correct because the time eventually must come to be more practical about financial opportunities, if the effects from an economic collapse are ever to end.

However, as time passes, this new generation gradually becomes excessively liberal—a counter-reaction to the overly restrictive attitude of the older generation. Eventually the new generation has infiltrated the ranks of financial institutions, becoming CEO's of corporations and leaders of government. The overly conservative position of the past left a major vacuum in the economy, and the "new kids on the block" now rush in to fill it.

By this time, who can remember the crash of 40 or 50 years ago anyway? In fact, who cares about the old stories of how tough it was? Just like teenagers who are unable and unwilling to consider that they do not live forever, these new kids on the block refuse to believe that what goes up must someday also come down. They become infatuated with their boundless skills in making money and their new "systems and financial safeguards," denying the possibility of any future vulnerability. They come to think of themselves and their new era as an exception to the rule of economics, and that nothing can stop them! With this mind-set in place, the stage is then set for another depression caused by too much greedy confidence, too much easily printed money, and too many bad loans, made too foolishly for nearly anything to anybody.

This "can't lose" mode of thinking is presently afflicting today's financial arena, and from a historical perspective one can certainly predict the eventual outcome. Some have suggested that the overly extended "credit cycle" we have been in began to unwind when the 1987 stock market experienced a major drop, and that whether we like it or not, the worst is yet to come.

THE INEVITABLE RESULTS OF FINANCIAL EUPHORIA

Cited here are brief but profound statements drawn from a book written by John Kenneth Galbraith titled *A Short History of Financial Euphoria*. They state basic principles one should know and understand in order to chart his personal course in the economic systems of today.

• There can be few fields of human endeavor in which history counts for so little as in the world of finance. Past experience, to the extent that it is part of memory at all, is dismissed as the primitive refuge of those who do not have the insight to appreciate the incredible wonders of the present (p. 13).

• The world of finance hails the invention of the wheel over and over again, often in a slightly more unstable version. All financial innovations involve, in one form or another, the creation of debt secured in greater or lesser adequacy by real assets (p. 19).

• All crises have involved debt that, in one fashion or another, has become dangerously out of scale in relation to the underlying means of payment (p. 20).

• The circumstances that induce the recurrent lapses into financial dementia have not changed in any truly operative fashion since the Tulip-o-mania of 1636-1637 (p. 106).

• Individuals and institutions are captured by the wondrous satisfaction from accruing wealth (p. 106).

• The associated illusion of insight is protected, in turn, by the oft-noted public impression that intelligence, one's own and that of others, marches in close step with the possession of money (p. 106).

• Out of that belief, thus instilled, then comes action—the bidding up of values (p. 106).

• The upward movement confirms the commitment to personal and group wisdom. And so on to the moment of mass disillusion and the crash (p. 106).

• This last, it will now be sufficiently evident, never comes gently. It is always accompanied by a desperate and largely unsuccessful effort to get out (p. 106).

• And thus the rule, supported by the experience of centuries: the speculative episode always ends not with a whimper but with a bang (p. 4).

• A further rule is that when a mood of excitement pervades a market or surrounds an investment prospect, when there is a claim of unique opportunity based on special foresight, all sensible people should circle the wagons; it is the time for caution. "Perhaps, indeed, there is opportunity." "A rich history provides proof, however, that as often or more often, there is only delusion and self-delusion." (p. 109).

• When will come the next great speculative episode, and in what venue will it recur . . . there are no answers; no one knows, and anyone who presumes to answer does not know he doesn't know. But one thing is certain: there will be another of these episodes and yet more beyond. Fools, as it has long been said, are indeed separated, soon or eventually, from their money. So, alas, are those who, responding to a general mood of optimism, are captured by a sense of their own financial acumen. Thus it has been for centuries; thus in the long future it will also be (p. 110).

• Recurrent speculative insanity and the associated financial deprivation and larger devastation are, I am persuaded, inherent in the system. Perhaps it is better that this be recognized and accepted. The list of those who have descended abruptly from the heights is long. (p. viii).

• The euphoric episode is protected and sustained by the will of those who are involved [such as with derivatives or many available stocks], in order to justify the circumstances that are making them rich. And it is equally protected by the will to ignore, exorcise, or condemn those who express doubts (p. 11).

• Only after the speculative collapse does the truth emerge. What was thought to be unusual acuity turns out to be only a fortuitous and unfortunate association with assets (p. 17).

• Then will be rediscovered the oldest rule of Wall Street: Financial genius is before the fall (p. 98).

Perhaps it can all be summed up in the following observation:

What the wise do in the beginning fools do in the end (Warren Buffett).

REAL-LIFE TRAGEDIES RESULTING FROM MONETARY CATASTROPHES

We read and hear news reports of economic difficulties, but they seem so far away or so academic that we never personalize the problems. Yet, economic disasters affect real live people—people just like you and me. These people never believed it could ever happen to them, but it did, and similar experiences will continue to happen to others. The following example of inflation may seem worlds away, little more than an interesting historical note, but the heartaches were real to the people who lived through those unbelievable times. Of course we hope nothing similar will ever happen to any of us, but that wish may not necessarily come true, for no one's world is ever absolutely safe.

The following material regarding inflation in Germany was printed in the October, 1933 issue of *The Improvement Era*. It began with this note:

The article ought to be of interest just now when the gold dollar, unlike the leopard, has changed its "spots." (meaning that the United States had just gone off the gold standard.)

Comparative Depreciation Scale of the Mark: 1919 to 1923

Normal:	January, 1919—for $1.00,	4.2 marks
	January, 1920,	49.8;
	January, 1921,	75 marks for $1.00;

January, 1922,	188 marks;
June, 1922,	273;
December, 1922,	7,650;
January, 1923,	7,260;
Anticipated Recovery	
June, 1923,	75,000;
August, 1923,	1,100,000;
September, 1923,	9,700,000
October, 1923,	242,000,000
November, 1923,	130,000,000,000 [billion]
December, 1923,	
at the time the lid blew off,	4,200,000,000,000 [that's trillion]"

(All of the above relates to $1.00)

As we witness the current economic turmoil in the world about us with its riots, starvation, and political upheaval occurring in nation after nation, many of us are completely oblivious to what the average individual in those nations is truly experiencing. Most of us have no real appreciation as to what it feels like to truly be without food, shelter, clothing and the basic necessities of life, and further, no place to turn for help. Reading about another's life experiences can add a dimension to our understanding, but it will be nothing like having personally lived through such a overwhelming crisis.

The *Improvement Era* article continues:

The Story of One Family in Germany After WWI
An Economic Collapse, Germany—1923

Could inflation or other conditions ever raise the price of bread in the United States to one million dollars a loaf? "Impossible!" you cry. "Why, that's absurd."

Yet, years ago [prior to World War I] to have said in Germany that a loaf of bread would soon cost four million marks would have brought forth equally emphatic protests . . .

As the mark began to decrease in value, as compared to the dollar, *wages doubled, but commodities and foodstuffs jumped 5000 percent and more.* Bank clerks and other white-collar employees found that although their wages had been increased many times the pre-war rate, *they were still unable to purchase sufficient food for their families, let alone clothing and other necessities . . .*

Trebor H. Tims traveling in Germany in 1923 reported the following: "I saw former professional men, doctors, lawyers, and even ministers anxious to carry our luggage in the hope of earning a tip of 100 marks or so (less than one cent) which represented to them a good day's pay . . .

As more and more currency was printed less careful protection was shown in the engraving. Finally cheaper paper and a smaller size was used for the million mark note than for the 10,000 mark note. Instead of printing and protecting both sides of the banknote, the million mark note had one side entirely blank . . . *carrying so much currency was a real [problem]. In fact on one occasion I found it necessary to purchase a valise to accommodate change for $10.00 . . .*

Many tragedies resulted from the extreme inflation and there occurred at this time an *epidemic of suicides principally among the elderly persons who had scrimped throughout their lives to save sufficient to live a meager, but independent, old age.* Finding, say 20,000 marks left in the bank, they found this sum insufficient to purchase even a slice of bread. So, suicide seemed the only way out . . .

We learned of a widow, sick and unable to find work, who had two small children and an older daughter, the latter their sole support, working for a small pittance. The mother quietly let herself into the river one night that by her sacrifice the money ordinarily spent for her medicine might be used to buy food for the little ones.

Many of the older persons were saved the ignominy of suicide by *passing into a paralytic sleep, which changed into death because of lack of oil in their systems, meat and butter being too expensive for them . . .*

Inability to meet the constantly increasing taxes forced many property holders to *sell out to foreigners for insignificant sums,* in foreign exchange."

My German parents-in-law paid premiums to an insurance company from the time they were married until the wife died at about 70 years of age. The sum realized from the insurance was 10,000 marks, or a pre-war exchange of about $2,500.00. When the money was paid by the insurance company the mark stood at about 200,000 for the dollar and so the amount received was hardly the price of a loaf of bread . . .

The author notes that on a "cold drizzly January day in 1923," his wife was ill so he called the hotel staff to request heat for their room and water. He was told that he could not be accommodated because *it was too expensive to heat the whole hotel for one person.* Because he continued to complain the manager came to his room with the same facts. The author inquired how much it would cost to heat the hotel and was told that it would be 500,000 marks, quick calculations determined that it would cost about $1.00, thus, the hotel that night had plenty of heat for all guests (*The Improvement Era,* vol. 36, no. 12, October 1933, p. 720).

Perhaps it would be helpful if we took a look at a time and place that is a little closer to home.

Russia, 1998

Lest we jump to the conclusion that the afore-cited incidents of events in Germany could never happen in America, consider the following condition in Russia today. Here is a people who only a few years ago would also have denied that the following could ever be even remotely possible in their country:

Angry coal miners, who in some cases *have not seen any real wage payment in a solid year,* are threatening to flood the mines. They recently locked management in a room supplied with the "miners diet"—bread and water.

A specific focus of their protests has been *the "barter mafia,"* a group which has made secret deals with mine managements wherein they are granted the right to collect payments for coal delivered to private and industrial consumers—at manipulated prices.

The Russian mafia accepts *payment in goods*—refrigerators, medication, and the like. Then, in turn, they give these goods to the management of the mines who must sell them if they are to pay the miners' wages. Because this process is often so complicated, the miners accept the "goods" in lieu of wages and try to sell them in order to recoup some of the wages owed them. This practice is so common that real wage payments have become the exception.

It was recently reported that *the Russian people have been able to survive their current economic situation because 80% of them have access to a place to raise their own food.* They either have access to government land, or relatives who have land sufficient to raise food which minimally meets their survival needs (a situation that most often does not exist in the United States today).

A recent letter (September 9, 1998) from Sister Tessa Gardner, a missionary serving in Russia, gives some added insight. It reads as follows:

I feel like I'm writing to you from another century or in the middle of a really strange dream. You probably already know but *the ruble has drastically fallen*—the last we knew you could get 28 rubles for one dollar—if you have a dollar, that is. The trouble started about 2 weeks ago—well, really over a century ago—ok, since the beginning of Russia's history she's had one crisis after another. But, this particular insanity started about 2 weeks ago when we noticed that the dollar was at 7 rubles instead of the normal 6. It's been steadily getting worse since then.

What does that mean? Well, a whole heck of a lot and none of it good. There are no dollars in Russia, anywhere—unless Yeltsin has them, which is a possibility no one is willing to rule out. *The people who have been working* (who *haven't been paid for months* on end—the *pensions for the elderly also haven't come* for about 3-4 months)—*are steadily losing their jobs.* People are scrambling to buy enough dry products with what money they have—but the *stores are running out of products* and of course are not being restocked—how do you restock without adequate funds? *Prices are rising,* but it doesn't really matter since there *soon won't be anything to buy and nothing to buy it with*—that is, if things don't improve . . .

Don't worry—president's at the helm and God is calling the shots for his missionaries in Russia. . . . It's the Russians you need to fast and pray for—ask others to do it, too . . . *Ask for stability, ask for bread.* And then, *get our family prepared.* Tell everyone to be prepared—*tell them to get a year's supply, learn to fix stuff with your own hands, plant a garden.* Tell them that no one is safe.

Russia is experiencing an "early winter of discontent" while America is enjoying "the best economic climate in 10 years." [Not so,] America is going to fall on its [backside] someday and we have got to be ready because there is no time. I know we as a family have never had much, but we've always had somewhere to go and something to eat. *It's amazing how fast you prioritized when you have no one, nothing, nowhere,—and no money to buy bread.* No bread. When was the last time America was grateful for bread?

We were at a member's, Mapuha, and she'd just lost her job (still fed us however) and had been *scrounging the streets looking for work.* Factories already closed years ago, the markets are closing—there's nothing. She laughs. She laughed and said that she was grateful they'd had a good harvest of potatoes. She watched her 12 year old son play with his mega-rainbow slinky on a ladder made out of books and I could literally read her eyes—all they could say were, "How am I going to feed you?" She has no options. "But she said, we can be at the meeting this Sunday!" (because she doesn't have to work).

We just scraped the last of our money together to get Bolodua on a plane to Armenia in order to pick up his wife and see and bury his daughter who just died. She was two years old and . . . died last Saturday night. Bolodua is such a good man—I've never seen such heartbreak before. His wife was thousands of miles away, his child just died (the 2nd of two to do so—the first died along with 50 other babies in Armenia due to food poisoning from some American milk company) and his boss refused to pay. Again, a person with no options. With only enough money for transportation and bread, the missionaries stood in a little circle feeling that God is great, after Bolodua and the president of our branch headed off for the airport. Helping was good.

But now we have nothing material left to give and are standing helpless as *those impossible stories are multiplying every day—people we love are destitute.* We didn't really think it could get any worse than it already was—until it did.

Everyday I'm so grateful that we bring people the gospel—the gospel will save a man—*give him an immaterial instinct to save his soul and a will to fight, to find bread and save his body.* The gospel is an amazing thing—it still takes me by surprise how practical and useful it is in every day we live in this insanity. Mapuha said that this isn't Russia anymore, it's an insane asylum. *In extremities a man either turns to God or denys him—grey areas are lost to the starving.* The proud are so . . . proud and the humble are so amazingly humble. I think it was Winston Churchill that said, "*You can judge a man by the decisions he makes under pressure.*" "Oh, yes, you can" . . .

I don't know if any of this is making sense or if I can adequately describe what's happening here. Even if tomorrow everything is cool, even if tomorrow the country collapses, the truth will still be truth.

Spend your time, spend your energy getting prepared. We're in a war zone, collect the rations. Prepare the garden. *Prepare others to prepare themselves.* Prepare grandpa. We have no time, there's just no . . . time.

Desperation is everywhere. On the streets I see the same faces having the same conversations—a vicious circle of "if" and "what" because there are no immediate answers—not even an end either way. The strangest autumn of my life is settling in around us. The trees are quietly changing from green to golden and the air is taking on a slightly pinkish glow of leaf fires and rainstorms. The Volga herself has lost her summer and is now a mirror of the rain clouds. Nature always seems to carry herself in accordance, however aloof from, the tide of the human story. Or maybe its just us that throw our connections over her like a fish net—it keeps us grounded in this sense, we are all fishermen—casting and pulling and casting and pulling in an endless cycle, hoping that in the endless cycle, hoping that in the rhythm we will find a sense of self and some kind of sanity.

I don't know when the harvest will ever come for this country but I know that God loves her. I know His great heart breaks for her. *I think the Lord is weeping for her in much the same way as he wept for Jerusalem.* I don't know if the missionaries will be forced to leave for awhile, but I do know the [gospel] will grow in this country until temples dot the face of it.

Every day is such a roller coaster—every day is such a battle. We fight fatigue, laziness, trunkiness, sickness—we fight the Devil. Every day, every minute—we fight and fight. And this is why we do it, this is why we stay—because we are an army. We make a difference one person at a time—every day, every minute.

Don't worry about me—worry about the kingdom of our home. Secure our kingdom—get them ready—expect miracles—expect the unexpected—expect anything.

It is hard for us to believe that only a short while ago Russia was competing with the United States as a world power, yet today it is caught up in a hyper-inflationary depression. Families are starving, medical care has all but disappeared. Engineers, doctors and other professional and blue-collar workers are groveling in the frozen soil to find a missed potato. The once-mighty Russian military is dangerously poised, like a caged animal, waiting for the moment that they can reclaim their place amongst world military powers.

The Russian experiment in so-called capitalistic democracy has, for all intents and purposes, failed. The world's biggest banks, trading firms, mutual and hedge funds, as well as corporations, have lost billions of dollars as Russia defaulted on its financial notes, yet—incredibly—the U.S. ambassador to Russia recently declared it a safe place to invest!

All of this has taken place in a nation that holds some of the world's largest stockpiles of oil, gold and diamonds, along with strategic metals such as platinum, palladium and titanium—metals the world cannot do without. Yet, with all of its natural wealth, it is bankrupt and calling upon the International Monetary Fund for billions to help bail it out of trouble—a process which has had little more effect than feeding a "Black Hole."

If you are thinking, "Well, that's Russia not the United States," be patient—our turn is coming. No country in this world is an island secure unto itself. This is especially true of the United States, the largest debtor nation on the planet. A recent government accounting report indicated that internal budget expenditures, property accounting and national debt is so complicated that no one really knows where all the money goes nor what this nation actually owes. What is known is that *the trade deficit for 1998 was the largest in history and growing ever faster, and that the government must borrow at least 50 billion dollars a month in foreign bailouts to just finance our trade/government debt.* This does not take into consideration the capitol required to service our huge consumer and corporate debt demands.

There is an ever-increasing need for every family to follow the teachings of the Lord to be prepared. We also need to pray for our nation, it's government and our people. Strangely, many of us living in this nation seem only dimly aware the United States is in serious economic trouble. As a people we have not cherished our freedom, we have simply taken it for granted, and all the while many have greedily and unscrupulously used their opportunities and freedoms to meet their personal selfish needs at the expense of others. It would seem extremely important that this nation awaken to what is happening around us and safeguard what we have before there are no choices remaining—and above all—Prepare . . . PREPARE . . . PREPARE!!

COUNT THE COSTS

Until somewhere in the 1970's, most American families were able to make it with one adult working outside the home. Then in the 1970's, 80's and 90's, mothers and wives got paying jobs with the idea that they were going to bring to their families extra income. Now try this. Add up the total taxes your household pays; look carefully because some of these taxes are hidden. There are state and federal income tax, sales tax, social security tax, property tax, gas tax (about 35 cents a gallon), and don't overlook "fees" that used to be taxes but now have been reworded by the government as a means of taxing under another name.

After doing this, compare your total governmental tax with one of the total wages earned. The odds are you will find there is still basically only one wage earner supporting the family while the other one is supporting the government. The second wage earner originally went to work so that the family could have something "extra" but now "must" work in order for the family to survive financially.

Thomas Jefferson warned that those who rely on government for food ". . . will soon want bread."

President *Ezra Taft Benson*, speaking at BYU, quoted this powerful statement by Thomas Jefferson on national debt:

> Thomas Jefferson, while President of the United States, expressed what I hope and pray is the conviction of all of us. Mark carefully his wise declaration. "I have sworn upon the alter of God eternal hostility against any form of tyranny over the minds and lives of men. *To preserve our independence, we must not let our rulers load us with perpetual debt. We must take our choice between economy and liberty, or profusion and servitude. If we run into such debts, we must be taxed in our meat and drink, in our necessities and in our comforts, in our labors and in our amusements. If we can prevent the government from wasting the labor of the people under the pretense of caring for them, they will be happy."* That government is best which governs the least, so taught the courageous founders of this nation. . . . The opposite philosophy leads inevitably to moral decay (*BYU Speeches*, February 28, 1962, pp. 4-5).

And *George Washington*, our first President, warned, "Government is not reason, it is not eloquence, it is force! Like fire, it is a dangerous servant and a fearful master."

THE DANGERS OF A PRECARIOUS ECONOMY

Perhaps some of what you have read appears to be so unbelievable that it almost seems like fiction. It is difficult to comprehend that not just one or two nations are *going* broke but, with very few exceptions, the nations of the world *are* broke. This is true whether it is the very biggest and most advanced nations, or the poorest and most underdeveloped ones. Global leaders from Washington, London, Berlin, Tokyo, Hong Kong, South America, Africa, and Asia, are all running to and fro looking for "the" answer and, politically, there is none to be found. They have no permanent solution, and everything they try, frustratingly, only holds for "a moment" before things begin to unravel again.

While sharing an awareness of how fragile our economic world really is, there has also been an underlying question running throughout this addendum, which is: what are you and I going to do about it? Just a few short years ago the Russian people were making it. During those years the Japanese were very well off and, along with many others in the rest of Asia, had became a very wealthy people.

As you ponder about that, the question which comes to mind is, can you and I survive what has happened to them? How long can your savings maintain you (should you have access to them)? What happens to you if your stock, money market funds, IRA, retirement plan or even your salary suddenly is greatly diminished or entirely disappears? What will you do if your bank, after you endlessly stand in line, won't give you but a portion of your money, and your credit cards cease to function? What will you do if the stores are suddenly empty?

You could say to me that this will never happen in America, but we all know it has happened before—far too many times—and it seems perfectly clear it will happen again. Perhaps you will say that you have noticed over the past few years that the world seems to be extremely troubled, but you think nothing serious will come of it here at home—after all, our experts tell us not to worry, everything is "coming up roses." If you feel secure with this you will not be the first to have passively harbored such an illusion.

If your world truly is going to go sideways and fall apart in a major way, what could have been shared with you that would have caused you to stop and seriously review what your circumstances would be if difficult times—or worse yet, tumultuous times quickly came upon you? Could you pay your rent or mortgage, obtain the necessary food and medical supplies, and provide clothing for your family?

Ask yourself, why would the Prophet make the specific suggestion that each of us to get out of debt, as he did recently in General Conference, if we are not headed for serious economic problems? Why did President Hinckley close his remarks with this firm declaration—"I wish to say it with all the emphasis of which I am capable" if he didn't mean for the Saints to truly "set their houses in order?"

The special thing about preparing for negative events is that if they never occur you haven't done anything that would severely damage you financially. But if the time came and you were without, really economically totally destitute, you would be so very grateful for having put forth the extended effort to be prepared.

Have you ever noticed that before a severe storm hits there is often a rather quiet time which proceeds it? In the distance you can see the storm clouds gathering, but all around you there is quietness. Often the wind settles to a slight movement in the trees, birds can be heard giving an occasional chirp or flutter as they settle in, and all seems well with the world. For some, this may be a time that lulls them into a false sense of security, as though the storm is intentionally setting them up so as to catch them unguarded. To others, it is a signal from nature that they have only a brief time to make preparations, a time to settle into a secure, protected place without interference from her.

Likewise, it is easy to look into the distance and see dark clouds of an economic storm gathering, although here at home, at least for the moment, things seem to be unusually positive. The message may be that now is the time to set things in order with preparation for an on-coming devastating storm. Should you prepare for a storm and for some reason it passes by, you need not regret having prepared, for there will be other storms. And in the event the impending storm or another storm suddenly comes upon you, then most likely you will feel a sense of gratitude, appreciation and peace of mind for having put forth the extended effort to be ready for it.

For those of you who haven't taken the time to look off into the distance, go quickly and take a look, and see for yourself what is appearing on the horizon. If what you see gives you reason for even a little concern, then perhaps you should take advantage of the time remaining to prepare your family's needs.

THINGS THAT ARE HARD TO HEAR

No one wants to look at where we are, as a people. Who wants to believe that the nations of the world are all nearly broke, dangerously close to being bankrupt, and that we as a people here in America are also personally bankrupt? Who wants to believe the words of a so-called "doom and gloomer" when so many people are getting richer on electronic paper: Everyone knows that all these people making money can't be mistaken—or can they? How do you apply the Prophet's admonition, *"There is a portent of stormy weather ahead to which we had better give heed"*? How do you translate that into your own life? For those of us that are uncertain of or unwilling to consider what "portent" means, the dictionary states it is "something that foreshadows a coming event, especially a momentous or calamitous event."

The challenge is before you. How you respond to the gathering storm clouds is strictly up to you. My desire is that the Lord will bless you with the spirit of obedience to His counsel such that your heart will be sufficiently touched that it moves you to action. Becoming prepared with a year's supply of food and essentials is not an overwhelming task once you have set your mind to it. In fact, it could become a memorable experience for you and your family as you witness the doors the Lord opens and the hurdles He moves out of your way, because He, too, wishes for you to be prepared. The effort put forth, the challenges experienced, and blessings received while preparing, have the potential to become one of those experiences your family may talk about for many generations. Why not give it a try and let the Lord decide how it eventually unfolds. I feel certain that if you will wisely do your part, you can count on Him doing his part.

Remember what President **Brigham Young** said: *"My faith is, when we have done all we can, then the Lord is under obligation, and will not disappoint the faithful; he will perform the rest"* (*Discourses of Brigham Young*, p. 155).

CHAPTER
16
CONCLUSION

In the Church we speak about great challenges related to the second coming of the Savior as though that specific event should be the point of our concern. The fact is, the actual appearance of Jesus Christ will be as great a relief to the hearts of this generation as it was to the Saints in Book of Mormon times. Their real struggle was to survive the events that preceded the appearance of the resurrected Christ, and so it will be with those of this generation. However, the problems preceding the Savior's second coming will take a great deal more time than the three hours of destruction which took place here in the Americas. This will necessitate that the time and circumstances we need to prepare for them will necessarily require a greater commitment, sacrifice and more extensive planning.

As Elder *Neal A. Maxwell* has observed, "A worldwide millennium is impending, *preceded by much misery and destruction, not total world annihilation*" (*Meek and Lowly*, p. 43).

A TIME TO PREPARE

We of pioneer stock know of the challenges that faced our ancestors as they assisted in the restoration of the gospel—challenges that we can only vaguely appreciate. Yet, we have been told that this, our generation, will face even more critical events than any previous generation has had to face. There is no doubt that the Lord will eventually have a prepared people. The question facing us is whether or not the children of Israel will respond to "gentle" counsel to bring order to their lives, or will we require chastisement, plagues and famine, as in times past, to bring us to the point of obedience?

Will the Lord's chosen people use this present time of relative prosperity to prepare, or will we wait until our required preparations come in times of great turmoil, distress and personal desperation? In either event, ultimately the Lord will have a people prepared to greet him, yet the circumstances by which we will individually ready ourselves and our families (if at all) is left for us to decide. We have ultimately arrived at our "significant point in time" where we no longer have the luxury of putting off what we must do if we are to become prepared as counseled. The events which will determine who the five wise and five foolish virgins are cannot be put off indefinitely.

The Lord has counseled us this way:

Ye are called to bring to pass the gathering of mine elect; for *mine elect hear my voice and harden not their hearts;*

Wherefore the decree hath gone forth from the Father that they shall be gathered . . . , *to prepare their hearts and be prepared in all things against the day when tribulation and desolation are sent forth upon the wicked* (D&C 29:7-8).

WHAT WOULD THE LORD HAVE ME DO TODAY?

Finally, human nature being what it is, most of us find it difficult to take on a new project, such as food storage, especially when there appears to be no apparent pressing circumstances to initiate it. It takes time, planning, and probably the thing that is most difficult for many, a need to budget and sacrifice in order to put together a food storage program.

The human mind tends to interpret new information, such as the counsel to store food, in terms of one's current circumstances. Actually, this is a normal response since we are seldom able to immediately enter everything new into our daily routine. Because of this, we filter what we encounter by means of what we believe to be true and of most importance in carrying out our daily activities. Our willingness to emotionally and physically integrate the essential aspects of new information depends on how well it conforms to our current perception of the world in which we live and how this adjustment would impact upon us.

For example, if we are feeling overwhelmed with life, we could be seriously tempted to tune out essential counsel from the Lord because it may require rearrangement of our priorities, extra energy, and even sacrifice. However, it is important to remember that objective truth exists regardless of our personal belief, feelings, energy level, or our willingness to respond to it. This means that the requirement to maintain a year's supply of food is not conditional upon our acceptance or rejection of prophetic direction. This counsel to BE prepared and REMAIN prepared applies to everyone, and the time to start is now—not at some undefined time in the future. I've often wondered how hollow the excuses will seem to those who procrastinated too long because they "just couldn't seem to find the time, means or the room to store anything."

In order to avoid having those things that are least important interfere with what is most important, we need to daily pose this question to ourselves: "What would the Lord have me do today?" Perhaps we could ask more specifically, "Today, or during this week's activities, what would the Lord have me do about obtaining essential foods for storage?" How we answer these questions will ultimately determine our response to the Lord's counsel to be prepared.

It is interesting that most people who would never consider living without health insurance, fire insurance, and automobile insurance (which have to be renewed every year) would willingly neglect their "obedience" insurance. The special thing about permanent food storage is that once it is in place it takes minimal time, effort and very little expense to keep it maintained—for all intents and purposes it is a once-in-a-lifetime investment. When we think about it in that light, doesn't it seem extraordinarily foolish for anyone to neglect their "obedience" insurance?

ATTITUDE—DIFFERENCE BETWEEN THE WISE AND THE FOOLISH

Elder **Bernard P. Brockbank** has noted that a lack of preparation places us in the same category as the five foolish virgins:

> Take note that the Lord was not talking about five thieves and sinners and five good people; he was talking about ten virgins, ten pure people who believed in God and had a desire to enter into the kingdom of heaven. *The five foolish virgins had failed to prepare. Their lights were out; they were in darkness. Their urgent pleas and hasty preparation were not sufficient*, and they heard these words from the lips of their God: ["Ye never knew me."] (*Ensign*, January 1973, p. 45).

The significant difference between the five wise and the five foolish virgins, described by the Savior, was their attitude regarding the need to prepare for the coming of the bridegroom. In both cases they were equally aware that there was a need to prepare, but their response to this awareness was significantly different. The five foolish virgins felt no obvious pressing need to immediately began the process of "trimming their lamps," consequently they assumed the classic Scarlet O'Hara attitude of "I'll think about that tomorrow."

In the case of the five wise virgins, however, the response was one of placing preparation high on the list of priorities. There was a willingness to be obedient, even though the need did not appear pressing at the moment. When the bridegroom came at an unexpected time, the scrambling of the five foolish virgins to somehow get their lives and lamps immediately in order identified the degree of their real inner commitment to the bridegroom.

President **Spencer W. Kimball** taught us that the 10 virgins spoken of in the Biblical parable are members of the Church:

> *I believe that the Ten Virgins represent the people of the Church of Jesus Christ and not the rank and file of the world.* All of the virgins, wise and foolish, *had accepted the invitation to the wedding supper; they had knowledge of the program and had been warned of the important day to come.* They were not the gentiles or the heathen or the pagans, nor were they necessarily corrupt and reprobate, but they were know-

ing people who were foolishly unprepared for the vital happenings that were to affect their eternal lives.

Rushing for their lamps to light their way through the blackness, half of them found them empty. *They had cheated themselves. They were fools,* these five unprepared virgins. Apparently, the bridegroom had tarried for reasons sufficient and good. Time had passed, and He had not come. They had heard of His coming for so long, so many times, that the statement seemingly became meaningless to them. Would He ever come? So long had it been since they began expecting Him that they were rationalizing that He would never appear. Perhaps it was a myth.

Hundreds of thousands of us today are in this position. Confidence has been dulled and patience worn thin. It is so hard to wait and be prepared always. But we cannot allow ourselves to slumber. The Lord has given us this parable as a special warning.

In the daytime, wise and unwise seemed alike; *midnight is the time of test and judgement* (*Faith Precedes the Miracle*, pp. 253-254).

Bishop *Vaughn J. Featherstone*, speaking in 1976, observed that the lives of many of the Saints are symbolized by the parable of the five foolish virgins. Then, he outlined a simple program for the Saints to use in obtaining their food storage:

For twenty-six years, since I was fifteen, I was involved in the grocery industry. I learned much about human nature during those years. I remember the effects that strikes, earthquakes, and rumors of war had on many very active Latter-day Saints. Like the five foolish virgins, they rushed to the store to buy food, caught in the panic of knowing that direction had been given by the prophet but not having followed that direction—fearful that maybe they had procrastinated until it was everlastingly too late.

It was interesting because only in Latter-day Saint communities did people seem to buy with abandon. It was not a few Latter-day Saints—it was a significant number. It caused great increases in sales. One such experience came when a so-called prophecy by someone outside the Church was greatly publicized.

How foolish we can sometimes be! We have a living prophet: we have God's living oracles, the First Presidency and the Council of the Twelve Apostles. Let us follow the Brethren and be constant. We need have no fear if we are prepared.

This morning I would like to discuss food storage. Let me suggest four things we can do. *Start by taking an inventory*—take a physical count of all your reserves. . . . We need to know where we are. Every family should take an inventory—get all the facts.

Second, decide what is needed to bring your present reserve levels to a year's supply. Then make a list and prepare a plan.

Now that you know where you are and where you need to be, *the third step is to work out a time schedule for when you will reach your goal.* I suggest that one year from today we ought to have a year's supply of food in all active—and many inactive—members' homes in the Church (*Ensign*, May 1976, p. 116).

Each of us has to decide in which group, wise or foolish, we will eventually find ourselves. Whether it is oil obtained for our lamps, living the gospel in our homes, a personal relationship with Heavenly Father and the Savior, or food placed in storage, the outcome will eventually be the same. When the unexpected accountability comes crashing upon us, the foolish will always panic trying to find someone or someway to get "bailed out." Hunger, disease, financial disasters, and war can be terrible motivators. All the while, the wise can move confidently and quietly forward because they are prepared through obedience. The end result—actions which were or weren't taken—for both groups is a reflection of simple obedience, not merely an accounting of whether or not someone believed prophetic counsel to be true.

Simply stated, a belief that food storage is essential, necessary, important, or a good idea only has validity in our life if it is correspondingly acted upon. If we have, indeed, taken the Holy Ghost to be our guide, we will be aware that it is the obedient action resulting from the exercise of one's agency which is the sanctifying element.

In the parable, we are not led to believe that the wise virgins had gone forth with great fanfare regarding their preparation. Rather, they had but quietly proceeded to obtain sufficient oil for their lamps as they had been counseled to do. Where some was used, it was immediately replenished so that they could remain prepared. So it is with those of this generation. We too, should quietly move forward, obedient to the counsel of the prophets which will always be confirmed by the spirit of the Holy Ghost if we are willing to let Him be our guide.

Please, don't miss the point of all of this. There will be five foolish virgins from among those who claim to "know" the Savior. The only question facing each of us is "will we be one of them?" When the Lord concluded His comments regarding His coming and that of the millennium, He made the following observation regarding the foolish virgins:

> And *until that hour there will be foolish virgins among the wise;* and at that hour cometh an entire separation of the righteous and the wicked: and in that day will I send mine angels to pluck out the wicked and cast them into unquenchable fire (D&C 63:54)

ZION SHALL ESCAPE IF WE ARE OBEDIENT

President *Joseph Fielding Smith* made this observation regarding the challenging days that are before us:

> I do not know when He is going to come. No man knows. Even the angels in heaven are in the dark in regard to that great truth. But this I know, that *the signs that have been pointed out are here.* The earth is full of calamity, of trouble. The hearts of men are failing them. *We see the signs as we see the fig tree putting forth her leaves; and*

knowing this time is near, it behooves me and it behooves you, and all men upon the face of the earth, to pay heed to the words of Christ, to his apostles and watch, for we know not the day nor the hour. But I tell you this, it shall come as a thief in the night, when many of us will not be ready for it *(Doctrines of Salvation,* vol. III, p. 52).

By being obedient in following the prophetic counsel to prepare, you and your family can lay claim upon the following promise the Lord made to Enoch:

. . . As I live, even so will I come in the last days, in the days of wickedness and vengeance, *to fulfill the oath which I have made unto you* concerning the children of Noah;

And the day shall come that the earth shall rest, but before that day the heavens shall be darkened, and a veil of darkness shall cover the earth; and the heavens shall shake, and also the earth; and great tribulation shall be among the children of men, *but my people will I preserve* (Moses 7:60-61).

If we can come to understand how the Lord fulfilled his promise to "preserve" his people from great tribulation in the days of Enoch, perhaps that awareness can increase our faith that the Lord will also provide for each of us a way to escape in our day. The Lord stated: *"Zion shall escape if she observe to do all things whatsoever I have commanded her"* (D&C 97:25).

President *Joseph Fielding Smith* explained how the righteous escaped in the days of Enoch:

Let me call your attention to a condition which prevailed in the days of Enoch which makes all the difference in the world. In his day the Lord gathered together all the righteous and *they with Enoch were taken from the earth, and later before the flood if any repented and accepted the truth they too were caught up* to the people of Enoch, so that when the time came to cleanse the earth with water, only Noah and his family remained of the righteous, and they were left that the race of mankind might be perpetuated after the flood *(The Signs of the Times,* p. 7).

In our day we know that we must prepare as Noah was prepared (a place of shelter with sufficient food), and then hold Zion in our hearts and let its precepts govern our lives if we are to find safety and peace in the coming storm. None of us know the ultimate purpose the Lord has in mind for those who keep a year's supply of food on hand. Perhaps it is the Lord's equivalent to us of entering the Ark or moving to the City of Zion, as were the alternatives offered to his children in the days of Enoch and Noah. In any case, whether or not you obtain a year's supply of food for yourself and your family, you may well be staking your family's life on your decision.

Far too many individuals and families live by the principle of "relative deprivation," which simply means that we see ourselves in relationship to the world environment wherein we live. For many, it is not a matter of what they have that meets their personal aspirations and needs, so much as how it measure up to those they live amongst. Therefore, what they want and what they truly need becomes confused. Individuals thus influenced tend to consistently live beyond their financial means in an effort to keep up appearances. The end results is that food storage, which has no particular social status, never quite materializes as a need. Thus as a want or a good idea it forever remains on the back burner—something that is "almost" but never quite taken care of.

TAKE DECISIVE ACTION NOW

If, after reading so much of the detailed instruction given by the Lord and the Brethren, you feel a little confused concerning how to personally respond, perhaps it would help if you could keep focused upon this thought from President Lee as he spoke about food storage: *"Think . . . of what it would take to keep alive."*

Perhaps the following suggestion made by Bishop **Vaughn J. Featherstone** would help:

> *Decide as a family this year that 25 or 50 percent of your Christmas will be spent on a year's supply. . . .* Half or part of these Christmas monies will go a long way toward purchasing the basics. I recall the Scotsman who went to the doctor and had an X-ray taken of his chest. Then he had the X-ray gift-wrapped and gave it to his wife for their anniversary. He couldn't afford a gift, but he wanted her to know his heart was in the right place. *Brethren, give your wife a year's supply of wheat for Christmas,* and she'll know your heart is in the right place (*Ensign,* May 1976, p. 117).

At the October 1992 general conference, Elder Harold B. Lee shared a parable which **President McKay** had given at a regional Church welfare meeting:

> An engineer pulled his train into a station one dark and stormey night, and while the engineer was out oiling his engine and getting ready for the next run, a timid passenger left his place in the train and walked up to the engineer and asked, "Aren't you afraid to pull your train out into the dark tonight, raining and storming like it is?" Without looking up, the engineer replied, "I am not pulling my engine out into the dark tonight." "Why," said the passenger, "it's pitch dark outside the lights of the station. I should think that with the responsibility of these four or five hundred passengers depending upon your handling of the train, you would be a nervous wreck."
>
> For an answer the engineer pointed up to the bright headlight and he said, "Do you see that light up there? That throws out an intense white light a thousand yards ahead on the track. When I pull out of the station tonight, *I will be running my engine only to the first circle of that light, a thousand yards away, and when I get to the outer circle of that light it will still be out another thousand yards in front of me. All through this dark night I will not be running in one foot of darkness all the way."*

Then President Lee said,

Now, brethren, . . . all through this night of uncertainty when we are trying to establish the security of our people in a temporal way, *this Church will be running in light of the revelations that come from God, all the way* (*Conference Report*, October 1962, pp. 79-80).

The point of this parable is for each of us to always stay, "all the way" within the "circle of light," ie. the revelations given by the Lord to his prophets. Since they have told us that the Lord desires for us to be prepared with food storage for at least a year ahead, then if we are obedient, we shall have the same confidence held by the engineer as he moved forward within the light. However, If we elect to ignore the counsel we are then left to feel, with uncertain feet, our way forward through the "dark and stormy" experiences of life, fearfully on our own.

For whatever reason, should you not feel the spirit of preparation, perhaps you need to read the preceding counsel again and again if necessary, until you sense the Lord's "light" and love for each of us and understand his great desire to protect us from harmful events that must surely come to pass. Once you receive a testimony regarding the need to stay prepared, many of the hurdles discouraging you will either disappear or be greatly diminished, and you will see by the "light" the way to move forward.

RIGHTEOUSNESS, OBEDIENCE AND PREPARATION

Panic preparation is not what the Lord has in mind, He wants us to prepare not because of a Y2K or similar scare but to prepare simply because He asked us to prepare. Isn't it interesting that some of the Saints would scramble to prepare because of something like a possible problem resulting from Y2K and yet had remained unprepared for years after a prophet had counseled them to get things in order? If history is any indicator, the Saints that prepare in a panic will go back to their previous pattern after Y2K, eat up their food storage, and then wait until someone in the world again announces another panic. They consistently ignore the Lord's statement that the "bridegroom" will come unexpectedly and that they should always be prepared.

Nephi witnessed our day and made some very pointed comments regarding the challenges to be faced by the Saints:

. . . they have all gone astray save it be a few who are the humble followers of Christ; nevertheless, they are led, that *in many instances they do err because they are taught by the precepts of men* (See 2 Nephi 28:14).

Then Nephi speaks of another group:

And others will he pacify, and *lull them away into carnal security that they will say: All is well in Zion; Zion prospereth, all is well*—and thus the devil cheateth their souls, and leadeth them away carefully down to hell . . . And behold, *others he flattereth away* (See 2 Nephi 28:21-22).

Nephi then gives this warning:

Therefore, *wo be unto him that is at ease in Zion!* Wo be unto him that crieth: All is well! (See 2 Nephi 28:24-25).

The "few" faithful Saints who desire not to "err" will follow King Benjamin's admonition:

See that all these things are done in wisdom and order; for it is not requisite that a man should run faster than he has strength. And again, *it is expedient that he should be diligent, that thereby he might win the prize; therefore, all things must be done* [not in a panic but] in order (Mosiah 4:27).

Having reviewed, in this treatise, many aspects of our physical and spiritual welfare, of counsels and instructions given, and prophecies proclaimed, it becomes obvious that there is much for us to consider, plan for and act upon. To this end may each of us eventually succeed in our earnest efforts to stand obedient and independent in the world before the Lord.

Although dark days and trying circumstances, "significant moments in time," are predicted for the future, yet there is the bright and gentle light of the gospel that can shine upon us through it all. As children of a loving Heavenly Father, and as Saints in Zion, we can still have peace of mind, but only to the extent that we are righteous, obedient, and prepared.

Righteousness—entitles us to promised guidance and personal revelation, so that as we heed the prompting of the Holy Ghost we can make wise and proper decisions.

Obedience—allows us safety as we reap the blessings of a caring Heavenly Father, who desires to spare us much of the tribulation that must come upon this earth.

Preparation—brings to us temporal and spiritual security as Heavenly Father instructs us regarding the measures we must take if we are to find peace of mind in an unsafe world.

The above three basic principles endow upon us the peace we need to walk with confidence in our sojourn upon the earth.

However, if given directions concerning how to prepare we yet fail to heed that counsel, we are then in many ways left to ourselves. We must remember the Lord wants, indeed, needs the children of Israel to have "strong faith," to be a happy, healthy, safe and righteous people—prepared to endure the tribulations which the earth must pass through in order for the Lord's Millennial Era to be ushered in and our Savior assume His rightful reign.

Elder *Richard L. Evans* taught that

We must have faith in the future regardless of the ultimate eventualities. There could be no greater calamity in this world than the calamity of sitting down and waiting for calamity. *We must not let the things which we can't do keep us from doing the things we can do. . . . The future will always be better for those who are best prepared* (*Church News,* June 25, 1988, p. 2).

I add my personal testimony that Heavenly Father will bless us all to whatever extent we allow Him. May you find joy and strength through obedience, my dear Brothers and Sisters. To this end has this work been compiled, that you might be prepared.

BIBLIOGRAPHY

LATTER-DAY SAINT SCRIPTURES

The Book of Mormon. (trans.) Joseph Smith, Salt Lake City, Utah: The Church of Jesus Christ of Latter-day Saints, 1981.

The Doctrine and Covenants of The Church of Jesus Christ of Latter-day Saints, 1981.

The Holy Bible. King James Version; Salt Lake City, Utah: The Church of Jesus Christ of Latter-day Saints, 1979.

The Pearl of Great Price. Salt Lake City, Utah: The Church of Jesus Christ of Latter-day Saints, 1981.

LATTER-DAY SAINT HISTORICAL SOURCES

Benson, Ezra Taft. *God—Family—Country.* Salt Lake City, Utah: Deseret Book Co., 1974

Benson, Ezra Taft. *The Teachings of Ezra Taft Benson.* Salt Lake City, Utah: Bookcraft, Inc., 1988.

Berrett, William Edwin. *The Restored Church.* 16th ed.; Salt Lake City, Utah: Deseret Book Company, 1961.

Crowther, Duane S. *Inspired Prophetic Warnings.* 4th ed.; Bountiful, Utah: Horizon Publishers, 1996.

Crowther, Duane S. *Prophecy, Key to the Future.* 2nd ed.; Salt Lake City, Utah: Bookcraft Inc., 1962.

Journal of Discourses. Volumes 1-26. Liverpool: F.D. and S.W. Richards, 1854-1886.

Journal History. Salt Lake City, Utah: The Church of Jesus Christ of Latter-day Saints, Historical Department Archives, 23 Sept. 1855.

Kimball, Edward L. Edited by. *The Teaching of Spencer W. Kimball.* Salt Lake City, Utah: Bookcraft, 1982.

Kimball, Spencer W. *The Miracle of Forgiveness.* 12th ed.; Salt Lake City, Utah: Bookcraft Inc., 1969.

Lee, Harold B. *Stand Ye In Holy Places.* 4 Volumes; Salt Lake City, Utah: Deseret Book Co., 1974.

Ludlow, Daniel H. Edited by. *Encyclopedia of Mormonism.* 3 Volumes; New York : Macmillan Publishing Co. 1992.

Maxwell, Neal A. *For The Power Is In Them.* Salt Lake City, Utah: Deseret Book Company, 1970.

Maxwell, Neal A. *All These Things Shall Give Thee Experience.* Salt Lake City, Utah: Deseret Book Company, 1980.

Maxwell, Neal A. *Wherefore, Ye Must Press Forward.* Salt Lake City, Utah: Deseret Book
 Company, 1977.

McConkie, Bruce R. *Doctrinal New Testament Commentary.* 3 Volumes; Salt Lake City, Utah:
 Bookcraft, 1973.

McConkie, Bruce R. *Mormon Doctrine.* Salt Lake City, Utah: Bookcraft, 1958.

McConkie, Bruce R. *The Promised Messiah.* Salt Lake City, Utah: Deseret Book
 Company, 1978.

McKay, David O. *Gospel Ideals.* Salt Lake City, Utah: An *Improvement Era* Publication, 1953.

Nibley, Preston. *Pioneer Stories.* Salt Lake City, Utah: Deseret New Press, 1940.

Rich, Russell R. *Ensign to the Nations.* 5th ed.; Provo, Utah; Brigham Young University
 Publications, 1979.

Rudd, Glen L. *Pure Religion.* Salt Lake City, Utah: The Church of Jesus Christ of
 Latter-day Saints, 1995.

Smith, Joseph. *History of the Church.* 7 Volumes; 2nd ed.; Salt Lake City, Utah: Deseret News
 Press, 1951.

Smith, Joseph Fielding. *Doctrines of Salvation.* 3 Volumes; Salt Lake City, Utah: Bookcraft,
 1954.

Smith, Joseph Fielding. *Essentials in Church History.* 13th ed.; Salt Lake City, Utah: Deseret
 News Press, 1959.

Smith, Joseph Fielding. *Teachings of the Prophet Joseph Smith.* 13th ed.; Salt Lake City, Utah:
 Deseret Book Company, 1963.

Smith, Joseph Fielding. *The Signs of the Times.* Salt Lake City, Utah: Deseret Book
 Company, 1952.

Stuy, Brian H. Compiled and Edited by. *Collected Discourses.* 5 Volumes; Sandy, Utah:
 B.H.S. Publishing, 1987.

Whitney, Orson F. *Life of Heber C. Kimball.* 3rd ed.; Salt Lake City, Utah: Bookcraft Inc., 1967.

Whitney, Orson F. *Saturday Night Thoughts.* Rev. ed.; Salt Lake City, Utah: Deseret Book
 Company, 1927.

Widtsoe, John A. Selected by. *Discourses of Brigham Young.;* Salt Lake City, Utah: Deseret
 Book Company, 1951.

SUGGESTED FOOD STORAGE FOR 12 MONTHS FOR VARIOUS AGE GROUPS, BY GENDER

	Unit	Male (over 18)	Male (7-18)	Female (over 18)	Female (12-18)	Female (7-11)	Child (under 7)
Grains Group							
Wheat	lbs	189	176	132	139	151	107
Flour, enriched white	lbs	17	16	12	12	14	10
Corn meal	lbs	42	39	29	31	34	24
Oats, rolled	lbs	42	39	29	31	34	24
Rice, white enriched	lbs	84	78	59	62	67	48
Barley, pearled	lbs	4	4	3	3	3	2
Spaghetti & *macaroni*	lbs	42	39	29	31	34	24
Totals		**420**	**391**	**293**	**309**	**337**	**239**
Legumes Group							
Beans (dry)	lbs	25	25	25	25	25	25
Beans, lima (dry)	lbs	1	1	1	1	1	1
Beans, soy (dry)	lbs	1	1	1	1	1	1
Peas, split (dry)	lbs	1	1	1	1	1	1
Lentils (dry)	lbs	1	1	1	1	1	1
Soup mix (dry)	lbs	5	5	5	5	5	5
Totals		**34**	**34**	**34**	**34**	**34**	**34**
Fats & Oils Group							
Vegetable Oil	gal	2	2	2	2	2	2
Shortening	lbs	4	4	4	4	4	4
Mayonnaise	qts	2	2	2	2	2	2
Salad Dressing (mayonnaise type)	qts	1	1	1	1	1	1
Peanut butter	lbs	4	4	4	4	4	4
Totals		**13**	**13**	**13**	**13**	**13**	**13**
Milk Group							
Milk, nonfat (dry)	lbs	14	14	14	14	14	14
Evaporated milk (12 oz. net wt.)	cans	12	12	12	12	12	12
Totals		**26**	**26**	**26**	**26**	**26**	**26**

	Unit	Male (over 18)	Male (7-18)	Female (over 18)	Female (12-18)	Female (7-11)	Child (under 7)
Sugars Group							
Sugar, granulated	lbs	40	40	40	40	40	40
Sugar, brown	lbs	3	3	3	3	3	3
Molasses	lbs	1	1	1	1	1	1
Honey	lbs	3	3	3	3	3	3
Corn syrup	lbs	3	3	3	3	3	3
Jams & preserves	lbs	3	3	3	3	3	3
Fruit drinks, powdered	lbs	6	6	6	6	6	6
Gelatin, flavored	lbs	1	1	1	1	1	1
Totals		**60**	**60**	**60**	**60**	**60**	**60**
Miscellaneous Group							
Yeast, dry	lbs	1	1	1	1	1	1
Soda	lbs	1	1	1	1	1	1
Baking powder	lbs	1	1	1	1	1	1
Vinegar	gal	1	1	1	1	1	1
Chlorine bleach	gal	1	1	1	1	1	1
Salt, iodized (8 lbs/person/year)	lbs	8	8	8	8	8	8
Totals		**13**	**13**	**13**	**13**	**13**	**13**
Water 2 gallons per day per person (56 gal/person/ for 4 weeks)	gal	56	56	56	56	56	56
Totals		**56**	**56**	**56**	**56**	**56**	**56**

INDEX

ABOUT THE AUTHOR

Neil H. Leash has lived a life filled with broad and varied experiences that uniquely qualify him to compile this particular work and commentary. He has served in a multitude of Church assignments, including callings as a Bishop on two occasions, and as a counselor in a Stake Presidency, service as a High Council member for decades, and as an Elders Quorum President, Seminary teacher, and in numerous other stake and ward auxiliary positions. In each of these callings he has had the responsibility to study and apply the teachings of the Prophets, including those related to food storage and personal and family preparedness.

Indeed, for extended periods in the past he has had specific assignments to assist members of the Church in gathering their food storage. His children speak with fond recollection of the "hideouts" their father arranged for them from wheat sacks, during those periods when large portions of the family living room was filled floor-to-ceiling with sacks of wheat and other foodstuffs, waiting to be picked up by the Saints who had chosen to become prepared.

His training and nearly 30 years experience as a licensed Marriage and Family Therapist (MFT) offer him further insight into those issues that underlie human nature, especially those which tend to either enhance or hinder the personal and family preparedness process. These insights were readily apparent in earlier authorship of a work entitled *The Unused Power of Self Mastery*, which explored ways to mold and shape one's own will and desires to more fully conform to those of the Savior.

Finally, his experience in developing counseling programs, Church programs, and as a much sought-after speaker, allow him to meaningfully address the otherwise rather pedantic and programmatic aspects of food storage with vivid illustrations and touching stories. Thus, his writing can help each of us more fully commit to being obedient to the counsel of the Prophets to become "a prepared people before the Lord."

Brother Leash received his Bachelor's and Master's degrees from California State University, Sacramento, and retired in 1993 after 34 years as a Supervising Probation Officer. Born and raised in Oakland, California, he was called at the age of 19 to serve as a missionary in the Eastern States Mission. Upon his return he served as an Army Medic during the Korean War, and shortly before discharge he married Velma D. Carraway in the Mesa Arizona temple. They are the parents of three children and reside in San Andreas, California.